SeaWorld Discovery Cove & Aquatica

Orlando's Salute to the Seas

Kelly Monaghan

SeaWorld, Discovery Cove & Aquatica

Orlando's Salute To The Seas

Published by The Intrepid Traveler
P.O. Box 531, Branford, CT 06405

Copyright © 2009 by Kelly Monaghan
First Edition
Printed in the United States
Book Jacket: George Foster, Foster & Foster, Inc.
Maps designed by MapGorilla.com
ISBN: 978-1-887140-80-5
LCCN: 2008929429

Publisher's Cataloguing in Publication Data.

Monaghan, Kelly

SeaWorld, Discovery Cove and Aquatica: Orlando's Salute to the Seas. Branford, CT: Intrepid Traveler, copyright 2009.

PARTIAL CONTENTS: SeaWorld Florida. -Discovery Cove. -Aquatica. -Busch Gardens Africa. -Resort Hotels.

1. Orlando region, Florida--Description and travel--Guidebooks. 2. Theme parks--Orlando region, Florida--Guidebooks. 3. Recreation--Orlando region, Florida. 4. SeaWorld, Florida--Description and travel--Guidebooks. 6. Busch Gardens Africa, Tampa, Florida--Description and travel--Guidebooks. 7. Hotels and Resorts--Orlando region, Florida--Guidebooks. 8. Discovery Cove, Florida--Description and travel--Guidebooks.

I. Title. II. Title: Orlando's Salute to the Seas. III. Title: Orlando IV. Intrepid Traveler.

917.5924

Trademarks, Etc.

Other Books by Kelly Monaghan

Universal Orlando:
The Ultimate Guide To The
Ultimate Theme Park Adventure

The Other Orlando:
What To Do When You've Done
Disney and Universal

Home-Based Travel Agent:
How To Succeed In Your Own
Travel Marketing Business

The Travel Agent's Complete Desk Reference

Air Courier Bargains:
How To Travel World-Wide For Next To Nothing

Fly Cheap!

Air Travel's Bargain Basement

Photo by SeaWorld

About the Author

Kelly Monaghan (on the left, above) has been covering the "other Orlando" since 1994. His interest in the many central Florida attractions beyond Disney World prompted him to write the groundbreaking *Orlando's **Other** Theme Parks: What To Do When You've Done Disney,* which included chapters on Universal Studios Florida and SeaWorld. When Universal literally exploded into a multi-park, multi-hotel destination, he spun off a new book, *Universal Orlando: The Ultimate Guide To The Ultimate Theme Park Adventure.* You are now holding the next step in the evolution of his continuing in-depth coverage of central Florida's theme parks. Over the years he has written other travel-oriented books about how to travel on the cheap and how to be a home-based travel agent. He offers a home study course for those who wish to expand their travel horizons with — and profit from — their own travel marketing business at . . .

www.HomeTravelAgency.com

Photo Credits

Front and back cover photos:

All interior photos are by the author, except as follows:

Courtesy Busch Entertainment Company: page 31 (middle); page 33 (top left & bottom); page 34; page 90; page 91 (top & middle); page 92 (bottom); page 109 (middle & bottom); page 110; page 124

Courtesy Marriott Corporation: page 126 (top)

Courtesy Peabody Orlando Hotel: page 141

Courtesy Rosen Shingle Creek Resort: page 150

Courtesy Jon Wassner: page 170

Table of Contents

List of Maps

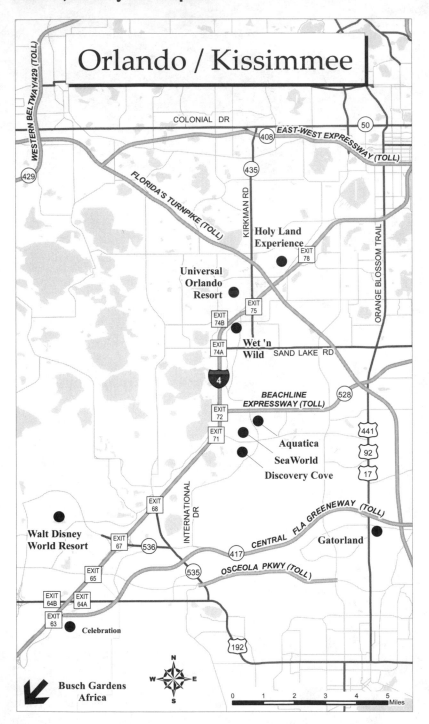

Orlando / Kissimmee

CHAPTER ONE:

Dive Right In!

BEFORE WE WADE INTO SEAWORLD AND ITS SISTER PARKS, LET'S GET our toes wet with some Orlando theme park history: Orlando's transformation into a tourist mecca began with the arrival of Walt Disney World, which opened near Orlando in 1971 as a new, improved version of California's Disneyland. With the luxury of 43 square miles in which to expand, the new park quickly eclipsed its West Coast namesake. Three more theme parks followed the Magic Kingdom — Epcot, Disney's Hollywood Studios, and Animal Kingdom. For good measure, Disney threw in a couple of water parks, a slew of themed resorts, and a sprawling shopping and entertainment district.

In 1990, Universal Studios opened Universal Studios Florida. Like Disney World, it was an outpost of a California original. It quickly became Orlando's number-two attraction. In 1999, Universal Studios Florida almost literally exploded, adding another theme park, a nighttime entertainment district and three superb resort hotels; in the process, it was renamed Universal Orlando. For the first time, Walt Disney World had competition worthy of the name and Orlando had its second multi-park, multi-resort, multi-activity, all-in-one, never-need-to-leave-the-property vacation destination.

Now something similar is happening with a trio of water-themed Orlando parks — SeaWorld, Discovery Cove, and Aquatica — that are part of the Worlds of Discovery family of theme parks. These are not all new parks, of course. SeaWorld opened in 1973, Discovery Cove in 2000, and Aquatica debuted in 2008. What *is* new is a growing awareness by the traveling public that these parks, along with another Worlds of Discovery park, Busch Gardens Africa in nearby Tampa, offer yet another opportunity for a multi-park, themed vacation experience. Each park is different, each has its own particular allure, yet all of them fit comfortably within the same "brand personality." Consumers see "Disney" and "Universal" as single brands comprising multiple parts; they are looking at Worlds of Discovery in much the same way.

Worlds of Discovery has encouraged this trend by offering multi-park ticket options (park hoppers, if you will) to encourage visitors to spend more time with their family of parks. This guidebook hopes to provide further encouragement by showcasing the special attractions of these parks to a wider audience.

Just What Is 'Worlds of Discovery'?

Worlds of Discovery is the brand name for a decidedly eclectic group of ten theme parks and water parks, located in five states scattered across the North American continent. Five of the ten parks are located in central Florida and form the subject of this book.

Worlds of Discovery

The parks included in the "Worlds of Discovery" brand are (an ★ indicates the parks covered in this book):

Adventure Island ★
Aquatica ★
Busch Gardens Africa★
    (Tampa)
Busch Gardens Europe
    (Williamsburg, VA)
Discovery Cove ★
SeaWorld Orlando ★
SeaWorld San Antonio
SeaWorld San Diego
Sesame Place
    (Langhorne, PA)
Water Country USA
    (Williamsburg, VA)

Unlike Walt Disney World and Universal Orlando, the Worlds of Discovery family of parks faces some unique marketing challenges, starting with its thematic and geographic diversity. Even in Florida, three of the parks are in Orlando, while the other two are an hour or so away in Tampa. The brand grew partly by acquisition of existing parks with existing names and more or less established brand identities and partly by internal expansion. So to the casual observer, there is no immediately apparent connection between SeaWorld in Orlando and Busch Gardens Africa in Tampa. Or even between SeaWorld and Discovery Cove.

The Florida outposts of Worlds of Discovery also do not have the advantage of large tracts of land on which to build its own, separate "world." All of the parks in central Florida are surrounded by and separated by public roads and other businesses over which it has no control. So they can't stage manage the visitor experience in the same way that Universal and Disney can. Nor can they offer the sort of on-property resort experience served up at the other megaparks, although, as we shall see, nearby posh resorts offer a terrific do-it-yourself alternative.

So what holds this all together? What makes SeaWorld and the other Worlds of Discovery parks in central Florida special and distinct from Disney and Universal? In a word: animals. At SeaWorld and the other Orlando parks, that means marine animals and the watery world they inhabit. Busch Gardens Africa, of course, means the magnificent beasts of the "Dark Continent."

In other words, the Worlds of Discovery parks celebrate the natural world and preach a subtle message about preserving it. (Animal conservation is a major beneficiary of the company's corporate philanthropy.) That's not to say that they neglect the fun, fantasy, and thrills aspects of the theme park experience. The parks in this book offer some of the best thrill rides in the state, indeed in the entire Southeast. Yet is the animals and the imaginative, often unique ways in which they are displayed and celebrated that set the tone.

Another thing that binds these parks together is the Worlds of Discovery system of "Passports" that allow multi-day access to several or all of the central Florida parks and, as we shall see, offer very good value for the money.

A Quick Overview

Each of the parks covered here has its own specialties and special features. It will help your planning to have a basic understanding of what each offers. Here they are in the order that they are covered in this book. I have provided the shortest URL (or Internet address) to get you to each park's web site, but you will have to do some more clicking to get to the information you want. In addition, all of these parks can be reached via . . .

www.worldsofdiscovery.com.

SeaWorld

In many ways the centerpiece of the Worlds of Discovery empire in central Florida, SeaWorld is dedicated to marine mammals, especially the orca (or killer whale) personified by Shamu, the park's star. The signature experiences here are a series of spectacular shows, starring whales, dolphins, sea lions, and other creatures, presented several times each day in large covered amphitheaters. There is also a small (but growing) selection of thrill rides, but they are more in the nature of an "extra added attraction" than the main order of business. There are some very nice dining options that lure annual passholders for frequent return visits.

www.seaworld.com

Discovery Cove

This upscale theme park limits daily attendance to just 1,000 guests and can best be likened to a visit to a Caribbean resort island, without having to bother leaving the conveniences of Orlando behind. The main lure here is the opportunity to swim with a live dolphin, an experience that's open to just 750 guests each day. It costs extra and requires booking well in advance.

Discovery Cove is unique in that it is not part of any multi-day, multi-park Passport. If you want to come another day, you pay another full day's admission. For this reason, most guests arrive when the park opens and leave only when the park closes, around dusk.

www.discoverycove.com

Aquatica

The newest Worlds of Discovery park is a water park with a difference that only SeaWorld could provide — marine mammals and tropical fish. Spacious and beautifully themed, Aquatica has fewer thrill rides and better dining options that most water parks, making it especially attractive to families and those who want a "day at the beach" experience but find Discovery Cove a little too pricey. There are two wave pools here, an enormous beach area, and a speedier version of that water park staple, the "lazy river" ride. But the signature attraction is a water slide that carries riders through a salt water pool filled with Commerson's dolphins — speedy, compact Shamu look-a-likes from Australian waters.

www.aquaticabyseaworld.com

Busch Gardens Africa

About an hour away, in Tampa, Busch Gardens Africa is a theme park that very nicely balances two distinct personalities — world class zoo and world class thrill park. The theme, of course, is the various ecosystems of Africa, from sun-baked Timbuktu to steamy Congo. Here you will find some of the most imaginatively designed animal habitats in the country, along with a collection of roller coasters that will satisfy even the most demanding thrill seekers. There is also a varied menu of stage entertainment, ranging from the amiable to the astonishing. All of this spread out over 355 beautifully landscaped and themed acres.

www.buschgardens.com

Adventure Island

Next door to Busch Gardens Africa is another water park. It is perhaps the most "ordinary" park reviewed in this book, but that's not to say it's not a lot of fun. It doesn't have the super themeing or marine mammals of Aquatica, but it offers more thrills for the teen set (among whom it is highly popular). Unlike Aquatica, Adventure Island is open only in the warmer months. It is the logical choice if a water park experience is on your to-do list and you can't make it to Aquatica.

www.adventureisland.com

Putting It All Together

In summary, then, the Worlds of Discovery in Orlando — SeaWorld, Discovery Cove, and Aquatica — offer a wide variety of sea-themed experiences, ranging from spectacular shows to hands-on interactions, interspersed with imaginative thrill rides. The dining and shopping options more than hold their own when compared to Universal and Walt Disney World, although with fewer high-end options. Plus, just a short distance away are some of Orlando's finest and poshest resort hotels, with fine restaurants of their own. Everything, in short, for the kind of all-in-one, upscale themed vacation experience that has long characterized visits to Disney and Universal. And as a sort of bonus, the special fun offered by Busch Gardens Africa, with its collection of amazing roller coasters and exotic animals, is just a short drive away; and Worlds of Discovery will even do the driving!

How This Book Is Organized

Each of the parks covered in this book is separate; each has its own parking lot. It is unlikely that you will be visiting more then one of them on the same day. Of course, it's possible, but I don't recommend it unless you have a multi-park Passport (discussed later), and even then, my personal feeling is that the parks lend themselves best to a one-at-a-time touring approach.

Because of the separate nature of the parks, I have included most of the introductory information about each park in the appropriate chapter. In this chapter, however, I cover a number of topics that apply to all the parks, such as timing your visit, a geographic overview, and the all-important (and rather complex) matter of multi-day, multi-park tickets. This approach may result in some duplication, but my goal is to save you the inconvenience of having to flip backwards and forward in the book to find the information you need.

The book first looks at the three Orlando parks — SeaWorld, Discovery Cove, and Aquatica — then examines the resort hotels near them. Finally, I cover the two Tampa parks, Busch Gardens Africa and Adventure Island.

When to Come

There are three major questions you must ask yourself when planning a visit to Orlando: How crowded will it be? What will the weather be like? When will my schedule allow me go? For most people, the third question will determine when they go, regardless of the answers to the other two. The dictates of business or the carved-in-stone school calendar will tend to dictate when you come to Orlando. For those who can be flexible, however, carefully picking the time of your visit will offer a number of benefits. And parents should bear in mind that school officials will often allow kids out of classes for a week if you ask nicely.

Let's take a look at these two variables: the tourist traffic and the weather. Then you can make a determination as to which dates will offer your ideal Orlando vacation.

Orlando's Tourist Traffic

Most tourist destinations have two seasons — high and low. For most of Florida, the high season stretches from late fall to early spring, the cooler months up North. Low season is the blisteringly hot summer, when Floridians who can afford it head North. Orlando, thanks to its multitude of family-oriented attractions, has five or six distinct "seasons," alternating between high and low, reflecting the vacation patterns of its prime customers — kids and their parents.

The heaviest tourist "season" is Christmas vacation, roughly from Christmas Eve through January first. Next comes Easter week and Thanksgiving weekend. The entire summer, from Memorial Day in late May to Labor Day in early September, is on a par with Easter and Thanksgiving. There are two other "spikes" in attendance: President's Week in February and College Spring Break. Various colleges have different dates for their Spring Break, which may or may not coincide with Easter; the result is that the period from mid-March through mid-April shows a larger than usual volume of tourist traffic. The slowest period is the lull between Thanksgiving and Christmas. Next slowest (excluding the holidays mentioned earlier) are the months of September, October, November, January, and February. Tourism starts to build again in March, spiking sharply upward for Easter/Spring Break, then dropping off somewhat until Memorial Day.

It would be nice to know how theme park attendance rises and falls from month to month. That information is a closely guarded trade secret, but fairly reliable annual estimates are available. Here are annual attendance figures for Orlando area parks for 2007 as estimated by the trade groups TEA and Economics Research Associates:

Rank*	Park	Attendance
1	The Magic Kingdom	17,060,000
3	EPCOT	10,930,000
4	Disney's Hollywood Studios	9,510,000
5	Disney's Animal Kingdom	9,490,000
6	Universal Studios Florida	6,200,000
7	SeaWorld Orlando	5,800,000

| 9 | Islands of Adventure | 5,430,000 |
| 11 | Busch Gardens Tampa | 4,400,000 |

*★Numbers represent the parks' **national** rankings. Disneyland, California, was number two, Disney's California Adventure was number seven, Universal Studios California was number ten.*

In other words, on any given day, the largest crowds will tend to be at the Disney and Universal parks. If you've been a Disney regular, the parks described in this book will seem quite manageable by comparison.

The best advice is to avoid the absolutely busiest times of the year if possible. I find the slow months of fall and spring to be ideal. I even enjoy January, but I'm not the sunbathing type, and winter presents special challenges, as noted in the next section. If you come during the summer, as many families must, plan to deal with crowds when you arrive and console yourself with the thought that, in bypassing Disney (and, to a lesser extent, Universal), you've automatically avoided the worst crowds.

Orlando's Weather

Orlando's average annual temperature is a lovely 72.4 degrees. But as we've already noted, averages are deceptive. Here are the generally cited "average" figures for temperature and rainfall throughout the year:

	High (°F)	Low (°F)	Rain (in.)
January	71	49	2.3
February	73	50	2.8
March	78	55	3.2
April	83	59	1.8
May	88	66	3.6
June	91	72	7.3
July	92	73	7.3
August	92	73	6.8
September	90	73	6.0
October	85	66	2.4
November	79	58	2.3
December	73	51	2.2

(Source: Orlando/Orange County Convention & Visitors Bureau)

Use these figures as general guidelines rather than guarantees. While the average monthly rainfall in January might be 2.3 inches over the course of many years, in 1994 there were 4.9 inches of rain that month and in 1996 almost 4 inches fell in the first two days alone. In June of 2005, Orlando International Airport recorded 16.74 inches of rain, over twice the historic average. The same holds for temperatures, especially in the winter months. January of 1996 and 2001 saw lows dip into the twenties.

I find Orlando's weather most predictable in the summer when "hot, humid, in the low nineties, with a chance of afternoon thunderstorms" becomes something of a mantra for the TV weather report. Winter weather tends to be more unpredictable with "killer" freezes a possibility. I cannot, in good conscience, recommend a wintertime visit if you are planning on visiting Aquatica or Discovery Cove. Both parks are open year round and never lack for paying customers, but swimming on a chilly day presents challenges for most of us. The temperature is less a factor when visiting SeaWorld or Busch Gardens Africa, although both parks have attractions that can get you very, very wet and that can be extremely uncomfortable in cold weather. As to those summer thunderstorms, they tend to be localized and mercifully brief (although occasionally quite intense) and needn't disrupt your touring schedule too much. Another thing to bear in mind is that June through September is hurricane season, with late August and early September the most likely time for severe weather.

Getting Oriented

SeaWorld, Discovery Cove, and Aquatica are located close together at the southern end of Orlando's tourist district. They lie just east of Interstate 4 and just south of State Route 528, the so-called Bee Line Expressway (its official name is the Martin Andersen Beachline Expressway), which connects Orlando International Airport to the Interstate.

Note: Although I-4 runs east-west across the state, it runs almost exactly north-south as it passes SeaWorld.

Another handy geographical referent is International Drive (or I-Drive as it's known locally), which is the gaudy spine of Orlando's tourist quarter; Universal Orlando lies at the north end of I-Drive and SeaWorld toward the south end. It runs roughly parallel to I-4.

From International Drive

If you are staying in one of the many hotels in the International Drive area, your obvious approach is down I-Drive, which takes you past the entrance to Aquatica to Central Florida Parkway, where you turn right to reach Discovery Cove (on your left) and SeaWorld (a little farther along on your right).

From the south on I-4

Coming from the south (that is, traveling "east" on I-4), take Exit 71, which leads directly onto Central Florida Parkway heading east. From here, SeaWorld is directly ahead on your left, while Discovery Cove is just a short distance farther on your right. To reach Aquatica, continue to International Drive and turn left; Aquatica will be on your right.

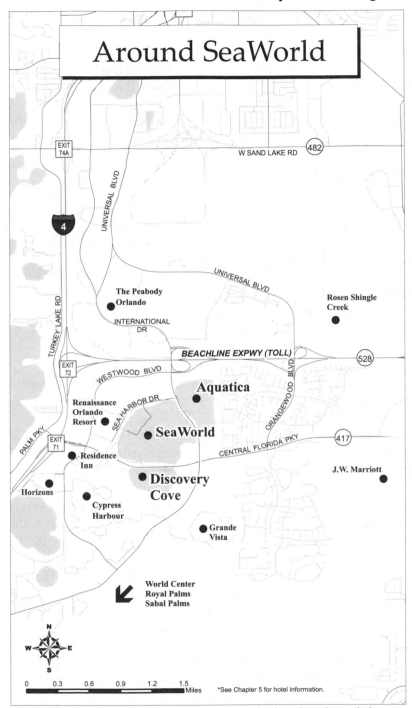

Around SeaWorld

Note: See *Chapter Five* for information on the hotels indicated above.

Note: There is no northbound reentry to I-4 at this exit.

From the north on I-4

Visitors approaching from the north (that is, traveling "west" on I-4), can take Exit 72 onto the Bee Line Expressway (State Route 528). This is a toll road, but you will be exiting before the first toll booth. Take the first exit, which loops around to International Drive. Turn left and follow the I-Drive directions above.

From the airport

If you have picked up your rental car at Orlando International Airport, take the north exit from the airport and get on State Route 528, the Bee Line Expressway, going west. You will pay a toll on this route, but it is modest. Get off at Exit 1, just before you reach Interstate 4. Turn left onto International Drive and follow the I-Drive directions from there.

The Tampa Parks

Directions to Busch Gardens Africa and Adventure Island are provided in *Chapters Six* and *Seven*, respectively.

Alternatives To Driving

Depending on where you are staying, it is possible to reach at least some of the Orlando parks without driving. The Renaissance Resort (described in *Chapter Five: Resort Hotels*) is just across the street from the entrance to SeaWorld, and a few other hotels are within reasonable walking distance. Walking to Aquatica from some of these hotels is also possible, but sidewalks are at a premium, and since you have to walk around to the other side of Aquatica to reach the main entrance, I can't wholeheartedly recommend this as an alternative. Reaching Discovery Cove on foot requires covering a greater distance and, since parking is included in the price of admission, there is no economic incentive to hoofing it.

If you are staying farther away, but still relatively close, look into shuttle service from your hotel. If it is available, shuttle service will most likely take you to SeaWorld but not to Aquatica or Discovery Cove. SeaWorld operates its own shuttle service to Aquatica (but not Discovery Cove). The service is typically **free** to guests, but some hotels may charge a small fee. In theory, you must be a guest of a participating hotel to use this service, but this is seldom if ever enforced. Hotels near a pickup point cheerfully send their guests next door to catch the shuttle. Shuttle service is usually limited to a few runs to the parks in the morning and another few return trips in the early evening

Unfortunately, information on routes, schedules, and which hotels are currently offering this service is hard to come by. The best bet is to ask the hotel you are planning to book whether they participate in the program.

If you are staying along the International Drive corridor, you can hop on the **I-Ride Trolley** to either SeaWorld or Aquatica (but, again, not Discovery Cove, although it gets close). The trolley is $1 for those 13 and older and 25 cents for those 65 and older. Kids 12 and under ride **free**. Exact change is required. All-day and multi-day passes, which are a good deal if you want to explore I-Drive, are available at many hotels and retail shops along I-Drive, but not on the trolleys. For more information, call toll-free (866) 243-7483 or view a route map on the Internet at www.iridetrolley.com.

You can also reach the parks via public transportation; Orlando's **Lynx buses** cost just $1.75 (85 cents for seniors 65 and older), exact change required. A weekly bus pass costs $12. Route 50 links Walt Disney World's Ticket and Transportation Center with SeaWorld and Route 43 links Universal Orlando and SeaWorld and continues on to the Florida Mall. For more information, call (407) 841-5969 or visit www.golynx.com on the Internet. On the web site you will be able to download maps of the routes that interest you; there is also a "Trip Planner" that lets you plot a route from anywhere in Orlando to SeaWorld, but I find it cumbersome to use and the results hard to decipher.

Otherwise, Mears Transportation offers walk up shuttle van service from the airport to hotels near SeaWorld for $28 round trip per person, $21 for children 4 to 11. No reservation is necessary. Taxi fare from the airport to these hotels runs roughly $30.

All of the above applies to the Orlando parks only. As for the Tampa parks, you pretty much have to drive, although a few modest hotels are within (long) walking distance of Busch Gardens. Details will be found in *Chapters Six* and *Seven*.

The Price of Admission

Five different parks are reviewed in this book and each offers a one-day admission option. If you are only visiting one park for one day, check the appropriate chapter for ticket information.

If you are planning on visiting more than one park during your Florida vacation (and if you are reading this book, you probably are) then your choices quickly become more complicated. At its simplest, the ticket you buy will be determined by the answers to two questions:

Which parks do you want to visit?

How long do you want to stay?

Multipark Tickets

If you are planning on being in central Florida for a week or less, then the "Length of Stay" ticket may be your best bet. You can create your own ticket by choosing up to three parks from the following four — SeaWorld, Aquatica, Busch Gardens Africa and Adventure Island. There is no option to include all four parks and some combinations (for example, Aquatica and Adventure Island or Busch Gardens and Aquatica) are not available.

These options allow for seven days of unlimited entry to the parks included on the ticket; parking is not included.

Here is what's currently on offer:

SeaWorld - Aquatica
Adults:	$95.80
Children (3 to 9):	$85.15

SeaWorld - Busch Gardens
Adults:	$106.45
Children (3 to 9):	$97.80

SeaWorld - Aquatica - Busch Gardens
Adults:	$143.72
Children (3 to 9):	$133.07

Busch Gardens - Adventure Island
Adults:	$85.15
Children (3 to 9):	$74.50

If you purchase on the Internet, you can get the adult ticket at the child's price. Each park's web site offers slightly different selections of ticket packages; for example, the Busch Gardens-Adventure Island option is only available on the Busch Gardens site. Use the URLs given above to get started; with a little poking around, you will find the order pages. Tickets can also be purchased at park gates and on the phone at (800) 327-2420 or (407) 363-2559.

Florida Resident Specials

If you are lucky enough to live in Florida (and can prove it with government-issued photo ID), the Worlds of Discovery parks have a very special deal for you. You can buy any of the multi-day tickets listed above, for the same price and on the same terms (that is, you can get the adult ticket at the kid's price online). But instead of seven days, you can return to the parks on your tickets as often as you like for the next year. Clearly Worlds of Discovery has recognized that folks who live within commuting distance of the parks will return again and again (and spend money on food, drink, and merchandise) if given sufficient incentive to do so. Florida resident deals are *not* available for the Orlando FlexTicket or the annual Passports discussed below.

The Orlando FlexTicket

If you will be in Florida for more than seven days, you may want to consider the Orlando FlexTicket. In fact, this can be a good choice even if you will be staying for a shorter visit, since it offers admission to some non-Worlds of Discovery parks as well.

Several of the non-Disney theme parks, namely Universal Orlando, SeaWorld, Aquatica, Wet 'n Wild, and Busch Gardens Africa, have banded together to offer multi-day, multi-park passes at an extremely attractive price. This option is called the Orlando FlexTicket and it works like this:

Five-Park, Fourteen-Day Orlando FlexTicket:

(Universal Studios Florida, Islands of Adventure, SeaWorld, Aquatica, Wet 'n Wild)

Adults:	$250.22
Children (3 to 9):	$207.62

Six-Park, Fourteen-Day Orlando FlexTicket:

(adds Busch Gardens Africa in Tampa)

Adults:	$298.14
Children (3 to 9):	$250.22

These passes are valid for fourteen *consecutive* days, beginning on the day you first use them. They offer unlimited visits to the parks they cover. As for parking, you pay at the first park you visit on any given day. Then show your parking ticket and Orlando FlexTicket at the other parks on the same day for complimentary parking. The six-park option includes free bus transportation from SeaWorld to Busch Gardens.

Remember, these tickets expire. That is, if you use an Orlando FlexTicket for only five days, you can't return a month later and use the remaining nine days. These passes offer excellent value for the dollar; the five-park adult pass works out to less than $18 a day if you use all 14 days! Even if you only stay a week, we're talking less than $36 a day. On top of that, they offer the come and go as you please convenience of Passports, albeit for a much shorter time. Passes may be purchased on the various Worlds of Discovery park web sites at any of the participating parks' ticket booths, or through your travel agent before coming.

Passports (a.k.a. Annual Passes)

If you are going to be in central Florida for an extended period of time or if you plan to visit several times within the next year or two, it may be worth your while to look into an annual pass. Worlds of Discovery calls its annual passes Passports. They are good for one year (Silver) or two years (Gold). Four parks are included in the Passport program: SeaWorld, Aquatica, Busch Gardens Africa (in Tampa), and Adventure Island (also in Tampa). You can "build" your own Passport to include one, two, three, or all four parks. However, some combinations are not available and, to further complicate matters, the price of combinations that include water parks differ according to *which* water park you choose. In the chart below, I try to sort it all out. Current pricing is as follows (including 6.5% tax):

	1 Year (Silver)	2 Years (Gold)
SW **or** BG	$106.44	$159.69
SW **and** BG	$170.34	$255.54
BG + AI	$170.35	$255.55
SW + Aq	$191.65	$287.50
SW+BG+AI	$212.95	$319.45
SW+BG+Aq	$234.25	$351.40
All 4 parks	$276.85	$415.30

(SW=SeaWorld, BG=Busch Gardens Africa, Aq=Aquatica, AI=Adventure Island)

Prices for children and seniors (65+) are $10 less than the adult price in each category. This pricing structure assumes that many people will want to use just one water park, presumably the one nearest to where they live; it also implies that Worlds of Discovery sees Aquatica as the superior of the two water parks, which may not be everyone's judgement. And, of course, these prices may change.

Passport holders enjoy a number of benefits. These include:
- Free parking.
- Modest discounts on guest tickets.
- A 10% discount on food and merchandise in the parks.
- Discounts on guided tours and other special park activities.
- 50% off preferred parking rates.
- Discounts on Discovery Cove admission.

Note: These perks apply only to those parks included in the Passport. If you drop in on another park for the day, your Passport won't work for parking or discounts.

Passports make sense for those who will be in Orlando more than once over the course of the Passport's term. If you take three one-week vacations in Orlando over the course of two years, the effective per day cost of a three-park Gold Passport is less than $15 a day!

The Platinum Passport

There is yet another Passport option that might appeal to some people depending, I suspect, on where they live and how widely they travel. The

Platinum Passport is valid for two years and costs $457.90 for adults, tax included. (Children 3 to 9 and seniors 65 years old and up get $10 off the pre-tax price.)

Although it is just some $43 more expensive than the two-year, four-park Passport mentioned above, it offers unlimited admission to *all ten* of the Worlds of Discovery parks across the country, including Busch Gardens Europe (Williamsburg, VA) and Sesame Place (Langhorne, PA). In addition, there are some nifty perks at the Orlando parks:

- Reserved seating at all SeaWorld shows.
- Reserved seating at Busch Gardens Africa's Moroccan Palace.
- "Ride again" privileges at SeaWorld's thrill rides and Busch Gardens Africa's roller coasters.

If these appeal and you are already considering the four-park, two-year Gold Passport, you might want to give the Platinum option a closer look.

EZ Pay

If you were tempted by those Passports, but hesitated at the price, perhaps EZ Pay will tip the scales. Opt for **EZ Pay** and you pay for your annual pass on a monthly basis, interest-free, over the life of the pass. Payments are charged to your credit card; no fees are added, just tax. With EZ Pay, a Platinum Passport is just $17.29 a month!

EZ Pay applies only to annual Passports and cannot be used to spread out payments for any other ticket options.

The Discovery Cove Ultimate Package

You will notice that Discovery Cove has been conspicuously absent from these various multi-day and Passport options. That's because the "special occasion" nature of a day at Discovery Cove does not lend itself to the come and go as you please model of multi-day or annual tickets.

Most people treat a visit to Discovery Cove as a separate item on their vacation menu, but the **Discovery Cove Ultimate** package is well worth considering if you'd like to visit other parks. For just $50 more than the cost of your day at Discovery Cove, you will receive a pass to visit SeaWorld, Aquatica, and Busch Gardens Africa for 14 consecutive days — that's well under $4 a day!

Even if you don't opt for this add-on, your admission to Discovery Cove comes with a pass for seven consecutive days at SeaWorld or Busch Gardens Africa, but not both. Full details will be found in *Chapter Three: Discovery Cove*.

Buying Tickets

Your best bet is to buy tickets on the Internet before you come to

Florida. Worlds of Discovery offers some attractive online-only ticket deals to encourage you to do just that, including adult tickets at child's prices and early admission to Aquatica.

At press time, all online ticketing options let you print out your ticket at home, ready to take to the park, but there are some subtle differences. If you purchase a single or multi-day ticket online, you can print out a ticket at home and head straight for the turnstile, where you will have to verify your identity.

If you purchased a Passport online, you can still print out a voucher, but when you arrive at the park, head for one of the electronic kiosks near the entrance. It will scan the bar code on your voucher and print out a ticket for you. If you opted for EZ Pay, you will have to stop into the office near the gate that handles annual passes.

Note: Everyone 16 years of age or older will be required to produce a photo ID when redeeming a voucher either at Guest Services or at the park turnstile.

If you prefer to have the tickets you bought online sent to you, UPS Ground shipping (6 to 8 business days in the U.S. only) is $5. Faster Fed-Ex shipping (3 to 4 business days) is available for $10, as is overseas delivery.

You can also buy tickets and Passports at the parks, in person or at one of the electronic kiosks. You will not get the online deals if you do. If you go this route, I suggest you buy your tickets on a day you won't be using them; that way, the time your spend purchasing your ticket won't cut into your park touring time.

If you use a travel agent, allow several weeks to receive your tickets. You can also visit your local AAA office if you are a member, or try the services of Ticketmania, described later.

Which Price Is Right?

This is an extremely difficult question to answer, given the number of variables and the wide variety of visitors, from families with several active kids to seniors. However, I will offer some observations, which I hope will be of assistance as you weigh your options.

If you are planning to visit Discovery Cove then I strongly recommend the **Discovery Cove Ultimate** option. For just $50 more you get 14 days at all the other Worlds of Discovery parks in central Florida, except Adventure Island. And since you'll be going to Aquatica, that shouldn't prove to be too much of a sacrifice.

If Discovery Cove doesn't fit into your budget, then a **multi-day ticket** that includes SeaWorld, Aquatica, and Busch Gardens Africa is the best option in my opinion. You have just seven days, but that gives you enough time to spend two days in each park with a seventh for a return visit to your favorite.

The **Orlando FlexTicket** is a good option for people who would like to include the razzle-dazzle of Universal Orlando in their vacation mix. It's more expensive, but it provides 14 days of fun for a per-day cost of roughly $18, which is a lot of entertainment bang for the buck.

Finally, the various **Passports** are worth considering if you will be spending more than one vacation in Florida over the next year or two. If you can use a three-park Silver Passport for two seven-day vacations, you not only save more than $50 over the cost of two seven-day "Length of Stay" tickets, but you get free parking and a 10% discount on food and merchandise thrown in.

Discounts

Getting a discount to the parks covered in this book is a good bit harder than it used to be, but it is still possible to save a few bucks. Here's how.

Order online. As noted earlier, if you order online at one of the Worlds of Discovery web sites, you can purchase some adult tickets at the child's price. This often represents a larger savings than you can get elsewhere.

AAA. Members of the American Automobile Association can buy their tickets through a local AAA club office, which will save between $3 and $10 depending on the park and the ticket packages and might vary from club to club. You can also use your card at the gate for a modest discount. AAA cards are not good for discounts at restaurants or shops inside the parks.

Coupons. The Orlando area is awash in throwaway publications aimed at the tourist trade. They all contain discount coupons for many attractions in the area, including the major theme parks. When coupons are available for these parks, which seems to be less and less these days, a typical discount is $2.50 off for each of up to six people. Discount coupons must be presented at the ticket windows at the parks and do not apply to Passports. If you can purchase your tickets online, you'll usually get a better deal than you would using a coupon.

Ticket Brokers. Another major source of discounts is ticket brokers. There are dozens of them scattered around the tourist areas, many of them located in hotel lobbies. Ticket brokers concentrate on the major attractions and the dinner shows that are an Orlando staple. Discounts for the major theme parks aren't as good as they used to be. At most you will be able to shave a few bucks off the price of admission. At worst, you will pay full price in exchange for the convenience of not waiting in a long ticket line at the parks.

One place worth checking out is the Official Visitors Center at 8723 International Drive, which is operated by the Orlando/Orange County Convention and Visitors Bureau and is about three miles north of SeaWorld. There you will find plenty of discount tickets, coupon books, and the free

Orlando Magicard, which offers a broad array of discounts at hotels, restaurants, and attractions.

Ticket brokers on the Internet. Ticket brokers are cropping up on the Internet. One of them, Ticketmania, offers SeaWorld, Aquatica, and Busch Gardens Africa tickets for about $5 off the gate price, depending on the pass. To this they add a $13 per order minimum shipping fee ($25 for delivery outside the United States), although from time to time they offer free shipping. Other options include picking up your tickets at their Orlando location (free) or having them delivered to your hotel (for a $10 fee). Usually, you can do better using the Worlds of Discovery sites given above and getting the online discount. The Ticketmania web site is www.ticketmania.com.

Vacation Packages. If you purchase a vacation package from your travel agent, one that includes airfare, hotel, and a rental car, as well as passes to the parks you are probably getting a very good buy on the tickets. If you are making SeaWorld and its sister parks the primary focus of your trip, these package deals offer excellent value and make a lot of sense. *Chapter Five* has more information about packages available from Marriott Hotels that include length of stay admission the Orlando parks.

Good Things To Know About

Here are some general notes that apply to all of the parks covered in this book. Notes that are specific to individual parks are included in appropriate chapter.

All Day Dining Deal

In the summer of 2008, SeaWorld, Aquatica, and Busch Gardens Africa tested a dining program that lets you eat as often as you want at a selection of park restaurants for a single price ($26 for adults, $12 for kids). Participants are fitted with an identifying bracelet that entitles them to one entree, one side dish, and on soft drink each time through the line. The restaurants included in the deal are all cafeteria-style eateries that don't open until 10:00 a.m. or 11:00 a.m. (so that early breakfast is out). Still, the selection of restaurants is generous (all the eateries at Aquatica are included, for example) and only a few food items like baby back ribs are excluded. If you eat two meals, the program should pay for itself. And as I read the rules, you can go back for seconds (and thirds) on dessert. Eat your heart out, Jenny Craig!

Drinking

The legal drinking age in Florida is 21 and is strictly enforced. If you are asked to present ID, try to feel flattered rather than annoyed.

Leaving the Parks

All the parks allow you to leave and return on the same day. Unless you have a Passport (an annual pass), you will need to get your hand stamped to facilitate your reentry. At Discovery Cove, the laminated ID tag you are issued will identify you for readmission.

Money

Major credit cards are accepted at all parks, everywhere but at the smallest outdoor snack stands. Likewise, all parks thoughtfully provide ATMs (with hefty fees) just in case you run out of cash.

Pets

Both SeaWorld and Busch Gardens Africa provide a Pet Care Center located near the main entrance. These simple facilities charges $6 per pet ($5 for Passport holders). They provide water; you provide food. If your pet needs walking during the day, that is your responsibility. In Orlando, visitors to Discovery Cove and Aquatica can leave their pets at SeaWorld; in Tampa, visitors to Adventure Island can use the Busch Gardens Africa facility.

Smoking

Florida state law prohibits smoking in all restaurants. Smoking is also not permitted in attraction lines or within the attractions themselves. Moreover, the parks restrict smoking even outdoors, providing designated areas in which smokers are permitted to light up.

A Note on Costs

Let's face it, visiting a theme park resort destination is not precisely a budget vacation, and the Worlds of Discovery parks are no exception. Of course, compared to other forms of entertainment, theme parks offer excellent value for the dollar, as most people will agree.

Nonetheless, most of us must keep an eye on how much money we are spending, so throughout the book I have tried to give you a quick idea of how much things like restaurants and hotels cost using dollar signs.

For restaurants, I have tried to estimate the cost of an average meal, without alcoholic beverages. In the case of full-service restaurants, I have based my estimate on a "full" meal consisting of an appetizer or salad, an entree, and dessert. In *Chapter Five: Resort Hotels*, I cover a number of upscale Orlando hotels in some depth, but I also include more moderate options that are convenient to the parks. For those hotels, I have tried to estimate the cost of one night's stay in a double room. The cost rankings are as follows:

	Restaurants	**Hotels**
$	Under $15	Under $100
$$	$15 – $25	$100 – $150
$$$	$25 – $40	$150 – $200
$$$$	Over $40	Over $200

Accuracy and Other Impossible Dreams

While I have tried to be as accurate, comprehensive, and up-to-date as possible, these are all unattainable goals. Any theme park worth its salt is constantly changing and upgrading its attractions. Restaurants change their menus; shops revamp their choice of merchandise with the seasons and even the theme of the shop itself.

In fact, as this book goes to press, there was some talk that Worlds of Discovery might be sold. If so, some references to the parks' current owner, Anheuser-Busch, may be obsolete by the time you read this.

What are most likely to change, alas, are prices. Like any business, Worlds of Discovery reserves the right to change its prices at any time without notice, so it's possible that prices will be revised after the deadline for this book. If you do run into price increases, they will typically be modest.

The Intrepid Traveler, the publisher of this book, maintains an entire web site with updated information about all non-Disney attractions in the Orlando area. Log on to the blog for the latest on prices and new rides and attractions:

http://www.TheOtherOrlando.com/blog

The SeaWorld lighthouse

Above: Every bit as scary as it looks. (Kraken)

Right:Like they say, you _will_ get wet! (Journey to Atlantis)

Below left: Here be puffins. (Penguin Encounter)

Below right: Gourmet dining (Sharks Underwater Grill)

Above: "I'm a Clydesdale. I'm a Clydesdale."
(Clydesdale Hamlet)

Left: Pearl divers on display.
(The Waterfront)

Below: Tourists aren't the only ones who need a break.
(Pacific Point Preserve)

Above Left: Swimming with Shamu. (Believe at Shamu Stadium)

Above Right: Street performers keep thing hoppin'.

Below: Another way to ride Shamu. (Shamu Express)

Cirque du Soleil meets Flipper.
(Blue Horizons at Key West Dolphin Stadium)

Chapter Two:

SeaWorld

"I'VE BEEN TO DISNEY," PEOPLE WILL TELL YOU, "BUT Y'KNOW WHAT I THINK is the best thing they've got down there in Orlando? SeaWorld!" I heard it over and over again. In a way this reaction was somewhat surprising. After all, compared to the Magic Kingdom or Universal, SeaWorld is downright modest, with only a smattering of thrill rides.

Of course, this "I-liked-SeaWorld-best" attitude may be one-upmanship — that quirk of human nature that makes us want to look superior. After all, SeaWorld is educational and how much more flattering it is to depict yourself as someone who prefers educational nature shows to mindless carnival rides that merely provide "fun." I'm just enough of a cynic about human nature to give some credence to this theory.

However, I think the real reason lies elsewhere. No matter how well imagined and perfectly realized the attractions at Universal or Disney might be, the wonders on display at SeaWorld were produced by a creative intelligence of an altogether higher order. The animated robotics guys can tinker all they want and the bean-counters in Hollywood can give them ever higher budgets and they still will never produce anything that can match the awe generated by a killer whale soaring 30 feet in the air with his human trainer perched on his snout. No matter how much we are entertained by Universal and Disney, at SeaWorld we cannot help but be reminded, however subliminally, that there are wonders in our world that humankind simply cannot duplicate, let alone surpass.

It's a feeling of which many visitors probably aren't consciously aware. Even if they are, they'd probably feel a little awkward trying to express it. But I am convinced it is there for everyone — believer, agnostic, or atheist. It's the core experience that makes SeaWorld so popular; it's the reason people will tell you they liked SeaWorld best of all. To paraphrase Joyce Kilmer's magnificent cliché about human inadequacy,

> *I think that Walt will never do*
> *A wonder greater than Shamu.*

Before You Come

You can get up-to-date information on hours and prices by calling (407) 351-3600 and pressing "2." Between 8:00 a.m. and 8:00 p.m., you can speak to a SeaWorld representative at this number.

For the latest on SeaWorld's animals, you can check out the Anheuser-Busch Adventure Parks animal information site on the World Wide Web. The address is www.seaworld.org. For Shamu fans the site to check out is www.shamu.com. Yet another web site provides information for both SeaWorld Orlando and its sister park, Busch Gardens Africa. The address is www.4adventure.com.

When's the Best Time to Come?

This is a tough call. Many people like to come to Orlando when the tourist traffic is thinner (see *Chapter One*), but SeaWorld stays open later and adds extra evening shows during the summer months and over Christmas. Some of them are terrific and it would be a shame to miss them. Even at the height of summer the crowds at SeaWorld are quite manageable compared to those you'll encounter at, say, Disney. Crowds in January are negligible and the weather cool to moderate, perfect viewing conditions for the outdoor shows, although it can get quite chilly.

Even if you come when the parks are open late, I would recommend arriving early and planning to stay until the park closes. There are two reasons for this. Early arrivals breeze right in; as the morning wears on, the lines at the attractions lengthen. As for staying until the bitter end, all of the added summer shows are performed in the hour or two just before closing. Compensate for the long day with a leisurely lunch.

Getting There

SeaWorld is located just off I-4 on Central Florida Parkway. If you're coming from the south (i.e. traveling east on I-4) you will use Exit 71 and find yourself pointed directly towards the SeaWorld entrance, about half a mile along on your left. Because there is no exit directly to Central Florida Parkway from Westbound I-4, those coming from the north (i.e. traveling west on I-4) must get off at Exit 72, onto the Bee Line Expressway (Route 528). Don't worry about the sign that says it's a toll road; you won't have to pay one. Take the first exit and loop around to International Drive. Turn left and proceed to Central Florida Parkway and turn right. It's all very clearly marked. This route, by the way, offers a nice backstage peek at *Kraken*, Sea-World's roller coaster. As you get close to SeaWorld, tune your AM radio to 1540 for a steady stream of information about the park. This will help while away the time spent waiting in line at the parking lot.

Arriving at SeaWorld

Parking fees are $10 for cars and $12 for RVs and trailers and are collected at toll booths at the entrance. If you'd like to park close to the front entrance, you can opt for Shamu's Preferred Parking, available for cars only, for $15. Annual passholders pay nothing for regular parking and pay $7 for preferred parking.

Handicapped Parking. Several rows of extra large spaces near the main entrance are provided for the convenience of handicapped visitors. Alert the attendant to your need for handicapped parking and you will be directed accordingly.

Valet Parking. At press time, SeaWorld was experimenting with valet parking. They were testing charges of $20 and $25.

The SeaWorld parking lot is divided into sections, and you will be ushered to your space in a very efficiently controlled manner. While the lot is not huge, it's still a very good idea to make a note of which lettered section and numbered row you're parked in. If you are parked any distance from the entrance, you may be directed to a tram that will whisk you to the main entrance, although trams don't run as often as they used to. If you arrive after noon, however, you may find yourself on your own. Fortunately, the farthest row is never too far from the park perimeter. You can orient yourself by looking for the centrally located *Sky Tower;* it's the blue spire with the large American flag at the summit.

Once you reach the beautifully designed main entrance, you will find a group of thoughtfully shaded ticket booths where you will purchase your admission. To the left of the ticket windows are the Guest Relations window and the annual pass center. Once inside the park, walk straight ahead to the Information Desk. There you can pick up a large map of the park. On the back you will find a schedule of the day's shows as well as information on any special events happening that day.

Opening and Closing Times

SeaWorld operates seven days a week, 365 days a year. The park opens at 9:00 a.m. and remains open until 6:00, 7:00, 8:00, 9:00, 10:00, or 11:00 p.m. — or even until 1:00 a.m. — depending on the time of year. Unlike Universal and Disney, SeaWorld does not practice soft openings (admitting guests early). During very busy periods, they will start admitting people at 8:30, but these early arrivals are held in the Entrance Plaza (or "mall") just inside the gates, until the park proper opens at 9:00. By the time the last scheduled shows are starting (about 45 minutes to an hour prior to the posted closing time), most of the park's other attractions have either shut down or are in the process of doing so.

One-Day Admission

SeaWorld has several ticket options, including some that offer admission to its sister park, Busch Gardens, in nearby Tampa. Most visitors will be looking at either a one-day admission or the Orlando FlexTicket. At press time, one-day admission prices (including sales tax) were as follows:

One-Day Admission:

Adults:	$65.97
Children (3 to 9):	$54.20

Children under age 3 are admitted **free**.

Value Ticket:

(One day each at SeaWorld and Busch Gardens Africa.)

Adults:	$106.45
Children & Seniors:	$95.80

Adults pay the same price as children when ordering either one-day or value tickets online seven days in advance. Special deals for Florida residents are announced on the web site.

Information on "Length of Stay" tickets, which combine two or more parks; the Orlando FlexTicket, which includes five or six parks; and "Passports" (annual passes), which also offer access to multiple parks, will be found in *Chapter One: Dive Right In!*

The Discovery Cove Option

If you are also planning to visit Discovery Cove (described in *Chapter Three*), be aware that your admission fee there includes a seven-day pass to SeaWorld (or Busch Gardens Africa, if you prefer). The pass is valid for seven consecutive days, starting the day of your first visit, and can be activated either before or after your Discovery Cove visit. To get the pass, stop into Guest Relations and show your Discovery Cove confirmation letter. You will be issued a nontransferable credit-card-sized pass. You may be required to produce a photo ID each time you enter the park using this pass.

Adventure Express

For those short on time and long on cash, SeaWorld offers a guided six-hour VIP touring option that guarantees you will hit the highlights and be treated like a celebrity along the way. You'll get to feed stingrays, dolphins, and sea lions and pet a Magellanic penguin. You will also be given reserved seats at the Shamu show, which means very good seats indeed. Similar preferred seating is offered at either the sea lion or dolphin show, depending on scheduling on the day of your visit. Guests on the Adventure Express who meet the minimum height requirements (see ride reviews, below) also get one-time front of the line privileges at the big thrill rides, *Kraken, Journey to Atlantis*, and *Wild Arctic*.

None of this comes cheap. The cost is $89 for adults and $79 for children 3 to 9 (younger children tour free) — and that's in addition to the regular price of admission! At least tax and lunch with a choice of sandwich, salad, dessert, and soft drink are included in these prices. There are only 16 spaces available for the Adventure Express, so you may want to reserve a spot by calling (800) 327-2244. Tours leave at varying times in the late morning; there may just be one tour a day during slower periods and as many as four or five during the busier tourist seasons.

If that's not exclusive enough, you can opt for a private version of Adventure Express, dubbed Elite Adventure Express. This private tour offers the same privileges, but is limited exclusively to your party. The tab is $1,100 including tax and lunch for up to 12 guests, plus the regular one-day admission. Book at least two weeks ahead for the Elite Express at (866) 781-1333.

Eating at SeaWorld

Dining at SeaWorld is almost entirely of the fast-food and cafeteria variety, a lot of it quite good. There is only one full-service restaurant, **Sharks Underwater Grill**, but it is a winner. I review all the restaurants a little later. SeaWorld also offers a number of what might be called "dinner shows," including a Polynesian luau. They are reviewed in a separate section near the end of the chapter.

There is beer to be had at most eateries, as you might expect at a park owned by Anheuser-Busch. In fact, there is precious little else on offer. If you have a hankering for a glass of wine or a mixed drink, you'll have to head for the Sharks Underwater Grill.

You can also get great desserts here. They're made right on the premises and most of the casual eateries offer them. I especially recommend the chocolate cherry and carrot cakes, but those whose taste runs to fruit for dessert won't be disappointed. Fresh strawberries are readily available.

Virtually every cafeteria style restaurant offers a moderately priced (under $10) "Kid's Meal." The main component varies from place to place, but the selection leans heavily to hot dogs and chicken fingers. Kids Meals are served in a reusable Shamu souvenir lunchbox.

SeaWorld lets you eat while waiting for or watching the big outdoor stadium shows; there are even snack bars (offering ice cream bars and nachos) conveniently located near the entrances to the stands, but I've seen people bringing in trays from restaurants some distance away. Not all eating establishments are open throughout the park's operating hours. A "Dining Guide," listing the various restaurants and their operating hours, is available at the Information Desk in the Entrance Plaza.

Shopping at SeaWorld

Of course, SeaWorld is dotted with strategically located gift and souvenir shops ready to help you lessen the heavy load in your wallet. The merchandise in the various shops, not to mention the shops themselves, change with such regularity that SeaWorld has given up on listing them on the park map. So rather than attempt a shop-by-shop or section-by-section description, I will touch on the overall shopping scene here and call out a few shops that I feel are deserving of special note.

Most of the wares on display are of the standard tourist variety but some items deserve special mention. Many of SeaWorld's shops offer some very attractive figurines and small sculptures. They range from quite small objects suitable for a bric-a-brac shelf to fairly large pieces (with fairly large price tags) that are surely displayed with pride by those who buy them. Prices range from under $20 to well over $2,000. If you're in the market for a special gift or are a collector yourself, you will want to give these items more than a cursory look. Among the shops to seek out for these art objects are **Shamu's Emporium** in the main entrance plaza and **Under the Sun** and **Artisan's Hall** in the Waterfront.

Another, more affordable souvenir is a Shamu-themed beach towel (which can come in handy after sitting in the splash zone at Shamu Stadium!) or one of the many plush dolls for kids, many of which are irresistible. The animals you will encounter depend on which attraction you've just exited, each of which seems to have its own gift shop. My personal favorites are the polar bears and baby seals in the **Arctic Shop** at the exit to *Wild Arctic*.

The shops in the **Waterfront** section, that flow one into another, offer some very nice clothing items. Most of it is for women, but men might score a good quality Hawaiian-style shirt. Also in these shops is a constantly changing variety of decorative items for the home that might make good gifts for you or someone you love.

A shop that will draw the curious as well as shoppers is **The Oyster's Secret**. Here you can watch through underwater windows as divers plunge downwards in search of pearl-bearing oysters. And if you decide to buy one and want it placed in a custom setting, you will be accommodated. There is also a good selection of pearl jewelry. Some of it quite expensive, but the small, irregular shaped fresh water pearls worked into intricate necklaces are both attractive and affordable.

Most of the shops offer a free package pick-up service that lets you collect your purchases near the front entrance on your way out, so you needn't worry about lugging things about for half the day. Inveterate shoppers can soothe their conscience with the thought that a percentage of the money they drop at SeaWorld goes towards helping rescue and care for stranded sea mammals.

Good Things to Know About ...

See the *Good Things to Know About ...* section in *Chapter One* for notes that apply to all the parks. These notes apply specifically to SeaWorld.

Access for the Disabled

All parts of SeaWorld are accessible to disabled guests and all the stadium shows have sections set aside for those in wheelchairs. These are some of the best seats in the house. Wheelchairs are available for rent at $10 per day. Electric carts are $38 per day.

Babies

Little ones under three are admitted free and strollers are available for rent if you don't have your own. Single strollers are $10 for the day, double strollers are $17. There are also diaper changing stations in all the major restrooms (men's and women's). In addition, there are "non-gender changing areas" at *Wild Arctic*, the Friends of the Wild shop, and the *Anheuser-Busch Hospitality Center* where you will find diaper vending machines. There are nursing areas near the Friends of the Wild shop and at the Baby Care station near *Shamu's Happy Harbor*, where you can also buy a limited menu of baby food and baby care products.

Education Staff

It's hard to say too much in praise of the education staff at SeaWorld. There are some 100 employees whose job it is to hang around and answer your questions. They are invariably friendly, enthusiastic, and more than happy to share their considerable knowledge with you. Don't be shy. Taking advantage of this wonderful human resource will immeasurably increase the enjoyment and value of your visit to SeaWorld. Just look for the word "Education" on the employee's name tag. In fact, even employees who are not with the Education Department will likely have the answer to your question.

Emergencies

As a general rule, the moment something goes amiss speak with the nearest SeaWorld employee. They will contact security or medical assistance and get the ball rolling towards a solution. There is a first aid station in a tent behind *Stingray Lagoon* in the North End of the park and another near *Shamu's Happy Harbor* in the South End.

Feeding Times

Feeding time is an especially interesting time to visit any of the aquatic habitats. Unfortunately, there is no rigid schedule. By varying feeding times, the trainers more closely approximate the animals' experience in the wild and avoid, to some extent, the repetitive behaviors that characterize many animals in captivity. However, you can simply ask one of the education staff at the exhibit when the animals will next be fed. If your schedule permits, I would recommend returning for this enjoyable spectacle.

Of course, at some exhibits — the dolphins, stingrays, and sea lions — you can feed the animals yourself — for a fee!

Kids' ID System

SeaWorld may be less crowded than Disney World, but it's still remarkably easy to lose track of your little ones here. Stop by Guest Services to pick up wristbands for your young children -- Guest Services will label them with your name and cell phone number so staff members can easily get hold of you if they encounter your child on the loose. Wristbands are available free of charge, and are uniquely numbered, so that even if the writing on the wristband smears, they can still use this number to look up your information back at Guest Services, should the need arise.

Lockers

Lockers are available just outside the main entrance and in the Entrance Plaza across from Cypress Bakery. The fee is $1 for small lockers, $1.50 for large (quarters only). Once you open your locker, you will have to insert another four or six quarters to lock it again. A change machine is located in the Entrance Plaza locker area. Lockers are also available near the thrill rides *Kraken* and *Journey to Atlantis*.

Shamu's Smartguide

If the paper park map is too 20th century for you, rent Shamu's SMARTGUIDE for $18 (plus tax) for a more 21st century approach to getting around. It's a GPS gadget with a big screen that serves up an interactive version of the park map along with information about whatever you happen to be near at the time. It also provides some park discounts.

Special Diets

Vegetarians can stop at the Information Desk and request the Food Services staff's list of meatless dishes and the restaurants that serve them. Similar lists of seafood and low-fat selections and other dietary notes are available from the same source.

Splash Zones

All of the stadium shows give the adventuresome the opportunity to get wet — in some cases very wet. One advantage of the splash zones is that they are some of the best seats at SeaWorld. But the threat is very, very real.

I am a believer in splash zones for those who come prepared. Those inexpensive rain ponchos that are sold at every major park will hold the damage to a minimum (although there is probably no real way to guard against a direct hit from Shamu!). Kids, especially young boys, will enjoy the exquisite machismo of getting thoroughly soaked.

One word of warning: In the cooler periods of the year, a full soaking will be extremely uncomfortable, and may be courting a cold, or worse. Bring a big towel and a change of clothes, or be prepared to shell out for new duds at the SeaWorld shops.

Sailing the Sea: Your Day at SeaWorld

SeaWorld can be seen quite comfortably in a single day, without rushing madly around or otherwise driving yourself crazy. This is especially true if you've arrived during one of Orlando's slack periods or if you will be forgoing the thrill rides. But even during the most crowded times, SeaWorld is still more manageable than other parks in the area.

SeaWorld is not a large park, but its comfortable layout and the large Bayside Lagoon at its center make it seem larger than it is. Much of the North End of the park is lushly landscaped with large shady trees and bird-filled pools along the walkways. The South End, on the other side of the Lagoon, is open and airy with a gently rolling landscape. In look and feel, it is quite a contrast to the more tightly crammed spaces of the Magic Kingdom and Universal Orlando. Many parts of SeaWorld have the feel of a particularly gracious public park or botanical garden.

One of SeaWorld's key differentiators is the fact that the vast majority of its attractions are either shows that take place in large, sometimes huge, outdoor auditoriums or "continuous viewing" exhibits through which people pass pretty much at their own pace. My observation is that most people pass through pretty quickly so even if there's a line, the wait won't be unbearable. Once inside you can take your own sweet time. Here, briefly, are the different kinds of attractions at SeaWorld:

Rides. There are just four "rides" at SeaWorld but they are doozies.

Outdoor Auditorium Shows. These are SeaWorld's primo attractions — Shamu, the sea lions, the dolphins, and some lesser events. There are plenty of shaded seats for these shows (anywhere from 2,400 to 5,500), but even in slower periods they fill up, which should tell you something about how good the shows are. It is possible to enter these auditoriums after the show has begun if they are not full.

Indoor Theater Shows. Some shows take place indoors, in darkened air-conditioned theaters. None of them involves sea mammals and none of them falls into the must-see category. When these shows begin, the doors close and latecomers must wait for the next performance. Be aware that it is difficult to leave these shows in the middle.

Seasonal Shows. Some shows are only put on when the park is open late, which means summer and Christmas. They are designed for twilight or after dark viewing and thus run only in the hours just before park close. I have called these shows out in the reviews in this chapter.

Aquatic Habitats. This is SeaWorld's term for its continuous viewing exhibits of live marine animals. The habitats range from huge tanks like those you may have seen at aquariums to elaborate stage sets the likes of which I can almost guarantee you've never seen before.

Guided Tours. These are small group experiences that operate on a limited schedule and charge a moderate additional fee. They offer unique access to SeaWorld's "backstage" areas and a chance to learn a bit more about some of the park's most interesting inhabitants.

Catch of the Day

If you had very little time to spend at SeaWorld, I would venture to suggest that you could see just a handful of attractions and still feel you got your money's worth — if you picked the right ones. Here, then, is my list of the very best that SeaWorld has to offer:

The three major open-air animal shows — **Believe**, **Clyde & Seamore**, and **Blue Horizons** — are the heart and soul of SeaWorld. Anyone missing these should have his or her head examined.

Close behind are the major "aquatic habitats" — **Wild Arctic** (and the ride that introduces the experience), **Shark Encounter**, **Key West at Sea-**

World, and **Manatee Rescue.** I have omitted **Pacific Point Preserve** and **Penguin Encounter** (both marvelous) only because you are likely to see their close equivalents elsewhere.

If you have the time, the **Pets Ahoy** and **Odyssea** shows are very entertaining and hold up to repeat viewing. Finally, for thrill seekers, there are the stupendous roller coasters, **Kraken** and **Manta**.

The One-Day Stay

1. Get up early, but not as early as you would if you were heading for Disney or Universal. Remember, when SeaWorld says the park proper opens at 9:00, it means it. Get there a little earlier perhaps (you can get a bite to eat or browse the shops in the Entrance Plaza starting at 8:30 a.m.), but there's no need to kill yourself.

2. After purchasing your tickets and entering the park, thrill seekers and ride freaks should head immediately to *Manta*, followed by *Kraken* and *Journey to Atlantis*. (Bear left after the entrance mall and follow the signs and the running kids.) Then plan on doing *Wild Arctic* and its exciting ride later in the day, preferably during a Shamu show when the lines for *Wild Arctic* tend to thin out.

If, for one reason or another you are taking a pass on the thrill rides, proceed immediately to *Wild Arctic*. (Just keep bearing right until you see the Lagoon and circle it in a counterclockwise direction.) If you're not interested in taking the ride, the line for the stationary version is always a good deal shorter, so coming later may be okay. Also, if you'd like to skip the ride portion altogether, it is possible to slip quietly in through the exit in the gift shop and just see the animals.

3. Now's the time to review the schedule printed on the back of the map you got when you entered. First, check the times of the "big three" shows — *Believe, Clyde & Seamore,* and *Blue Horizons.* Whatever you do, don't miss these. Don't try to see two shows that start less than an hour apart. Yes, it can be done but you will be making sacrifices.

Instead, schedule your day so you can arrive at the stadium about 20 minutes before show time, perhaps longer during busier seasons. That way you can get a good seat, like dead center for *Believe* or in a splash zone for the kids. There is almost always some sort of pre-show entertainment starting 10 or 15 minutes before the show. It's always fun and, in the case of the warm-up to the sea lion show, often hilarious.

4. Use your time between shows to visit the aquatic habitats. Use the descriptions in the next section and geographical proximity to guide your choices. For example, you can leave the dolphin show and go right into the manatee exhibit. Or you can visit the penguins just before seeing *Clyde &*

Seamore and visit *Shark Encounter* immediately after.

5. If you have kids with you, you will miss *Shamu's Happy Harbor* at your peril. Adults, of course, can give it a miss.

6. Fill in the rest of the day with the lesser attractions or return visits to habitats you particularly enjoyed. In my opinion, several of the non–animal shows and attractions can be missed altogether with little sacrifice. If your time is really limited (e.g. you got to the park late), I strongly urge you to take my advice. You can always come back another day and prove me wrong.

7. If you stay until the end, as I recommend, you will not want to miss *Sea Lions Tonight* and *Shamu Rocks* (if they're playing during your visit).

This plan should allow you to see everything you truly want to see in one day and maybe even some attractions you wished you hadn't bothered with.

The Two-Day Stay

If you have the luxury of spending two or more days visiting SeaWorld (Discovery Cove visitors and Passport holders take note), I would recommend relaxing your pace, perhaps leaving the park early on one day to freshen up and catch a dinner show elsewhere. With two days, even a very relaxed pace should allow you to see everything in the park, several of them more than once.

Another strategy to adopt is to use the first day to concentrate on the shows and the second day to concentrate on the rides, the animal habitats and, perhaps, take a guided tour or two.

THE NORTH END

SeaWorld is not neatly divided into "lands" like some other theme parks I might mention (although Key West and the Waterfront are a step in that direction). However, a convenient division of the park is provided by Bayside Lagoon. If you look at the map you collected on arriving at the park, you will notice that the vertical line formed by the *Sky Tower* effectively divides the park in two: the larger northern side ("The North End") is to the left of the Tower; the southern side including most of the Lagoon ("The South End") is to the right. In this chapter I have adopted this North End/South End division. Please remember that this is my terminology and not SeaWorld's. If you stop a SeaWorld employee and ask, "How do I get to the North?" you may be told to get on a plane and fly to Philadelphia.

The layout and open landscaping of the southern half, combined with the sheer size of the stadiums located there, make getting your bearings relatively easy. In the northern half, however, the layout and lusher landscaping, while pleasing to the eye, can be confusing. When traveling from Point A to

Point B in the northern half of the park, use the map to get you started in the right general direction. Then rely on the directional signs, which are posted at nearly every turning, to guide you to your destination.

I begin with the northern half of the park for the simple reason that this is where you enter the park past the Shamu lighthouse in the artificial harbor that graces the airy entrance area. I describe the attractions in geographical, rather than thematic order, starting with *The Waterfront*. From there I proceed in a roughly clockwise direction, returning full-circle to *The Waterfront* and the fabulous *Pets Ahoy* show located there.

The Waterfront

Rating:	★ ★ ★
Type:	Themed shopping and dining venue
Time:	Continuous viewing
Kelly says:	Lovely to look at

Although it is home to two major attractions — *Sky Tower* and *Pets Ahoy*, *The Waterfront* is primarily a place to dine, stroll, and shop. Themed beautifully as a fantasy Mediterranean seaside village esplanade, this area is the gateway to the sole walkway across Bayside Lagoon to the southern end of the park.

The Waterfront is home to three large restaurants, **Voyagers Wood Fired Pizza**, **Seafire Grill** and **The Spice Mill.** All are cafeteria style, all are moderately priced, and all are reviewed a little later.

Between these lies a series of shops offering some of the nicest merchandise in SeaWorld. Each has its own entrance but they are all linked inside, making for seamless, not to mention cool, shopping. Outside is the esplanade, dotted with coffee stands and snack kiosks and the setting for periodic street shows. On the lower level is a children's water play area and a sea wall where waves crash every few minutes, soaking the delighted kids who gather there precisely for that reason.

Just off shore, on a tiny island at the base of the *Sky Tower*, is the **Sand Bar**, an outdoor bar and one of the nicest places in Orlando to sip a beer al fresco.

Sky Tower

Rating:	★ ★ ★
Type:	Bird's-eye view of Orlando
Time:	Six and half minutes
Kelly says:	For those who've seen everything else they want to see at SeaWorld

Riding the *Sky Tower* will set you back an additional $3, unless you have an annual pass, in which case it's free. You'll have to decide whether the

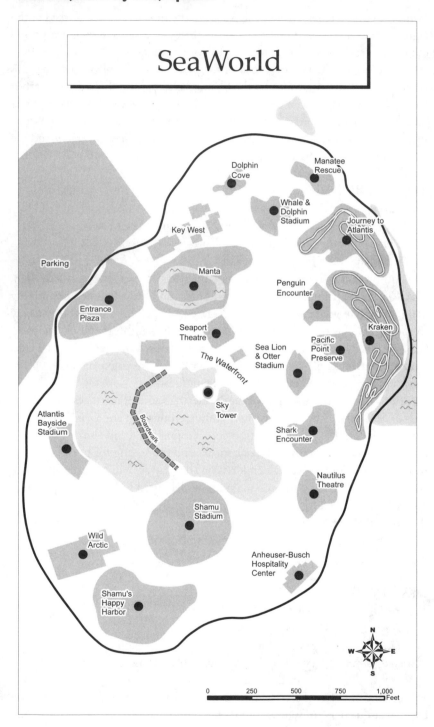

SeaWorld

Parking

Dolphin Cove

Manatee Rescue

Whale & Dolphin Stadium

Key West

Journey to Atlantis

Manta

Penguin Encounter

Entrance Plaza

Seaport Theatre

Kraken

Sea Lion & Otter Stadium

Pacific Point Preserve

The Waterfront

Boardwalk

Sky Tower

Atlantis Bayside Stadium

Shark Encounter

Nautilus Theatre

Shamu Stadium

Wild Arctic

Anheuser-Busch Hospitality Center

Shamu's Happy Harbor

0   250   500   750   1,000 Feet

six-and-a-half-minute glimpse of Orlando from on high is worth the extra charge. I regularly see people answering that question in the negative.

The *Sky Tower* is a circular viewing platform that rotates slowly while rising from lagoon level to a height of 400 feet. From there you can see the dome of *Spaceship Earth* at Epcot and *Space Mountain* at the Magic Kingdom, as well as some of the Orlando area's other high-rise buildings. Closer by, you will get a superb view of the layout of *Kraken* and, across the street, Aquatica. If your timing is right you will get to see a load of terrified riders make a complete circuit on the awesome coaster.

There are two levels, each offering a single row of glassed-in seating that circles the capsule. You pick the level of your choice as you enter. The upper level would seem the better choice, and most people head that way, but it only gives you a 10-foot height advantage that doesn't really affect your enjoyment of the experience.

Riding the *Sky Tower* is an enjoyable enough way to kill some time if you aren't eager to see anything else and don't mind paying the extra charge. Seeing SeaWorld from the air can be fascinating. You will also gain an appreciation for the cunning way the park is laid out and see why you've been having difficulty navigating from place to place in the North End.

The *Sky Tower* ride is at the mercy of the elements. Any hint of lightning in the area closes it down, as do high winds, which might buffet the top of the tower even when it's perfectly calm on the ground.

Pets Ahoy (at Seaport Theatre)

Rating: ★ ★ ★ ★
Type: Indoor theater show
Time: 25 minutes
Kelly says: A must for pet lovers

If you saw *Animal Actors* at Universal Studios Florida, you might be tempted to skip this one. However, if you are a pet lover, you'll want to put this charming show on your list. It offers a pleasant break from the hot Florida sun.

The SeaWorld twist here is that almost all the animals in the show were found in Central Florida animal shelters and rescued from an uncertain fate. As a result, the cast list runs heavily to cats and dogs, although there is an amusing pig, a skunk, and even a mouse.

Ace trainer Joel Slaven (of *Ace Ventura: Pet Detective* fame) has done an amazing job here, especially with the cats. Not only do Slaven's pussycats do every doggie trick and do them better but there is a cat who does a tightwire act and one who bounds over the heads of the audience, jumping from one tiny platform to another.

Abby and Elmo's Treasure Hunt (Seasonal)

Rating: ★ ★ ★
Type: Indoor theater show
Time: 25 minutes
Kelly says: Strictly for tots

During the summer months, the characters from Sesame Place, a Worlds of Discovery sister park in Pennsylvania, come south to entertain the hordes of kids in Orlando at the Seaport Theatre. There are typically three shows a day, in the morning and very early afternoon.

This one promotes reading with a silly story about finding clues to a riddle that will allow Elmo, Abby, Rosita, Grover and Cookie Monster to open a talking trunk filled with kids' books. There's plenty of loud music and the characters run into the audience, much to the delight of their tiny fans.

Entertainment at The Waterfront

Rating: ★ ★ ★
Type: Indoor and outdoor acts
Time: Irregular and unpredictable
Kelly says: Pleasant enough

There is a regular and ever-changing menu of entertainment on tap in and around the Waterfront. Some of the entertainment takes the form of street acts that could be animal show and tell, strolling musicians, or cut-up physical comedy. Fairly typical is **Groove Chefs**, an act that has shown some staying power. Three young guys, who are ostensibly chefs at the nearby Seafire Grill, take a break with garbage cans, pots, pans, and drumsticks and rustle up a rhythmic ragout that is sure to get your toes tapping. The rhythms are intricate, the footwork fancy, and the variety of sounds that emerge from their oddball collection of implements quite amusing.

There's indoor entertainment, too, on the stage in the back room of the Seafire Grill. The acts that appear here are unpredictable and tend to be in the variety show tradition. Most recently, there was a show called **Wild Things** that showcased exotic animals like kinkajoos, African crested porcupines, and young kangaroos in an easy going show and tell format. The best part is that you can either enjoy these shows while eating or stroll in just for the show. Sometimes these shows are listed in the show schedule on your map.

Dolphin Nursery

Rating: ★ ★ ★
Type: Small shaded outdoor pool
Time: Continuous viewing
Kelly says: Not much to see but hard to resist

This is where dolphin moms get to enjoy a little maternity leave with their newborns during the bonding process. A barrier fence prevents you from getting right to the pool's edge, so at best you will just be able to glimpse the little ones as they swim by in close formation with mom.

Still, even a glimpse of a baby dolphin is a hard lure to resist and you will probably want to pause here for a look. Education staffers are on hand to answer your questions. Feedings usually take place in the morning and late afternoon, making those the best times to visit.

Manta

Rating:	Not yet rated
Type:	Flying roller coaster
Time:	Not yet known
Kelly says:	First of its kind in Orlando

In Summer of 2009, SeaWorld will unveil its latest entry in the ongoing Orlando roller coaster sweepstakes. This is not a "me-too" coaster but another new departure that is sure to draw coaster enthusiasts in the thousands.

Manta celebrates the ray, one of the sea's most majestic and graceful creatures. The queue line for the coaster (from which non-riders will be able to gracefully exit) begins with a total immersion in an aquarium filled with 300 rays of all descriptions — shark rays, spotted eagles rays, leopard rays, cownose rays, and oscillate river rays.

Then you get a chance to actually be a ray, a supercharged one, in fact. The business part of *Manta* is a so-called "flying" roller coaster, the ride vehicles themed to resemble the creatures they celebrate. Just before the coaster takes off, the seats tilt downward, giving the distinct sensation of zooming, superhero-like through the air. The ride, which will feature elaborate lighting and sound effects, as well as rushing waterfalls, promises to take riders high overhead, then speed them to within inches of the simulated sea below.

Sounds like another winner to me.

Key West at SeaWorld

Key West at SeaWorld is not so much an attraction as a collection of related attractions wrapped in a single theme. The attractions here are aquatic habitats featuring the denizens of warmer waters and the theme, of course, is the casual sophistication and good times atmosphere for which Key West has become famous. On both scores, SeaWorld acquits itself admirably.

Turtle Point

Rating:	★ ★ ★
Type:	Aquatic habitat

Time: Continuous viewing

Kelly says: Best when a staffer is present

Turtle Point is small by SeaWorld standards, a shallow sea water pool fringed by white sand beaches. It is home to four species — loggerhead, Kemp's ridley, hawksbill, and green sea turtles, all of them rescued animals.

Turtles, it must be said, are not the most lively creatures SeaWorld has on display. No leaps and twirls here. So, for most folks, this habitat will warrant no more than a quick look. Fortunately, SeaWorld staffers are often hanging out by the pool ready to answer questions. When a group of people gathers and starts exercising its curiosity, a visit to *Turtle Point* can be quite interesting.

Stingray Lagoon

Rating: ★ ★ ★ ★

Type: Aquatic habitat

Time: Continuous viewing

Kelly says: Your best shot at touching a SeaWorld critter

Under a shading roof lies a long, shallow pool with a smaller "nursery pool" in one corner. Its edge is at waist height for easy viewing and interaction. Scores of stingrays lazily circle the main pool, while their "pups" navigate the nursery pool. The mature rays may look scary, but they are remarkably gentle creatures that will tolerate being petted (they feel a bit like slimy felt) and will almost always appreciate a free handout. A small tray of tiny fish called silversides can be purchased for $4 ($7 for two, $10 for three and $13 for four; annual passholders get a $1 discount). No credit cards are accepted. Once again, SeaWorld education staffers make regular appearances here, providing a steady stream of information about these fascinating creatures. The staffers are always ready to answer any questions you might have.

Thanks to the accessibility of the stingrays, this is a very popular attraction. If the pool edge is packed, be patient. Eventually you will be able to make your way forward where your patience is sure to be rewarded.

Dolphin Cove

Rating: ★ ★ ★ ★ +

Type: Aquatic habitat

Time: Continuous viewing

Kelly says: A spectacular SeaWorld habitat

Dolphin Cove lets you get up close to these delightful creatures — at a price. This extensive Key West habitat allows petting and feeding on one side and viewing on the other, from both a raised platform and an underwater observation post. Most people start at poolside.

Here you can lean over a low wall and reach out to touch a passing dolphin. Since dolphins are naturally curious and gregarious animals, they often pause to check out the curious tourists who are checking them out. For many people, passing their fingers along the sleek flanks of a passing dolphin is the highlight of their day at SeaWorld.

Unfortunately, if you want to grab the best viewing spot and maximize your chances of touching one of the inhabitants here, you will have to pay for the privilege — and queue up to do so! You see, dolphin feeding here is carried out by paying customers and a prime section of the water's edge is roped off for those who are performing this job. A line, often a long one, forms for the purpose of purchasing a small paper tray of three smelt-like fish for $6 ($5 for annual passholders). Only those who have purchased fish are allowed into the prime viewing area alongside the dolphin pool.

Note: The amount of fish sold is limited, because the staff wants to make sure the dolphins don't over-indulge — unlike the human guests who are, in fact, encouraged to eat to excess! So, while you can purchase more than one tray, there may be a limit on your total purchase depending on the size of the crowd.

If you don't wish to buy dolphin snacks, you are relegated to a much smaller viewing area at the far end of the pool, where your chances of interacting with a dolphin, while not precisely nil, are certainly much diminished.

Having fish to offer will definitely increase your chances of touching a dolphin, although they will occasionally swim close enough to the edge to allow a foodless hand to sweep along their flanks. But you can't just show up any old time and buy food. It's sold only at specified feeding times and only up to the quantity that SeaWorld's marine dietitians have determined is appropriate to keep the dolphin fit and not fat. If touching a dolphin is a priority for you or your child, I would advise checking out feeding times and arriving a bit early to get on line to purchase food. Otherwise, there is a good chance you will be disappointed.

A number of SeaWorld photographers roam the far shore and snap just about everyone who makes it to poolside. The photos can be previewed on video screens in the photo hut just a few yards away. A single 6-by-8-inch photo will set you back $20, but you can get every picture they took of you and your family on a CD for $60. There are frames, too, including one held by a plush doll dolphin for $20.

While touching dolphins seems to be the first order of business for most visitors, don't overlook the underwater viewing area (as many people obviously do). It offers a perspective on these graceful beasts that you just don't get from above and, not incidentally, is a wonderful place to wait out those afternoon summer thunderstorms for which Orlando is famous. It will also give you a deeper appreciation of the skill and craft that went into designing the reef-like pool in which the dolphins live. To get there from the petting and feeding area, walk around the pool to your left.

As at all the habitats, SeaWorld staffers make occasional educational presentations. There is usually a staffer sitting on a life guard's raised chair on the beach across from the petting area. Feel free to hail him or her from the sidelines if you have any questions.

Blue Horizons (at Key West Dolphin Stadium)

Rating:	★ ★ ★ ★ +
Type:	Live water show with dolphins, pseudorcas and acrobats
Time:	25 minutes
Kelly says:	Cirque du Soleil meets Flipper

This show, which rounds out the Key West experience, is Shamu in miniature, with a large dose of Cirque du Soleil-style pizazz thrown in for good measure. Instead of giant killer whales we have the far slimmer bottle-nosed dolphins and pseudorcas, or "false killer whales." The setting is a swirling, multi-level, multi-platform blue extravaganza of flying manta rays and sea foam over the large dolphin pool.

The show is conceived as the fantasy of Marina, a girl who dreams of "a place where our dreams come true." She dives out her window (don't try this at home) and finds herself in a watery world of wonder where she meets Delphis, a dolphin spirit who transforms into a hunky guy in an anatomically correct wet suit, and Aurora, a bird spirit in gaudy red plumage who soars overhead in an aerial ballet.

Dolphins, pseudorcas, acrobats, high divers, parrots and lorikeets, and even an immense buzzard get in on the act in what is one of SeaWorld's most elaborate spectacles. I counted 18 performers, nine dolphins, and two pseudorcas, as well as a passel of parrots.

The debt to Cirque du Soleil is obvious and they carry it off well. An elaborate aerial harness apparatus enables the performers to soar over the pool in graceful circles and gives the razzle-dazzle divers a quick route back to their high platforms for another spectacular leap.

The marine mammals are no slouches either. At one point, all nine dolphins are in the pool in a three-ring circus of amazing behaviors. At one point, two dolphins propel their trainer in a corkscrew pattern through the water. At another, Delphis and Marina take turns riding a pair of dolphins chariot style around the pool, a foot on the back of each animal.

The show ends with all the performers soaring and diving while the air is alive with multi-colored birds. It's a sure-fire crowd pleaser that marks yet another triumph for the SeaWorld creative team.

Manatee Rescue

Rating: ★ ★ ★ ★ ★
Type: Aquatic habitat
Time: 20 to 30 minutes
Kelly says: For everyone in the family

You don't expect a natural history exhibit to pack an emotional wallop, but this one sure does — and does it very deftly. It is unlikely that anyone in your family will emerge from this experience unaffected.

The manatee is a large, slow-moving marine mammal that favors the shallow brackish waterways along the Florida coast, the very same areas that have become a recreational paradise for boaters and fishermen. As man's presence in their habitat has increased, the manatees' numbers have dwindled. The good news is that, thanks in part to the rescue efforts of SeaWorld, the manatee population is on the rebound.

But manatees are not out of danger yet, a fact brought home when we realize that all of the small manatees in the exhibit are orphans and that some of the larger animals have been grievously wounded by their encounters with civilization. One has lost most of its tail, another a front flipper. One of the themes of this exhibit is SeaWorld's ongoing rescue efforts of manatees and other marine mammals. On video, we see a seriously wounded adult nursed back to health and released back into the wild. The news that at least one released manatee has reproduced in the wild seems like a major victory.

After viewing the manatees from above — in a pool that re-creates a coastal wetland, with egrets and ibises looking on — we walk down a spiraling walkway into an underground circular theater for a short and highly effective film containing a plea for conservation and protection of the manatee. From there, we pass into the underwater viewing area where the majesty and fragility of this odd beast become even more apparent. Their slow, graceful movements and their rather goofy faces make the manatee instantly appealing. The aquatic setting is lovely too.

Interactive touch-screen video monitors provide a self-guided wealth of additional information about manatees and the problems they face from habitat destruction and pollution. Staffers from SeaWorld's education department stroll the viewing area on a somewhat irregular schedule. If any are there when you visit, they will be more than happy to answer your questions.

I found this a profoundly moving experience and one to which I return eagerly on each visit. Signs along the exit ramp challenge you to make a personal commitment to help the manatee. What will you do?

Photo Op: As you leave the exhibit, look for the sculpture of the manatee cow and her calf floating artfully above the pavement. It makes an excellent backdrop for a family photograph.

Journey to Atlantis

Rating: ★ ★ ★ +
Type: Combination flume ride and roller coaster
Time: About 6 minutes
Kelly says: Wet and wild

It just goes to show you: always heed the warnings of crusty old Greek fishermen, no matter how crazy they seem. Of course, the tourist hordes ignore Stavros' sage advice and set sail on a tour of the ancient city of Atlantis which has mysteriously risen from the Aegean.

Rising some ten stories, Atlantis looks gaudily out of place at SeaWorld, but it sure looks pretty in the golden glow of the setting sun. But it's not the architecture that draws us here. It's the dizzyingly steep water flume emerging from the city walls and the happy screams of those plunging to a watery splashdown. Wend your way through the Greek-village-themed waiting line and be entertained by the news coverage of the eerie reappearance of Atlantis as you wait for your boat.

The voyage gets off to a peaceful start, but after a benign and quite lovely interlude, the boat is seized by the evil Allura, who I gather is a vengeful ancient spirit of some sort. You are winched higher and higher before being sent on a hair-raising journey that combines the scariest elements of a flume ride and a roller coaster. It's a nifty engineering feat but most people probably won't care as they plunge down the 60-foot flume into a tidal wave of water. Another slow ascent gives you a chance to catch your breath before you zip through a fiendishly hidden mini-roller coaster to another splashdown, as Allura cackles gleefully. It's all over quickly — too quickly for my taste — but you can always head immediately for the end of the inevitably long line for another go.

It must be said that the story line for this ride is a bit confusing and hard to follow, which bothers some purists. Most people don't seem to care.

Tip: This is a very wet ride, especially if you are in the front row of the eight-passenger boat that serves as the ride vehicle. An inexpensive poncho (which you can get at any of the theme parks) provides pretty good protection. Expensive cameras and other items that might not survive a soaking can be checked as you enter the boat, but they are placed in unlocked lockers and no guarantees are provided. Pay lockers are available near the entrance to the waiting line; they cost 50 cents and if you don't have the change you will have to walk over to the nearby lockers for *Kraken*, where a change machine is available.

As you exit the ride, don't miss the lovely **Jewels of the Sea Aquarium**, just off the inevitable gift shop. Hammerhead sharks and stingrays swim above you in a domed aquarium, while angelfish inhabit the aquarium beneath your feet. Around the walls, don't miss the moon jellyfish that glow enchantingly when you press the light button. Just outside the aquarium and gift shop, playful hidden fountains await to soak the unwary.

Photo Op: Just outside the Jewels of the Sea Aquarium is a plaza with a splendid view of the 60-foot flume plunge. If you don't want to take your own pictures, shots of every boatload of happily terrified cruisers are on sale at the ride exit.

Kraken

Rating:	★ ★ ★ ★ ★
Type:	Roller coaster
Time:	2 minutes
Kelly says:	Aieeee!

When *Kraken* opened, SeaWorld clearly set out to compete head to head with Universal and Disney for coaster bragging rights and, by Neptune, they've succeeded.

Kraken has several claims to fame. For starters, it is higher (at about 150 feet) and faster than any other coaster in Orlando. But the neatest (or scariest) thing about *Kraken* is that the seats are raised slightly so your feet dangle free. So even though the track is beneath your feet at all times, you don't have the same feeling of connectedness you get on other coasters. Nor do you have the comfort of the overhanging superstructure you get in an inverted coaster. The effect is subtle, yet undeniably terrifying.

For a coaster this fast (they claim speeds "in excess of" 65 miles per hour), *Kraken* is also remarkably smooth. Your head may be pressed against the headrest by the G-forces but it won't be buffeted about. Another thing you may notice (if you aren't screaming too loudly) is that *Kraken* is an unusually quiet coaster. Even if you are standing right next to the fence where *Kraken* dips underground at the end of its run, you can barely hear it. Farther away, it is only the shrieks of the riders you hear in the distance. Another item of note is that the ride designers have made a special effort to accommodate those with large upper torso measurements; specially modified seats in rows four and five of each car can handle those with chest measurements of up to 52 inches. There is also a minimum height requirement of 54 inches.

This is an extremely "aggressive" ride, to use the phrase preferred by the designers. They even have a sign urging those with prosthetic limbs to make sure they are securely fastened! So you will be well-advised to stow everything that's not firmly attached to your body in the pay lockers at the entrance to the ride. Smaller lockers are available at modest cost. A change machine is provided.

Now you're ready for the experience itself. As you make the excruciatingly slow climb to the 15-story apex of the first hill, show off just how cool you are by taking in the panoramic view of the park you get from the top. It may be the last time on this ride you have your eyes open.

As you enter the first drop, you begin to fully appreciate the exquisite horror afforded by *Kraken's* unique design. The effect is less like riding in a roller coaster than like being shot through the air on a jet-propelled chair, all the while turning and twisting head over heels. There are seven loops — at least I think there are seven loops, because I keep forgetting to count — as the coaster soars over water and dips below ground along over 4,000 feet of torturous turquoise and yellow track.

The 119-foot vertical loop, the 101-foot diving loop, the zero-gravity roll and the cobra roll may all have their equivalents on other coasters, but experiencing them in *Kraken's* raised, exposed seats adds a heightened level of sheer terror that beggars description.

As astonishing as the engineering is, one of the best moments of the ride occurs thanks to the scenic design. It occurs when the coaster dives underground into what is described as the "monster's lair," a tunnel that appears to be on the brink of being totally inundated by a thundering waterfall. But before you have a chance to drown, you are whipped back above the surface and into a flat spin before returning to the starting point. Truly amazing!

On the downside, the experience is short, about two minutes altogether and a full minute of that time is consumed getting you to the top of the first hill and returning you to the starting point after the coaster brakes at the end.

If you'd like to get a preview of *Kraken*, perhaps to decide if you want to subject yourself to its special brand of terror, there are two good vantage points. The first is just to the left of the main entrance, where a viewing area has thoughtfully been provided for the faint of heart. This spot gives you a good view of the first drop and the end of the ride. Over at *Pacific Point Preserve*, you can get a good view of the main section of the ride.

Photo Op: If you have high speed film and a fast shutter speed, you might try for a shot in the viewing area near the large Kraken head where the cars dip underground, just at the ride's end.

And speaking of photos, you can pick up one of you and your terrified fellow riders at the exit to the ride in a variety of mountings, including key chains and snow globes. For a fee, of course, which can run well over $20.

For those who care about such things, *Kraken* takes its name from a mythical sea creature that, in SeaWorld's version at least, looks a lot like a giant dragon eel, a multicolored cousin of the moray. In a cave near the viewing area by the main entrance, you can see actual dragon eels pretending to be embryos in giant Kraken eggs.

Penguin Encounter

Rating:　　　★ ★ ★ ★
Type:　　　　Aquatic habitat
Time:　　　　Continuous viewing (5 to 10 minutes)
Kelly says:　　Kids love this one

This is the only exhibit at SeaWorld that you smell first. It hits you the moment you enter but, for some reason, you get used to it very quickly. Soon you are facing a long glass wall behind which is a charming Antarctic diorama packed with penguins. If you bear to the right as you enter, you are funneled onto a moving conveyor belt that takes you at a steady pace past the viewing area; bearing to the left takes you to a raised, stationary, viewing area. Don't worry if you get on the conveyor belt and discover you want to dawdle; you can get back to the stationary section at the other end.

As you ride the conveyor, the water level is about at your chest, so you get an excellent view of the underwater antics of these remarkable birds as they almost literally "fly" through the water. On land, their movements are considerably less graceful, but their slow waddling has its own kind of grace, especially in the case of the larger king penguins with their yellow-accented faces. Overhead, artificial snow sprinkles down from hatches in the roof. The water temperature, an electronic readout informs us, is 45 degrees Fahrenheit, while the air temperature is maintained at 34 degrees. Chilly for us, perhaps, but these highly adapted creatures are used to a much deeper freeze, as we discover in the Learning Center immediately past the penguins.

Here, interactive teaching aids provide the curious with a wealth of additional information about gentoos, rockhoppers, and chinstraps. Here, too, you can watch informative videos about the hand-rearing of penguins and how they molt, the Antarctic environment and penguin predators, and Isla Noir, a Chilean island that is especially popular with penguins.

Just past the Learning Center is a smaller habitat featuring alcids, a group of birds, including the puffins and murres, that is the northern equivalent of the penguin. Unlike their Antarctic cousins, these birds fly in the air as well as beneath the sea. The alcid viewing area, like the penguin exhibit, is equally divided between land and sea and, if you're in luck, you will see murres "flying" to the bottom to scavenge smelt. As you leave the exhibit, you will have an opportunity to circle back to the penguin viewing area for another look.

Pacific Point Preserve

Rating:　　　★ ★ ★ ★
Type:　　　　Outdoor aquatic habitat
Time:　　　　Continuous viewing
Kelly says:　　Don't miss feeding the sea lions

Over 50 sea lions roar and bark with delight in this two-and-a-half-acre, open-air, sunken habitat. SeaWorld's design team traveled to the Pacific Northwest to take molds of the rock outcroppings along the coast to build this remarkable re-creation. Adding to the verisimilitude is a wave machine, similar to those used in the water theme parks, that creates waves of anywhere from a few inches to two feet in height. The viewing area extends entirely around the exhibit, and while the sea lions (and a smaller number of harbor seals) are safely out of reach, it's almost as if you can touch them.

But if you can't pet them, you can feed them. Small trays of fish are available at certain times for $4 a tray, $7 for two, and $10 for three, plus a free fourth tray (Passport holders get $1 off these prices) and their contents will very quickly disappear down a sea lion's gullet. It's all great fun and, if you aren't careful, you can very quickly squander your lunch money. The sea lions, for their part, have learned how to part you from your smelt and will bark furiously and even leap decoratively up onto the edge of the pool until their hunger is satisfied, which it never is. Fortunately, watching other people feed the sea lions is almost as entertaining as doing it yourself. The feeding stations are open regularly and it is only on extremely crowded days that the allotted ration of fish is sold out before closing time.

While their feeding behavior might lead you to believe these animals are tame, they are not. The sea lions you see perform in the *Clyde & Seamore* show just around the corner live separately from their cousins in Pacific Point. They have been trained for years and habituated to interacting with humans. The animals in *Pacific Point Preserve* are wild and like all wild animals unpredictable. In other words, don't dangle little Susie over the edge to get her within smelt-tossing range.

Tip: You might want to ask someone on the education staff when the main feeding will take place that day. While the public certainly helps with the feeding, the staff has to make sure that their charges are adequately fed. They do this by serving up fish by the bucketful at least once a day. This is a highly entertaining ritual so it's worthwhile to check the schedule. Also, the handlers have to hand-feed some of the older sea lions and seals who don't compete well for food with their younger rivals. You and your kids will undoubtedly find this part of the feeding particularly touching.

Clyde & Seamore Take Pirate Island (at Sea Lion & Otter Stadium)

Rating: ★ ★ ★ ★

Type: Live water show with sea lions, otters, and walruses.

Time: 25 minutes

Kelly says: The funniest show at SeaWorld

Forget about education. This one's all about high spirits and low humor and it's a sure-fire crowd pleaser. Clyde and Seamore are sea lion versions of Laurel and Hardy, or Ralph Kramden and Ed Norton, or maybe two of the Three Stooges. In any event, they're bumblers.

There's a plot about a search for gold (and fresh fish), a treacherous otter, and (of course) pirates, but it's almost beside the point. The real point of this show is watching Clyde and Seamore cavort up, down, and around the multilevel set and into and out of the pool that rings the lip of the stage. The humor is broad and the little kids love it. One thing that makes the show such a hoot is the slapdash way in which the human performers carry it off, bloopers and all. Some of the gaffes are due to the unpredictability of the animals but other boo-boos seem to be written into the script, although few will suspect as much unless they see the show several times.

If you are lucky, you might get to see a walrus or two make a cameo appearance. Walruses, I am told, are nowhere near as tractable as sea lions and, given their considerable bulk and potential for wreaking havoc, they only appear when they're in the mood. Even then, they may balk at performing, just like a Hollywood star, and the trainers know better than to argue with several tons of balky blubber. As usual, a small child is summoned from the audience to help out (and shake Clyde's flipper). And, of course, there are the usual dire warnings about splash zones, although the wetness quotient is far lower here than at the Shamu show.

Tip: If you arrive more than about 10 minutes early, you will be entertained by **The SeaWorld Mime**. If you arrive fewer than 10 minutes before show time, you may become one of his victims. This is not mime in the cutesy Marcel Marceau tradition — there's no getting trapped inside an invisible box or walking against an imaginary wind. This is mime with an attitude, that mimics, mocks, and plays pranks on the steady stream of people arriving for the show. Those familiar with the work of David Shiner, the clown prince of this genre, will know what to expect. For others, I don't want to give too much away. This is, far and away, the best of SeaWorld's pre-show entertainments. It is an attraction in its own right and not to be missed.

Sea Lions Tonight (Seasonal)

Rating: ★ ★ ★ ★ ★

Type: Live show

Time: 25 minutes

Kelly says: Hilarious sendup

As the title suggests, this show is performed only at night, only once a day, and only when the park is open late. If you are here when this show is being offered, don't miss it!

The goofy guys who brought you Clyde and Seamore let their hair down even farther to bring you this truly funny (and occasionally biting) satire on the *other* shows at SeaWorld. But instead of dolphins and whales, they use sea lions, walruses, and otters. The SeaWorld Mime is dragooned into the show and doesn't seem to be too happy about the dumb things he's called on to do, including standing in for the birds of *Blue Horizons* and donning a whale fluke headpiece for their version of *Believe*.

The show pokes good natured fun at the pretentiousness that lurks just below the surface of shows like *Blue Horizons* and *Believe*. Maybe there's a wee bit of jealousy involved, too. In one of the show's funniest bits, the cast members strut and preen as orca trainers, their wet suits bulging with artificially enhanced muscles, while an enormous lumbering walrus stands in for Shamu. There are jabs taken at *Pets Ahoy, Bayside Ski Jam*, and *Kraken* as well. All in all, it adds up to one of the best shows at SeaWorld.

Shark Encounter

Rating: ★ ★ ★ +
Type: Aquatic habitat
Time: 15 to 20 minutes
Kelly says: Up close and personal with some scary fish

In *Shark Encounter*, SeaWorld has very cleverly packaged an aquarium-style display of some of the seas' scariest, ugliest, and most dangerous creatures. The tone and lighting of this exhibit is dark and foreboding, with appropriately ominous soundtrack music, but you needn't worry about any unpleasant surprises. When you get right down to it, it's fish in tanks and far too fascinating to be truly scary to any except perhaps the most suggestible kids.

The attraction wraps around **Sharks Underwater Grill** and, in fact, the restaurant has commandeered what used to be the big attraction — a massive tank brimming with a variety of shark species, with huge picture window viewing areas. You still get a nifty view of the sharks, as we shall see, but something was lost from the attraction when the restaurant was added.

You enter this habitat to the left of the restaurant. A short corridor leads to a clear acrylic tunnel through an artificial tropical reef. This is home to the moray eels — nasty-looking snake-like fish. The moray's coating of yellow slime over its blue flesh gives it a sickly green tint. At first, all you see are the many varieties of reef fish swimming about, but closer inspection reveals the morays poking their heads out of their holes. The more you look, the more you see. There are dozens and dozens of the creatures hidden in the crevices of the reef. From time to time one swims free, undulating its long body right overhead. Looking up you see the surface of the water. The tank has been designed to mimic the natural habitat as closely as possible; the lighting comes from a single overhead source, standing in for the sun.

The tunnel curves around and into a viewing area in which several tanks hold specimens probably best kept separate. First is the delicate and intricately camouflaged lion fish. Looks are deceiving here, because the lion fish's feathery appendages are actually poisoned spines that are highly toxic to swimmers unfortunate enough to come in contact with them.

Tried any fugu at your local sushi bar? You may want to reconsider after viewing the puffer fish on display here. Fugu, as the fish is known in Japan, is one of the world's most poisonous fish. The Japanese consider its edible portions a delicacy, and licensed fugu chefs carefully pare away the poisonous organs. Despite their precautions, several people die each year from fugu poisoning. Swimming unconcernedly with the puffer fish are surgeon fish, a pretty species that carries the marine equivalent of switchblades concealed near the tail. When attacked (or grabbed by unwary fishermen), they lash out with their hidden weapon, inflicting a nasty gash. Across the way are barracuda, looking every bit as terrifying as when I first encountered them while snorkeling in the Caribbean. Had I been to SeaWorld first, I would have known that an attack was unlikely and probably would have made less of a fool of myself.

As you walk down the long tunnel toward the shark encounter that gives the attraction its name, wall displays fill you in on little known shark facts. For example, did you know that a shark's liver takes up nearly 90% of its body cavity and accounts for nearly a quarter of its weight? Scientists theorize that, since the liver contains a great deal of oil and since oil is lighter than water, the shark's huge liver may contribute to its buoyancy. Here, too, you will find smaller, temporary displays, such as a recent one about frogs.

Look for a series of rectangular windows on your right. Here you can get a glimpse of what the lucky diners in the restaurant are seeing. It's a spectacular sight, even from this somewhat restricted vantage point and it may be enough to make you decide to have lunch there.

At the bottom of the zig-zag tunnel, you reach the attraction's culmination — a slow, stately ride on a conveyer belt through a 124-foot tunnel that takes you right down the middle of the shark tank. About a foot thick, the clear acrylic walls of the tunnel are supporting 450 tons of man-made salt water over your head. Don't worry, you're perfectly safe; the acrylic can withstand a tromping by 372 elephants (as you are informed on exiting).

All around and above you swim small sawtooth sharks, brown sharks, nurse sharks, bull sharks, lemon sharks, and sandpiper sharks. There are no giants here but what the specimens lack in size they more than make up for in number. If you ever encounter sharks in the wild, hopefully there will be nowhere near this many of them.

The next stop is the exit and the blinding Florida sunshine. If you overlooked the pool at the entrance to Sharks Underwater Grill when you entered, take a moment to check it out as you leave. Look for the bridge over a shallow pool in which some of the smaller and less threatening shark specimens are displayed. Here are small hammerheads and nurse sharks along with a variety of rays, including the jet-black bat ray.

Tip: You can satisfy your curiosity and get a great view of the restaurant's shark viewing windows by heading for the bar and having a cool drink. It's seldom crowded at the bar and often you can walk right in, past families waiting for a table. If you're hungry, the full menu is served at the bar and at a number of nearby raised tables.

Odyssea (at Nautilus Theatre)

Rating: ★ ★ ★ ★
Type: Indoor stage show
Time: 25 minutes
Kelly says: A delightful dance and acrobatic fantasy

If you can't afford the astronomical ticket prices of Cirque de Soleil over at Disney, this wordless blend of acrobatics, mime, and dance makes a nice substitute.

The plot, such as it is, involves an amiable innocent with more curiosity than brains who gets sucked into a delightful underseas fantasy world filled with wondrous creatures who form the basis for a series of whimsical routines. Beautiful contortionists on the half-shell perform feats of balance with giant pearls, colorful tropical fish become spinning aerialists, and bizarre multi-colored worm-like critters bounce and wriggle in ways that make you scratch your head and ask, "How'd they do that?" The best is saved for last as a gaggle of zany penguins bounce, tumble, and twist at dizzying speed around their iceberg home.

This show takes a while to hit its stride, but your patience will be rewarded with a fun-filled extravaganza with gorgeous sets, costumes, and lighting that turn the Nautilus Theatre into a watery wonderland.

Note: From time to time, acts change. Contortionists become acrobats and vice versa. However, the overall shape of the show has remained remarkably stable since it first opened.

Paddle Boats

Rating: ★ ★ +
Type: Just what it says

Time: As long as you want, one half hour at a time
Kelly says: Can be skipped

In Bayside Lagoon you can rent large, pink, flamingo-shaped paddle boats for a leisurely outing on the lagoon. The boats seat two adults comfortably and cost $6 a half hour. If you have the time and enjoy this sort of activity, you may want to give them a go.

Life jackets come with your rental and are required wearing. You must be at least 56 inches tall to ride and you must be 16 or older to take a boat out alone. Check the park's daily calendar for opening hours, which vary.

Eating in the North End

Most of SeaWorld's dining options are located in the North end of the park. In fact, most of them are located in, or just a stone's throw from The Waterfront. The North end also is home to the park's only full-service sit-down restaurant, the eye-popping **Shark's Underwater Grill,** which is not only the best dining in the park, but one of Orlando's best restaurants, period.

Everything else is self-serve, cafeteria-style dining and most of it is pretty good when you take into consideration the limitations this style of serving places on the chefs and cooks. All of the cafeteria-style restaurants offer a kid's meal. Just about every place, except the snack bars and ice cream stands, serves beer, although only Shark's Underwater Grill serves wine.

In reviewing the eateries below, I follow a circuitous route from the front of the park, through The Waterfront, to Sharks Underwater Grill, then back towards Key West.

Cypress Bakery
What: Baked treats
Where: Near the front mall
Price Range: $

If you missed breakfast, you can find a high-calorie substitute here, close to the park entrance. Or, more sensibly, you can stop back later when you've worked off some of those self-same calories. The chocolate cherry and carrot cakes, which I have praised before, are reliable choices. The fruit tarts are pretty good, too. However, don't be surprised if some of the other options look better than they taste. Coffee is served to wash it down. All seating is outside, limited, and only partially shaded depending on the time of day.

Polar Parlor Ice Cream
What: Ice cream
Where: Near the front mall
Price Range: $

Right next door to the bakery are more high-calorie options, this time of the frozen variety. This small ice cream parlor is barely large enough for the serving lines. Both soft serve and regular ice cream is dished up here and the waffle cone sundaes are reliably tasty. Take your rapidly melting goodies to one of the small number of outdoor tables or eat it on the go.

Seafire Inn

What: Burgers, cafeteria-style
Where: On The Waterfront
Price Range: $

"Gourmet steakburgers" are the main draw at this functional cafeteria with its twin serving lines. The Waterfront Burger is essentially a bacon cheeseburger, the Tavern Burger is a variation on that theme with cheddar cheese and peppered bacon, and the Jalapeño Cheddar Burger is just what it says. The Seafire SteakBurger is a plain old cheeseburger.

Other choices include a tropical chicken stir fry, a "cordon bleu" club sandwich, a pulled pork sandwich, and a Caribbean club sandwich. The best dish is the mahi-mahi served over rice with a delicious piña colada sauce. Salads include a Greek salad and an antipasto salad.

Specialty coffees are served here in addition to the usual selection of soft drinks and Busch beers.

Seating indoors is somewhat limited and a little too close to the serving areas for my taste; a better choice when the weather's nice is the shaded outdoor seating. One reason that seating is limited is that only a portion of the place is open during the day. The Seafire closes up in the evening for the *Makahiki Luau,* reviewed later.

Tip: When you enter, head for the serving line that's farther away from the door; it's usually less crowded.

Voyagers Wood Fired Pizza

What: Pizza
Where: On The Waterfront
Price Range: $ - $$

Voyagers has a wonderful stone exterior, dominated by a tall parabolic arch framing massive wooden doors filled with windows. You enter, however, to the left, through less grandiose doorways. Inside is a large cafeteria with two serving islands, each containing two identical serving lines.

Pizza is the most prominent offering, all of them prepared in open ovens. The choices are four cheese (mozzarella, provolone, smoked gouda, and asiago) or pepperoni. The pizza is served as a large slice rather than an individual pie. One bit of overkill is a pizza and fries combo.

Barbecue is the other specialty and the choices include BBQ chicken in quarter- and half-chicken servings and half and full slabs of BBQ baby back ribs. Pasta primavera in marinara or alfredo sauce with penne is a vegetarian option, unless you add a grilled breast of chicken. The most elaborate offering is a pesto-flavored filet of grilled salmon served with fresh veggies and French fries.

Most of the seating is indoors, although there is some shaded seating outdoors as well. The interior takes its theme from the Age of Exploration, with murals depicting famous explorers. Overhead are curved wooden beams that evoke the skeleton of an old sailing vessel. Towards the back, slightly separated from the rest of the seating area is an often overlooked area that offers some respite from the usual din. Its tables are covered in colorful tiles or antique maps, while antique maps ring the walls; it's very attractive and my first choice when dining here.

The Sandbar

What: Outdoor bar with beer and soft drinks
Where: At the bottom of the *Sky Tower*
Price Range: $

Time was, you could get a nice mixed drink here, but recently the fare has been strictly beer and soft drinks, which doesn't seem to bother the thirsty folks who gather here.

Since you can get everything offered here elsewhere, the real draw is the location, which is around the back of the *Sky Tower,* overlooking the lagoon. Since it's a little out of the way and somewhat hidden, this can be a good place to get away from the crowds. All seating is outdoors, only some of it shaded.

The Spice Mill

What: Cafeteria dining with "spicy" entrees
Where: On The Waterfront
Price Range: $ - $$

The Spice Mill, with its pleasing Italian-Mediterranean decor, promises fare that has a little more zing than that being served up elsewhere, although nothing beside the "house specialty" Cajun Jambalaya is really all that spicy. More typical is the homestyle chicken tenders platter.

There is a nice selection of sandwiches, all served with fried and nicely seasoned (those spices again!) potatoes. They include grilled steak and cheese, Caribbean jerk chicken, and beer-battered fish. The hearty meal-in-a-bread-bowl option here is an Amber Bock chile con carne, the amber bock being a dark beer.

Other options include a chicken garden salad and a New Orleans-style muffaletta sandwich, chock full of salami, ham, mortadella, and Swiss cheese, served with a mustard-style potato salad. And, of course, there is a selection of beers, including several dark beer options not always found elsewhere.

There are two identical cafeteria lines to speed serving when things get busy. The Spice Mill's greatest asset is the shaded verandah seating overlooking the Lagoon. Diners are protected from marauding gulls by thin vertical wires that keep the birds out but let the view in just fine.

Shark's Underwater Grill

What: Fine dining in a dramatic setting
Where: In the *Shark Encounter* building
Price Range: $$ – $$$$

This is the crown jewel of SeaWorld dining and one of the most spectacular restaurants in Orlando. Even though the restaurant itself has no windows (there are a few in the bar area), the place has a spectacular view. That's because it looks directly in to the massive shark tank, filled with over 100 sharks and other fish. The effect is, quite literally, breathtaking.

The main dining area is long and narrow, so no table is very far from the massive glass walls of the tank. You can sit right next to the tank, but I prefer the banquette-like booths against the opposite wall, which afford some perspective on the amazing sight before you.

The food, which is styled as "Floribbean," has a tough act to follow and, by and large, it meets the challenge. You might expect seafood to dominate the menu here, but equal time is given to poultry and meat. Among the appetizers, I can recommend the Stuffed Mushroom Trio and the Land and Sea, which pairs cold, blackened tuna and a beef empañada.

Among the seafood entrees, you will find blackened scallops, crab cakes, salmon, and red snapper. An excellent choice is the Shark's Trio of shrimp, scallops, and tuna, either pan seared or blackened Cajun style. I am also partial to the Caribbean Seafood Ragout, served over penne.

For the diehard meat eater, there is a decent, if pricey, filet mignon and a New York strip steak. You can also find a chorizo-stuffed breast of chicken and Moho Pork, which is Cuban-style pork loin served with black beans and rice. Desserts are elaborate and extravagant.

This is the only place in the park where you can get a mixed drink, although the choice, both of drinks and liquor brands, is somewhat limited. There is a small but perfectly adequate wine list, with some good wines served by the glass, all at more than reasonable prices. Of course, you can always choose the beer of your choice, as long as it's made by Busch.

The pricing takes a quantum leap above that at other SeaWorld eateries, but the price of entrees is no more than you might expect at a restaurant of similar quality and none of those can beat the view here. I doubt that anyone who has dined here will feel they were overcharged, unless they let their little ones order from the grown up menu. (No "Kid's Meals" here, but there is a more moderately priced menu with entrees under $10 for those under 12.)

For obvious reasons, this is a popular dining spot and, unless you eat early, you will have a wait for a table. Your best bet is to call ahead for priority seating; the number is (407) 351-3600. Otherwise, you can stop by the restaurant early in the day (it opens at 11:00) and make arrangements for later in the day. The restaurant closes half an hour before the park.

Tip: The best-kept secret at Sharks is the bar area. The bar itself is pretty neat — it's top is a long shallow aquarium with tiny, brightly-colored fish swimming among simulated coral outcroppings. But the best news is that you can eat at the bar or at one of several raised tables around it. Just tell the greeter out front that you're heading for the bar; I have never encountered a wait. From the bar, you have a pretty good view of the shark tank; not as good as if you were sitting in the main dining area, but pretty good nonetheless. What's more, you can always visit the restrooms, a journey which will take you the length of the dining area. Take your time.

Smoky Creek

What:	Barbecue stand
Where:	Behind the Seaport Theater
Price Range:	$

If barbecue is your thing, I can wholeheartedly recommend this casual eatery, where the cafeteria-style serving line fits right in with the down home theme. I mean, what self-respecting barbecue joint serves up its food any other way?

There is chicken (quarters and halves), beef, and spareribs (half and whole slabs). If you have trouble making up your mind, there are combo platters. All with fries, of course, and there is beer with which to wash it down. I think most barbecue aficionados will agree that the quality is above average. The only thing lacking, perhaps, is the superior sauces for which the country's great barbecue places are famous.

All seating is outdoors, some of it under a large pavilion and all of it protected by wires from swooping birds of prey like sea gulls.

Mama's Kitchen

What:	"Healthy alternatives" cafeteria
Where:	Across from *Penguin Encounter*
Price Range:	$$

The decor here is retro-modern diner, with simple four-seater tables and padded booths. What also sets Mama's Kitchen apart is that is has the only menu at SeaWorld that specifies in excruciating detail just what your meal means to your body in terms of calories, fat, fiber and the like.

There is "homemade, low-fat, vegetable chili," which to my way of thinking is a double oxymoron, but I have to admit it tastes pretty good. Elsewhere on the menu (and without further editorial comment) is Mama's chef salad, a turkey sandwich on a whole wheat baguette, a seafood salad baguette, a meat version of the chili, and pan-seared chicken breast sandwich. There is also a variety of salads.

In keeping with the healthy theme, the Kid's Meal at Mama's consists of a turkey hot dog. They serve beer here, too, which confirms what I have long suspected — that, contrary to popular opinion, beer is actually good for you!

If you are trying to count your calories or watch your fat intake, Mama's is an excellent (in fact, your only) choice. Those trying to follow a currently trendy low-carb regimen, however, will find themselves pretty much restricted to the chef's salad.

Captain Pete's Island Eats

What: Walk-up stand
Where: In Key West
Price Range: $

I'm not sure what island they have in mind, unless maybe it's Coney. The fare here is limited to hot dogs, chicken fingers, and funnel cakes. There's beer, though, and after a few of those, who care's what island you're on?

THE SOUTH END

The southern half of SeaWorld lies to the right of the *Sky Tower* on the map, most of it across the wooden walkway that takes you over Bayside Lagoon to Shamu Stadium. The whole feel of this side of the park is quite a bit different, with its large open spaces between huge modern stadiums and buildings. Once again, I describe the attractions in geographical rather than thematic order, beginning with the *Hospitality Center* and continuing in a clockwise direction around Bayside Lagoon.

Clydesdale Hamlet

Rating: ★ ★ +
Type: Horse stables
Time: As long as you want
Kelly says: For horse lovers and Bud fans

Since Anheuser-Busch, the brewing giant, owns SeaWorld, you probably can't hold it against them for blowing their own horn a bit. And even if you find this sort of blatant self-promotion distasteful, you'll probably have to admit they do a pretty good (and fairly tasteful) job of it.

There are really two attractions here, *Clydesdale Hamlet*, the home of Budweiser's trademark Clydesdale beer wagon team, and the *Anheuser-Busch Hospitality Center*. *Clydesdale Hamlet* is actually a very upscale stable, impeccably clean and not in the least aromatically offensive. This is where the impressive Clydesdales hang out between appearances elsewhere in the park. Here you can usually queue up and have your photo taken with one of these steeds.

These steeds, from Scotland, were originally bred for the heavy work of hauling man's stuff from place to place, and while they may not have the magnificent grace of their racing cousins they are pretty impressive in their own right — all 2,000 pounds of them. They are also pampered, beautifully groomed, and obviously well-cared for. There are stable attendants always close at hand to make sure you don't slip them a sugar cube or a contraband carrot and to regale you with horse lore. Did you know, for example, that if you hold down the jaw of a supine Clydesdale, it will be unable to stand up? Seems they have to be able to raise their heads off the ground first before they begin the process of standing up.

Hospitality Center

Rating: ★ ★ ★ +
Type: Free beer!
Time: As long as you want
Kelly says: For Bud fans

Next door to the Clydesdales is the *Anheuser-Busch Hospitality Center*, a large, airy pavilion whose architecture reflects that of the stable. It's a lovely building surrounded by immaculate lawns. A comfortable outdoor seating area overlooks a crystal clear lake, fed by a babbling waterfall. It's the nicest place in the park to just sit and take your ease.

Inside you'll find **The Deli** (a fast-food restaurant) and the **Label Stable** (a souvenir shop). The centerpiece of the Center, however, is the free beer dispensing area that faces the main entrance and is backed by huge copper brewing kettles. That's right, free beer. The cups are on the small size (about 10 ounces) and there's a limit (one sample at a time, two per day), but it's still a gracious gesture. Most of Anheuser-Busch's brands are available, including the nonalcoholic O'Doul's.

Brewmaster's Club

Rating: ★ ★ ★ ★
Type: Yet more free beer!
Time: 30 to 40 minutes
Kelly says: For beer buffs

Also at the Hospitality Center, several times a day, you can attend the *Anheuser-Busch Brewmaster's Club*, which turns out to be a fascinating opportunity to take beer a little more seriously than you usually might and ask questions about the sometimes subtle differences between brands.

The premise is that beer deserves the same high-falutin' folderol that is usually accorded to wine, so there is much talk about "beer pairing," although if you want to know how Bud Light holds up to a fine steak you'll have to conduct your own tasting on your own dime. Here the fare is limited to little cubes of cheese, slices of fruit, and chocolate (yes, chocolate). The idea is a worthy one, but I suspect most people are lured here by the beer rather than the connoisseurship.

You and five fellow tipplers belly up to a semi-circular bar where a friendly bartender guides you through four "flights" of beer and pours samples into one of the four small glasses in front of you. You only get to sample one beer in each group, so of the 16 beers you will see, you only get to taste four — unless, of course, you cut a side deal with your neighbors to sample each other's selections. Many people do just that. Even so, a certain amount of care is taken to assure that you don't overindulge.

I'm not a big beer drinker, but I found the experience rewarding. There were Busch brands (some produced under private labeling arrangements) that I'd never heard of and beers (like blueberry flavored brew and sorghum beer) that I never knew existed. True beer lovers should not miss this one.

Samplings take place throughout the day. To guarantee a place at the bar, stop by the Hospitality Center early in the day and make a reservation. If you have kids in tow, they thoughtfully provide a glassed-in play area for the little ones.

Arcade and Midway Games

Rating: ★ +
Type: Video and "skill" games arcades
Time: As long as you want
Kelly says: For video game addicts

My feelings about these money-siphoning operations, located near the Shamu Stadium, can be summed up pretty easily — why bother? The main reason you paid good money to come to SeaWorld is just paces away and everything you can do here, you can do elsewhere for less money. That being said, these venues are clean and attractive and the prizes at Midway Games are better than most.

Believe

Rating:	★ ★ ★ ★ ★
Type:	Live stadium show
Time:	25 minutes
Kelly says:	The acme of the SeaWorld experience

Could there be a better job than being a killer whale trainer and being shot 30 feet into the air off the nose of a 5,000 pound orca? You won't think so after seeing this razzle-dazzle demonstration put on by the dashing young SeaWorld staffers who spend their time teaching the Shamu family some awesome tricks (although the trainers prefer the term "behaviors").

Actually, they aren't "tricks" at all in the common sense of the term. They are simply extensions of natural behaviors that have been reinforced by the whales' trainers with patient attention and liberal handfuls of smelt. Nor is *Believe* to be confused with mere entertainment. In keeping with SeaWorld's commitment to conserving the marine environment and saving endangered marine species, this show teaches important lessons about the realities of nature and the importance of the marine mammal husbandry practiced at SeaWorld Orlando and its sister parks around the country.

The stars of the show are members of the family *orsinus orca*, commonly known as killer whales and affectionately known by nearly everyone who visits SeaWorld as Shamu. The first killer whale ever captured was named Namu after a town in British Columbia. Shamu means "mate of Namu" in the language of British Columbia's native people. Of course, different whales appear in different shows, so the mammoth performers in this show are, in a sense, playing the role of Shamu.

The "stage" is a huge seven million-gallon pool filled with man-made salt water kept at a chilly 55 degrees (although the whales are used to much chillier water in their natural habitats) and completely filtered every 30 minutes. At the back is a small island platform for the trainers, above which looms a large structure in the shape of a killer whale's tail fluke and four video screens that move, merge, and spin as the moment requires. The front of the stage is formed by a six-foot high Lucite wall that gives those in the first several rows an underwater view. Downstage center is a shallow lip that allows Shamu to "beach" herself for our enjoyment.

On film, we are told the story of a young lad who carves a wooden pendant in the shape of a tail fluke and dreams of swimming with the orcas. When the focus switches from video screen to stage, we discover this kid has grown up to be a SeaWorld trainer. It's a touching story, but the real focus of the show is the awe-inspiring and absolutely delightful interaction of the whales and their trainers. The whales leap, glide, dive, and roll with a grace that belies their huge size. The trainers ride on their charges' bellies, surf the pool on their backs and, in the most breathtaking moments, soar high aloft, propelled off a whale's snout. Many times, two trainers working with two whales will perform in perfect synchronization. They make it look easy and natural, but my guess is that it is fiendishly difficult to pull these tandem tricks off.

The video backstory pays off in a segment toward the end of the show in which a future orca trainer is summoned from the audience to meet Shamu and the tail fluke pendant is passed to a new generation.

The warnings that precede the show's grand finale are in deadly earnest. If you're sitting in the first 14 rows, you'll likely get very, very, very wet. Actually, it's possible to sit in this section and escape a drenching — I've done it. But if you happen to be in the direct line of one of the salvos of chilly salt water hurled into the audience by the cupped rear fluke of a five-ton whale, you will be soaked to the skin. It's pretty much a matter of luck. Some of the biggest laughs come when people who have fled the "splash zone" for the higher ground of the first promenade get nailed anyway by a particularly forceful fluke-full of water.

The best seats in the house. Many kids (especially 9- to 13-year-old boys) will insist on sitting in the splash zone and will feel cheated if they don't get soaked. But adults should consider sitting here as well. If you wear a rain poncho (which you may already have from a visit to another park) you can protect yourself relatively well, and these seats do offer an excellent view, especially underwater. But the seats higher up, where you are assured of staying dry, offer excellent sight lines and the video coverage of the show assures that you won't miss anything.

Tip: Between shows, follow the pathways that ring Shamu Stadium to locate the ramp to the **Underwater Viewing Area** around back. This is a not-to-be-missed perspective on these magnificent creatures. Especially enchanting is the opportunity to watch Shamu and her much smaller calf, Baby Shamu, swimming gracefully in tandem. The whales are rotated through this viewing pool, so there's no guarantee that a specific whale will be there when you drop by. There are benches in front of the picture windows and if the crowds are thin enough you can watch while you rest.

Shamu Rocks (Seasonal)

Rating:	★ ★ ★ ★
Type:	Rock show with killer whales
Time:	20 minutes

Kelly says: Shamu and trainers at play

This is the last show of the day in Shamu Stadium when the park is open late. It is somewhat shorter and different in tone but no less exciting and enjoyable. This time around, there's little or no attempt to "educate" you. Instead, the focus is on ear-splitting rock (with a live guitarist making a splashy cameo appearance) and a dazzling computer-generated video show that really puts those spinning video screens through their paces. The trainers appear in glitzier wet suits, some with red sashes around their waists, and do some disco dance routines designed to coax the audience into joining in.

The whales seems almost an afterthought, which is too bad. Still, they do some amazing things like leaping in tandem or soaring completely out of the water and doing a back flip. In one amazing display, an orca corkscrews through the water while its trainer nimbly runs around its massive midsection, somehow managing to stay upright for the entire ride. I would have liked less rock and more Shamu, but you can't have everything.

Some things don't change, however. The show still ends with a barrage of water to the lower seating area. Why tamper with success?

Shamu's Happy Harbor

Rating: ★ ★ ★ ★ +
Type: Play area
Time: 30 minutes to an hour
Kelly says: Great for young kids, toddlers, and their
                long-suffering parents

If *Wild Arctic* (below) represents an attempt to reach out to the thrill-seeking segment of the tourist population, *Shamu's Happy Harbor* seeks to appeal to the youngster too antsy or uninterested to sit still for a fish — no matter how big it is. Here is a way for even very young children to be entertained in that most effective of ways — by doing things for themselves.

Shamu's Happy Harbor is dominated by a four-story, L-shaped, steel framework painted in shades of sea green and pink. At first glance it looks like a construction site gone very wrong. Closer inspection reveals it to be an intricate maze of cargo netting, plastic tubes, and slides that kids can climb up and through to their heart's content. Some chambers in this maze contain tire swings, just like the ones in backyards across America, except that these are two stories above ground level. The cargo netting is completely enclosed in smaller-mesh black netting. While there's no danger of falling, the upper reaches of the structure are quite high and some smaller children may become frightened.

It's not just for kids, either. Adults can join in, too, although some of the parents I watched obviously wished they weren't allowed. While the corridors of netting are big enough to accommodate anyone, the tubes are designed with smaller people in mind. Thus, the average sedentary grown-up will get quite a workout going through them. You're allowed to climb up but stairs are provided for the trip down. Too many middle-aged sprained ankles is my guess.

The larger structure of *Shamu's Happy Harbor* is complemented by any number of lesser activities, called "elements," all of them action-oriented. These will keep kids busy for hours unless you can drag them away to the next show at the Sea Lion and Otter Stadium. There are four-sided, canvas "mountains" that kids can climb with the help of knotted ropes and then slide down, and large inflated rooms in which kids 54 inches and shorter can bounce and tumble.

Standing in front of it all is a kid-sized schooner, the **Wahoo Two**, just waiting to be explored. Nearby, the **Water Works** offers a jumble of tubes and netting that is constantly splashed with jets of water. The perimeter of the Harbor is ringed with a series of smaller kiddie rides, the most elaborate of which is the **Sea Carousel**, a cute kiddie-friendly ride with a capacity of 64 aboard colorful sea creatures in four concentric rows. The choices of critter range from the cute to the rather scary, so guide your child accordingly. On the other side, you will find **Flying Fiddler** (42 in. minimum height) **Jazzy Jellies** (42 in. minimum), **Ocean Commotion** (42 in. minimum), **Swishy Fishies** (36 in. minimum), and, most interestingly, the **Shamu Express** (38 in. minimum), a kiddie roller coaster with cars cleverly themed with Shamu-like tail flukes. At the other end of the Harbor, you'll find **Shamu's Splash Attack**, where you can pay to sling water bombs at a friend. Buckets of seven water-filled balloons are two for $5, and **Op's Beat**, where kids can bang on hanging steel drums to their heart's content.

Shamu's Happy Harbor is an ideal place for parents to take the squirmy baby of the family when he or she gets restless with the more grown-up attractions at SeaWorld.

Photo Op: Just opposite *Shamu's Happy Harbor* is a made-to-order photo backdrop. It's a life-sized model of Shamu and Baby Shamu perfectly posed under a sun awning (to protect your shot from that annoying glare). Place your kid on Shamu's back and click away.

Wild Arctic

Rating:	★ ★ ★ ★ ★
Type:	Simulator ride plus a spectacular habitat
Time:	5 minutes for the ride; as long as you want for the habitat
Kelly says:	A SeaWorld must-see

That large, techno-modern, warehouse-like building near Shamu Stadium houses one of SeaWorld's most popular attractions — a devilishly clever combination of thrill ride with serene aquatic habitat. All in all, this is one of the most imaginative attractions in Orlando. Mercifully, the waiting line snakes through an area that is shielded from the blazing sun, because the lines can get long.

Tip: To avoid long waits, you will be well advised to see *Wild Arctic* early in the morning. Another option is to visit during performances at nearby Shamu Stadium. But time your visit carefully; the waiting line fills up very quickly when the Shamu show empties out.

During our wait, we are entertained by a fascinating video presentation on the lifestyle of the Inuit peoples who inhabit the frozen realm of the Arctic. And during our slow journey through the line, we are asked to make an important decision: Do we want to take the helicopter ride to the base station or do we want to go by land? It's a choice between "motion" and "non-motion" and it can be important.

The Wild Arctic Ride

If you choose to take the helicopter, be prepared for a whale of a simulator ride (you should pardon the expression). We begin our journey by crossing a metal bridge into the vehicle itself. Once all 59 voyagers are strapped in, the staff exits, the doors close, and the "helicopter" takes off.

The ride, which lasts all of about five minutes, simulates a flight aboard an amphibious (not to mention submersible) helicopter to a research station deep within the Arctic Circle. Despite the gale warnings crackling over the radio, our friendly pilot can't help doing a little sightseeing, including putting the rotors into "whisper mode" so we can drop in on a polar bear family, and dipping below the waves for a glimpse of a narwhal. But his unscheduled detours exact their price and soon we are caught in that gale. At first the pilot prudently puts down on a glacier to await a better reading on the weather but the glacier gives way and we plummet headlong towards the icy waters below.

At the last second, the pilot gets the rotors whirling and we zoom away from certain death. Next, he decides we'll be safer flying through a crevasse, away from the howling winds, but we fly straight into and through an avalanche. Finally, we break through into the clear and the Arctic base station lies dead ahead.

It's a real stomach-churner and remarkably realistic. As I write these words I realize that I'm becoming a little queasy just remembering it all. The action is fast, abrupt, and violent. You'll find yourself being tossed from side to side as you grip the armrests and scream — in excitement or terror, depending on your mood.

Those who choose the "non-motion" alternative for their voyage to the *Wild Arctic*, are escorted past the three simulators to a stationary room where they watch the same video, before entering the Arctic base station.

Tip: The non-motion line moves much, much faster than the line for the simulator ride. If you are pressed for time, you might want to consider making the ultimate sacrifice (or use this as an excuse for missing what can be a very scary ride).

Note: You may want to take an over the counter medication before you head for the park if you are prone to motion sickness but would like to experience the ride.

The Wild Arctic Aquatic Habitat

Once you wobble off the simulator ride, you enter SeaWorld's most elaborately conceived aquatic habitat, one that would have been a five-star attraction even without the exhilarating thrill ride that proceeds it.

The conceit here is that scientists have discovered the wrecked ships from the expedition of John Franklin, a real-life British explorer who disappeared in 1845 while searching for the nonexistent Northwest Passage. The wreck, it seems, has drawn a wide variety of wildlife seeking shelter and prey, so the scientists "stabilized" the wreck and constructed their observation station around it.

The first "room" of the habitat simulates an open-air space, with the domed ceiling standing in for the Arctic sky. A sign informs us that we are 2,967 miles from SeaWorld in Florida. Gray beluga whales (the name is derived from the Russian word for "white") are being fed in a pool directly in front of us. Thankfully, SeaWorld has not attempted to mimic Arctic temperatures.

Next, we enter the winding tunnels of the research station proper. The walls alternate between the ancient wood of the wrecked vessels and the corrugated steel of the modern structure. We view the animals through thick glass walls; on the other side, temperatures are maintained at comfortably frigid levels for their Arctic inhabitants.

Art imitates reality here in the form of the SeaWorld research assistants, clad in their distinctive red parkas. They are here to answer guests' questions but they are also carrying out valuable scientific research by painstakingly recording the behavior patterns of the polar bears and other animals in the exhibits in an attempt to find ways to short-circuit the repetitive motion patterns that befall many animals in captivity. One strategy has been to hide food in nooks and crannies of the habitat, encouraging the animals to use true-to-nature hunting behaviors to find their food. By the way, the fish swimming with the polar bears usually avoid winding up on the dinner table, although the bears sometimes just can't resist taking a swipe at them.

For most people, the highlight of this habitat will be the polar bears, including the famous twins Klondike and Snow, born in the Denver Zoo, abandoned by their mother, nursed through infancy by their zookeepers, and then placed with SeaWorld as the facility best equipped to nurture them to adulthood. They're adults now and usually aren't in the habitat at the same time.

There are also enormous walruses swimming lazily in a separate pool. Harbor seals appear in a video presentation showing the animals in their natural habitat. The narration is cleverly disguised as the radio transmissions of the scientists gathering the footage for research purposes.

After viewing the animals on the surface, we walk down a series of ramps to an underwater viewing area for a completely different and utterly fascinating perspective. Video monitors show what's happening on the surface and simple controls allow visitors to move the cameras remotely to follow the animals when they climb out of the pool. The set decoration below the surface is every bit as imaginative as it is above, simulating the Arctic Sea beneath the ice shelf.

There's much to explore here, including displays that let kids crawl through a simulated polar bear den or poke their heads through the ice, just like a seal. Dotted throughout the exhibit are touch-sensitive video monitors that let us learn more about the animals we are viewing and the environment in which they live. Just before the exit ramp, a small room offers a variety of interactive entertainments.

One lets you plan a six-week expedition to the North Pole, selecting the mode of transportation, date of departure, food supply, and wardrobe. Then you get to find out how wisely you planned. Another computer offers up a printout that tells, among other interesting facts, how many people have been born since the date of your birth.

Tip: The exit is through the Arctic Shop and a prominent sign says "No Re-Entry." However, late in the day, it appears to be easy to sneak back in through the back door if you'd like another peek at this fabulous habitat.

Bayside Ski Jam (Seasonal)

Rating:	★ ★ +
Type:	Ski show with music
Time:	20 minutes
Kelly says:	Aimed at tweens or so it seems

This boisterous, loud, and harmless show mixes some pretty good water skiing, a dash of jet ski, a little bit of derring-do, and a tween-friendly quartet to middling effect. It takes place in Atlantis Bayside Stadium and uses both the shore and the lagoon as a stage.

Some of the best bits are the simplest, as when two watercraft tow tiered kites that do a little aerial ballet. Then there's a truly impressive high dive off a teensy platform 80 feet up into water just a few feet from the shore; someone must have dug an awfully deep hole.

A highlight of the show is water skiing and wakeboarding. There's a bit of everything from aerial flips to adagio skiing with male-female teams. Best of all is a three-man front flip off the ski ramp.

It's all held together by an attractive young cast that puts its heart into the bland numbers it's called on to perform. I must say that "Play That Funky Music, White Boy" has seldom seemed less funky. Still, the young kids in the audience love it.

Tip: Catch the last show; it's more fun after sunset.

Mistify (Seasonal)

Rating: ★ ★ ★ ★
Type: Light show and fireworks
Time: 20 minutes
Kelly says: A fitting finale

SeaWorld has tried some of the elements in *Mistify* before, but now they have been all wrapped up in what's billed as the largest and most spectacular finale in the park's history.

Positioned as springing from the imagination of a child, *Mistify* is a phantasmagoria of water- and sea-themed special effects that unfold in the lagoon just offshore from *The Waterfront*. Hundred-foot-tall walls of water spray serve as screens on which laser images of the sea are projected, as flames erupt and fireworks shoot skyward. There are even underwater light effects. It's a joyful mishmash that's sure to delight and send folks off to the parking lots in a jolly mood.

Eating in the South End

There are far fewer dining choices at this end of the park and nothing rises to the size and relative sophistication of the eateries on The Waterfront. Still, the Deli and Mango Joe's are good choices for a quick and simple meal. In addition to the spots reviewed below, there are a number of permanent or seasonal snack shops or carts that offer quick snacks and soft drinks to go. The South End also houses **The Cove**, where a number of dinner attractions (reviewed a bit later) are offered on a by-reservation basis.

The Deli

What: Hearty cafeteria sandwiches

Where: In the *Hospitality Center*
Price Range: $

More of a walk-up stand than a cafeteria, this vest-pocket eatery is the first thing you encounter in the *Anheuser-Busch Hospitality Center* if you enter directly from the Clydesdale Stable next door. If you are coming through the main doors, head to your left. The quality of the hefty sandwiches served here belie the modest appearance.

The sandwich choices include turkey, "hand-carved" beef, bratwurst, and the Deli Club. There is also a nice warm entree, the Hospitality Beef Stew, which is served in a bowl carved out of a hearty loaf of bread.

For salad lovers, there is a grilled chicken Caesar along with the usual soft drink selection. You can also buy beer here, but you might want to avail yourself of the free samples being handed out just paces away.

There is a limited seating section just opposite the serving line, but a far better choice is the outdoor seating area overlooking the pool and beautifully landscaped grounds. There's plenty of it and it is perhaps the loveliest outdoor dining venue in the park.

Coconut Cove Snacks

What: Small selection of empty calories
Where: In *Shamu's Happy Harbor*
Price Range: $

This walk-up stand should be avoided like the plague by parents who want their kids to "eat healthy." The small selection includes such irresistible no-nos as cotton candy and Crackerjacks. The healthiest thing here is a strawberry-banana smoothie. Yum.

Mango Joe's Cafe

What: Fajitas, cafeteria style
Where: Near *Wild Arctic*
Price Range: $

Fajitas are the entree of choice here and they're not at all bad. Chicken, steak, or a combination, they are served with flour tortillas and served with the requisite sour cream, guacamole, grilled peppers and onions, and mildly spicy pico de gallo. The only downside is that they don't arrive sizzling on a griddle and by the time you make it through the cafeteria line and find your way to a table in the large shaded seating area that lies outside behind the restaurant, what warmth they had might have cooled a good bit.

Other options include a fajita salad, a veggie wrap, or a Southwestern wrap (chicken or steak); the wraps are served with potato salad. For the less adventurous, there are chicken fingers with fries and a dipping sauce.

A full range of Busch beers is available, along with the usual soft drinks and coffee.

Tip: There are two identical lines here, with entrances on opposite sides of the building. If one line looks daunting, check out the other side; often it is far shorter.

DINNER SHOWS

In addition to the restaurants and food stands I have already reviewed, SeaWorld offers a number of experiences that combine entertainment and food. They are like the dinner shows you find elsewhere in Orlando in that they operate on a fixed schedule, have an entry price, and involve all-you-can-eat buffets or table-served meals. Tips for servers are expected.

Dine With Shamu

Rating:	★ ★ ★ ★
What:	Nightly dinner show
Where:	At The Cove near Shamu Stadium
Reservations:	(800) 327-2424; (407) 351-3600
Prices:	Adults $39, children (3 to 9) $19. Plus tax and tip.
Times:	Varies, call the number above for info

After the stadium show, why not join the stars for a nice meal? That's essentially the opportunity afforded by *Dine With Shamu*. The large pool with the underwater viewing area (see above) doubles as an al fresco buffet restaurant for orcas and their guests. It's a pleasant way to get another, more relaxed look at those magnificent orcas. Tables have been set up along one side of the pool, under an awning and a small building behind the tables houses a buffet line.

The meal is scheduled for late afternoon at a time that varies somewhat with the season. If the park is open late, there may be two shows. It's advisable to check.

The buffet dinner is simple but plentiful. Typically there will be chicken, beef, seafood, and vegetarian main courses, with veggies, rolls and other side dishes. A separate buffet line caters to kids' tastes and both grown-ups and kids share a dessert buffet that includes puddings, brownies, cookies, and the like. Beer and wine, along with iced tea and lemonade are included in the price.

The meal I had was adequate, the entrees seeming almost purposely bland, but then the meal is not the main draw here. Shortly after the meal begins, the main business of the event gets under way — a pleasant encounter with one of the mammoth performers from the Shamu shows.

Typically, two trainers are involved. One works with the animal while the other stands on the opposite side of the pool from the dining area and keeps up a running patter filled with interesting factoids about orcas and how the staff works with them and cares for them. For example, did you know that SeaWorld's killer whales have their teeth brushed every day? Why? Because dental problems are the single biggest cause of orca fatalities in the wild.

There is much less of the flamboyant acrobatics of the main show. There are a few leaps and you are warned that you might get wet, but the trainers seem to keep things fairly subdued. Shamu does emerge onto a shallow slide-out area and seats here are good ones. The trainer encourages questions but you will have to shout them out to be heard.

The whole event from start to finish lasts less than an hour and will seem too short to most folks. I would recommend *Dine with Shamu* only for die-hard fans. For others, the price will seem a little steep for what you get.

Backstage at Believe

Rating: ★ ★
What: Buffet and a video
Where: At The Cove near Shamu Stadium
Reservations: (800) 327-2424; (407) 351-3600
Prices: Adults $25, children (3 to 9) $10. Plus tax and tip.
Times: Varies, call the number above

This meal is much like *Dine With Shamu* with the important distinction that you don't dine with Shamu. Instead, you are treated to a video about the making of Believe as you chow down. The screen is on the other side of the pool and, given the constant chatter of the kids who aren't paying the least bit of attention, you may find the video hard to follow. Besides, the video can be purchased at Shamu's Emporium on the way out of the park and, frankly, seeing the video at home might be a better experience.

The pool is open to the whales and one (or more) may choose to pop in during your meal, but there are no interactions scheduled. So don't come thinking you'll see Shamu; you might but it's not guaranteed. Knowing this will help you avoid any possible disappointment.

The real benefit to this show is the reserved seats that await you at Shamu Stadium after the meal. They are in the upper section, so if you have your heart set on sitting in the splash zones, your hopes will be dashed.

Shamu Rocks Dinner Buffet (Seasonal)

Rating: ★ ★
What: Pre-show buffet

Where: At The Cove near Shamu Stadium
Reservations: (800) 327-2424; (407) 351-3600
Prices: Adults $32 children (3 to 9) $17. Plus tax
                        and tip.
Times: In the evening, just before *Shamu Rocks*

In the summer, when the park is open late, this show offers you the chance to enjoy a buffet meal beside one of the pools of Shamu Stadium before seeing *Shamu Rocks*, the splashy nighttime show. As with, *Backstage at Believe*, there are no guarantees that you'll see even so much as a tail fluke and once again the real benefit is not having to get to Shamu Stadium 40 minutes early to snag a good seat.

Makahiki Luau

What: Nightly dinner show
Where: In the Seafire Inn at the Waterfront
Reservations: (800) 327-2424; (407) 351-3600
Prices: Adults $45.95, children (3 to 9) $29.95. Plus
                        tax and tip. Park admission not required.
Times: Daily at 6:00 p.m.; a late show is added at
                        busy times, call for info

At dusk, a ceremonial procession makes its way through the Waterfront, heralding the approach of a Polynesian tribal chieftain. A warrior blows a conch shell to announce the arrival of the Grand Kahuna. A welcoming ceremony complete with dancing briefly enlivens the wharfside while the park's visitors look on. Then, those who have ponied up for the luau are ushered into a spacious theater in the back of the nearby Seafire Grill restaurant where they are transported to the lush South Seas. Giant tikis flank the raised semicircular stage and family-style tables radiate outwards to give everyone a good view.

The show, which begins as the crowd settles in, is hosted by the Grand Kahuna himself, a sumo-sized mountain of a man, with the assistance of a guitar and ukulele trio singing songs of the island from the authentic to the hokey commercial variety.

Most of the show is given over to the dancers, five bare-chested men and four lissome young women who constantly reappear in new and ever more colorful costumes to evoke a variety of styles and moods. The dancing is never less than enchanting and in the war chant numbers rather exciting. What's more, the dancing never veers towards the offensive, making this a perfectly G-rated show.

The Grand Kahuna and his female counterpart are charming hosts as they take us on a guided tour of the folk dances of the islands of Polynesia, from Hawaii to New Zealand, with stops at Tonga and Fiji along the way. The show's standout is a Fire Dance that is literally incendiary, as a dancer wearing nothing but a loincloth twirls a flaming baton and rests the burning ends on his tongue and the soles of his feet.

All of this, our host explains, to illustrate "the light of life that shines in the sky and in every one of us." The sentiment is typical of the gentle spirit of this show, which is apparently a family affair. At one point, the Grand Kahuna introduces his son, who seems to be having just as much fun as the audience.

The food may not be quite as good as the show, but there is plenty of it, all served family style. First comes a salad, followed by three entrees, mahi-mahi in piña colada sauce, sweet and sour chicken, and BBQ spareribs, along with rice and mixed steamed vegetables. Dessert is the "Big Kahuna," a sort of peanut flavored bundt cake, accompanied by coffee. The admission price includes the meal, one complimentary cocktail, and complimentary soft drinks, coffee, or unlimited iced tea. For the drinkers in the crowd, a cash bar is available.

OTHER ADVENTURES

SeaWorld offers a number of "Behind the Scenes" guided tours, as well as animal interactions, and educational activities. The guided tours carry a nominal additional charge, over and above your admission price. The other activities range from moderately pricey to downright expensive but offer some opportunities to interact with or learn about the animals here that you'd be hard-pressed to find elsewhere.

Guided Tours

If you have the time and interest, these one-hour tours can be fascinating. The guides are members of the education staff and are all extremely knowledgeable, personable hosts. At this writing three guided tours are offered on a regular basis. The cost varies seasonally. Adults tickets are $10, $13, or $16 and tickets for kids 3 to 9 are $8, $10, or $12. Annual passholders get a modest discount. The schedules are somewhat erratic depending on the number of people expected to visit the park that day and other factors.

Since all tours limit the number of participants, signing up early is advisable. To enquire about schedules and availability, head for the tour desk when you arrive. You'll find it almost directly ahead as you pass through the entrance turnstiles. When you purchase your tours, you will be given a ticket with the name and time of your tour. This serves as your "ticket" and lets the guide know who belongs to the tour and who doesn't. Tours begin at different points in the park. The meeting points are marked with signs. You will be given directions to them when you sign up.

Polar Expedition

This tour has three stops. The first two take you "backstage" at *Wild Arctic*. The first stop is the beluga whale holding pool, where you may be lucky enough to see "off-duty" whales relaxing. Also in this area are some of the seals that keep the belugas company in the exhibit. Then it's off past the huge filtration tanks that keep the artificial salt water in the attraction sparkling clean, to the hidden "den" of the polar bears.

Whether you will actually see any bears depends on your luck with timing. Nothing happens on a rigid or even regular schedule with these animals. Their keepers don't want them to become habituated to a set routine and try to keep the daily sequence of events as it is in the wild — fairly random.

Even if you don't get to see bears through the glass in their den, you can see them on the remote video camera that is focused on their public habitat. You will also get a wealth of fascinating information about polar bears in the wild and the behind-the-scenes world of *Wild Arctic*. You might be told, for example, that the water in the exhibit is kept at 45 to 55 degrees Fahrenheit, just warm enough to prevent ice from forming on the bears' fur. When keepers must enter the water, they wear three wet suits and then can only stay in the water ten minutes before hypothermia starts to set in. You'll even get to pet polar bear fur (in the form of a pelt, not a live bear).

The next stop, after a short bus ride, is the chilly confines of the Avian Research lab, where you will have a chance to pet a Magellanic penguin (two fingers only, please!). Penguin mothers have a spotty record when it comes to parenting skills. Abandoned or abused chicks are brought here to be reared in a more caring environment. The center even hatches orphaned eggs. Depending on when you visit, you may see young chicks covered in their downy gray baby coats or molting into the more recognizable sleek black and white of their mature feathers. Penguins are gregarious and curious birds and they will take great interest in your visit, waddling over for a closer look and eyeing you with apparent curiosity. Careful of your fingers!

Predators!

Here's a great chance to pet a shark and find out more about these cartilaginous carnivores we all love to hate. For those who don't like to read, taking this tour can serve as an alternative to reading all that informational signage in the *Shark Encounter* exhibit.

You also get to visit the inner workings of the shark tank, where you can gain some appreciation of the water filtration system. Then comes a chance to examine shark jaws, shark skins, and sawfish bones up close. The piece de resistance is a close encounter with a shark — a small, docile critter, but a shark nonetheless. Reach out your hand and enjoy bragging rights back home.

Saving A Species

SeaWorld is far more than "just" a theme park. This engrossing and entertaining tour highlights SeaWorld's role as a major rescuer and rehabilitator of aquatic — and other — animals. What you see on this tour will depend on which animals are currently in the park's care. You will likely get to see manatees and sea turtles that have been injured, typically by the carelessness of Man. You may see some dolphins, but they are usually here for reasons other than injury. Thanks to its reputation, SeaWorld is sometimes given injured animals that are not part of its usual stock in trade — like snakes, rabbits, and exotic birds. These, too, are on display.

The areas you visit also include an aviary where you can hand feed the birds, as well as tanks used to quarantine sea animals that are new to Sea-World before they are introduced to the exhibits. If you've ever wondered how to rid sea animals of parasites, this is the place to find out. (Answer: Dip them in fresh water for a few seconds.)

Animal Interaction Programs

Yes, you can interact with the animals at SeaWorld — if you have the money and can meet these programs' age and height requirements. Sea-World offers four interaction programs, ranging in price from $40 to $399 including tax. One lets you swim with Shamu's cousin, the beluga whale, and learn some training commands. Another gives you an up-close look (but no real interaction, thankfully) with a bunch of sharks.

Despite the high prices, the programs are very much in demand and arrangements have to be made well in advance of your visit. Reservations for all these programs can be made by calling (800) 406-2244 or (407) 363-2380. Reservations can also be made at the Tour desk near the front entrance to the park. Most program fees are non-refundable, although you may be able to reschedule.

Dolphin Spotlight

If you're not including a visit to Discovery Cove (see *Chapter Three*) in your vacation, you can still interact with a dolphin, maybe two or three, by taking this informative one-hour tour. It has the additional advantage of being the least expensive of the interaction programs (at $40 per person) and having no age restrictions.

The experience begins when you step backstage at *Blue Horizons* to get a peek at the performers relaxing between shows and receive a briefing on the mechanics of staging this extravaganza. You'll also see the "med pool," a narrow space in which a dolphin or pseudorca can be isolated; then the slatted bottom can be raised, lifting the creature out of the water to facilitate various veterinary procedures.

Next it's off to the animal rehab section where dolphins, manatees, and sea turtles are cared for when they're sick or just need a little R&R. The education staffers who run these tours are extremely knowledgeable, so feel free to pepper them with questions; it's a great chance to get a free education on dolphin lore.

The culmination and undeniable highlight of the tour is a private visit to the dolphin feeding area at *Dolphin Cove*. The tour group is broken up into family units and each family gets plenty of face time with a dolphin or two. You will have an opportunity to touch, rub and scratch these delightful creatures, shake their flippers and have them respond to some simple commands. Feeding is handled by staffers. In it's own way, this experience is just as much fun as actually swimming with the dolphins at Discovery Cove. And photographers record it all for posterity.

Marine Mammal Keeper Experience

Think you'd like to rescue injured manatees or care for beluga whales, seals, and other marine mammals? If you've got $399 ($360 for silver and gold passholders, $349 for platinum), are at least 13 years old, 52 inches tall, and can climb a flight of stairs and lift 15 pounds, and can get yourself to the park by 6:30 a.m., here's your chance to find out. Up to four guests per day get to work with SeaWorld's caregivers, helping to prepare the mammals' food (each species has a special diet) and feed and care for them. The experience lasts eight hours (6:30 a.m. to 2:30 p.m.) and the price includes park admission, lunch, and a souvenir t-shirt.

Sharks Deep Dive

SeaWorld's coolest up-close and personal experience takes daring visitors on a leisurely 30-minute underwater tour of the mammoth shark tank at the *Shark Encounter* attraction. Participants don a wet suit (provided by SeaWorld) and climb into a submerged shark cage that travels, very slowly, along a 125-foot track through the tank. Specially designed helmets allow you to breathe (and talk!) underwater, even if you are not scuba certified. Along the way, guests will be able to ogle (but not touch) the 50 plus sharks in the tank. Also on display, dimly glimpsed through the depths, will be the diners in the Sharks Underwater Grill restaurant.

As you might have guessed, there is an additional charge for this attraction — $150 per person ($140 for silver and gold passholders, $135 for platinum). These prices include tax as well as a souvenir t-shirt and an informative booklet about sharks. Participants must be at least 10 years of age.

Reservations are required — the ride only accommodates two people — and can be made by calling (800) 406-2244 or (407) 363-2380. Reservations can also be made at the tour desk near the front entrance to the park.

Beluga Interaction Program

SeaWorld's latest animal encounter revolves around the snowy white beluga whales that inhabit the *Wild Arctic* exhibit. This innovative two-hour experience allows you to step into the artfully designed Arctic environment and actually dangle your feet in the chilly 55-degree water of SeaWorld's simulated Arctic Ocean.

The adventure begins when you and up to three other intrepid souls don a much needed wet suit and take a tour of the behind-the-scenes area of the exhibit. Then you become part of the show for the tourists as you step into the exhibit itself and sit on the simulated icy shore of the whale's tank. Under the watchful eyes of two trainers, you will have a chance to pet and feed Spooky, a 1,700-pound bundle of beluga. You'll even get a cold peck on the cheek. Sadly, or perhaps fortunately, you never get a chance to slip into the bone-chilling water.

The fee is $179 per person ($169 for silver and gold passholders, $164 for platinum). Participants must be at least 13 years old.

Family Adventures

SeaWorld offers a smorgasbord of special activities, day camps, and sleep-over programs for kids from kindergarten through the eighth grade (roughly ages 5 through 13). A five and a half hour birthday party with a Shamu theme costs $850 (including tax) for groups of up to 20 kids and adults and typically includes invitations, birthday cake, favors, reserved seats at Shamu Stadium, and the chance to feed some animals.

Adventure Camp is the umbrella name for a series of week-long half-day and full-day programs for kids of various ages. A variety of age-appropriate programs are offered during the year. **Day Camps** typically run from 9:00 a.m. to 5:00 p.m. (programs for younger kids end earlier). Prices, including tax, range from $250 for half-day programs to $350 for the full-day sessions. After-camp care, until 6:00 p.m., can be arranged for an additional fee. **Resident Camps**, where the kids stay overnight, can cost over $1,000 per child.

Year round sleep over programs offer bonding experiences for kids and their parents, including such treats as a Halloween outing to *Shark Encounter*. These overnight events cost about $75 to $80 per person (including tax).

For more information on these programs call (866) 479-2267 or (407) 363-2380; passport holders can call (800) 406-2244 for information on discounts. The email address is education@seaworld.org. A brochure spells out the registration process in some detail. A complete health history and medical release form must accompany all registrations.

Beluga Interaction program at Wild Arctic in SeaWorld.

Above: A newfound friend.
(Dolphin swim at Discovery Cove)

Left: Snorkeling with stingrays.
(Discovery Cove)

Below: The Caribbean? Tahiti?
No, you're still in Orlando.
(Discovery Cove)

Above: A 'pod' meets its dolphin.
(Dolphin swim at Discovery Cove)

Right: Hard at work in the Aviary.
(Discovery Cove Aviary)

Below: Raised by hand, so you
can feed them by hand.
(Discovery Cove Aviary)

Chapter Three:

Discovery Cove

As I write these words, the newspaper carries a short piece about a 14-year-old Italian boy saved from drowning in the Gulf of Manfredonia by a dolphin. The lad, a non-swimmer, fell off a sailboat and was sinking under the waves when he felt something pushing him upward. "When I realized it was Filippo, I hung on to him," the boy was quoted as saying. One can only assume that Filippo is Italian for Flipper!

This is only the latest example of a tale that has been told since antiquity. The frescoes of the ancient Minoan civilization of Crete are alive with playful dolphins, and Greek literature is peppered with accounts of dolphins saving wrecked sailors. So humankind's fascination with this playful and occasionally lifesaving creature has a long and honorable pedigree. And as the story about the boy from Manfredonia illustrates, *Flipper*, the hit TV show about a preternaturally precocious dolphin and his towheaded sidekick, clearly has a hold on the world's imagination many years after its original prime time run.

The marketing geniuses at SeaWorld were not blind to this intense fascination with the stars of their animal shows and some years ago instituted a program (now discontinued) that allowed a small number of guests to duck backstage at SeaWorld and actually meet and swim with the stars of the show. Out of this somewhat makeshift idea, SeaWorld has created Discovery Cove, a whole new class of theme park, the first one to be designed specifically for one-to-one human-animal interactions. At Discovery Cove you can not only swim with dolphins but cruise with stingrays, have tropical fish nibble at your fingers, and let exotic birds perch on your head and shoulders while you feed them by hand.

Because of its unique mission, Discovery Cove has been carefully designed to accommodate a limited number of visitors. Only 1,000 people can come to Discovery Cove each day and only 750 of them will be able to swim with the dolphins. Consequently, reservations are mandatory, whether you will be swimming with the dolphins or not. Discovery Cove will admit walk-ups for its "non-swim" program (i.e. you don't get to interact with the dolphins) *if* there is room. That is a very iffy proposition during the warmer months, but your odds of getting in on short notice improve dramatically in the winter.

This limited-capacity policy is, first and foremost, for the protection of the animals, but it has undeniable benefits for the human visitor. The park clearly has room for more than a thousand, so there is plenty of space to spread out on the expansive beaches. No scrambling for lounge chairs, no shoulder-to-shoulder sunbathing and only the very occasional traffic jam at prime snorkeling spots.

Before You Come

Because of its limited capacity and obvious popularity, a visit to Discovery Cove demands advance planning. Reservations are mandatory and making reservations six months or more in advance is not such a silly idea. In fact, reservations can be made up to a year in advance. Somewhat to the surprise of Discovery Cove's marketing people, more visitors (over 50%) want to swim with the dolphins than had been anticipated. So if a dolphin interaction is your goal, the sooner you book, the better your chances.

While it is extremely unlikely that you will be able to book a dolphin swim on short notice, it can happen, especially if you can be flexible on dates. Cancellations do occur. If you want to visit Discovery Cove and not swim with the dolphins, your chances of getting in at the last minute are only slightly better.

The best plan is to phone regularly before your visit and drop by in person once you have reached Orlando. Obviously, the more people in your party who want to swim with the dolphins, the less likely it is you will be successful. It is also possible that there will be openings for just two people when you have a party of four.

There are two ways to make reservations, by phone or on the Internet. The toll-free reservation line is (877) 434-7268. Overseas visitors can call (407) 370-1280. You can make a reservation for the day you visit but you cannot reserve a specific time to swim with the dolphins until you arrive at the park, which is a good incentive to arrive early on the day of your visit. More on this later. The Internet address is

www.discoverycove.com

When's the Best Time To Come?

Although I don't generally recommend coming to Orlando at the height of the summer if you can possibly avoid it, the tropical island beach resort ambiance of Discovery Cove makes it a delightful place to spend a blistering hot summer's day. The salt water pools are kept nice and cool for the animals and make for a bracing dip. Of course, summer brings with it the increased likelihood of stormy weather. Dolphin interactions will be held in the rain, but will be cancelled if there is lightning in the area.

In late spring and early fall, the weather should be closer to ideal. Winter in Orlando can range from the pleasant to the chilly. At this time of the year, the weather may not be ideal for lounging on the beach but the water temperature may be warmer than the air temperature. On the other hand, crowds are generally smaller during the cooler months and the non-swim package is discounted in January and February (see below). Wet suits are available to ease any discomfort of in-the-water activities.

Getting There

Discovery Cove is located just off I-4, near SeaWorld, on Central Florida Parkway so the driving directions are similar. From the south (i.e. traveling east on I-4) use Exit 71 and you will find yourself pointed directly toward Discovery Cove; it's a little more than half a mile along on your right, a short distance past the SeaWorld entrance on the left.

From the north (i.e. traveling west on I-4), get off at Exit 72, onto the Bee Line Expressway (Route 528). Take the first exit and loop around to International Drive. Turn left and proceed to Central Florida Parkway and turn right. The Discovery Cove entrance will be on your left, almost immediately after turning.

Arriving at Discovery Cove

Self-parking is free and just a short walk from the entrance. Unfortunately, there is no valet parking. You can drop members of your party at the front door, but you will then have to handle the parking chores yourself.

Opening and Closing Times

The official opening hours are 9:00 a.m. to 5:30 p.m. but since the first dolphin swim begins before 9:00 (as early as 7:30 or 8:00 during peak periods), the doors are open earlier. It is also possible to linger until 6:00 before you are politely pointed to the exit. My personal recommendation is to arrive early, about 8:00 or 8:15, if you are participating in the dolphin swim. I provide some more advice on timing your dolphin swim later. On the other hand, if you are coming in winter, when the first dolphin swim isn't until

10:00 a.m., you can afford to sleep in a bit. If you choose the 'Twilight Discovery' package, you don't have to arrive until three in the afternoon.

One-Day Admission

Prepare yourself for a shock. Discovery Cove is probably the most expensive theme park you will ever visit. But before you flip immediately to the next chapter, read on. On closer examination, Discovery Cove offers extremely good value for your investment. In my opinion, this very special park is worth every penny.

There are two "seasons" at Discovery Cove, with prices adjusted accordingly. Low season is from January through mid-March and from early November to about December 20. High season runs from mid-March through October and again from December 21 to 31. At press time, prices (including tax) for everyone over six years of age were as follows:

All-Inclusive Day Package (includes the dolphin swim):
Low season: $286.49
High season: $307.79

Non-Swim Day Package:
Low season: $179.99
High season: $201.29

'Twilight Discovery' Package:
This option was available in 2008, on Tuesday through Friday from June 3 to August 22 only; it ran from three in the afternoon until 9:00 p.m. Presumably, the 2009 schedule will be similar.

With dolphin wade: $286.49
Without dolphin wade: $201.29

Children under 3 are **free**, but all others are charged the same rate as adults. Children must be at least 6 years old to swim with the dolphins, so kids between 3 and 6 will pay the non-swim rate.

Note: In 2009, the low season rate for the dolphin and non-swim packages will rise to the 2008 high season rate. The 2009 high season rate had not been set at press time.

Is It Worth It?

In a word, yes. But if you need more convincing, bear in mind that the price of admission includes a continental breakfast, a very nice, all-you-can-eat lunch, and all your beverages (including beer and wine coolers) throughout the day. Admission also includes seven days admission to either SeaWorld or Busch Gardens Africa. For an additional fee of $50 (plus tax) you get 14 consecutive days admission to SeaWorld *and* Aquatica *and* Busch Gardens Tampa. If you are going to do Discovery Cove, this is your best buy to see the rest of the parks.

Trainer for a Day

If those prices didn't take your breath away, perhaps you'd like to upgrade to the "Trainer for a Day" program. For a mere $519.72 (including tax), or $498.42 during low season, you will be treated to a "enhanced dolphin interaction and training encounter" as well as a number of other behind-the-scenes activities. Participants must be at least six years of age and those under 13 must be accompanied by a paying adult.

Discounts

The best way to get a discount is to book early. Bookings made 100 days or more out qualify for a ten percent discount. Florida residents can also qualify for a discount as long as one member of their party does the dolphin swim. Discovery Cove has offered occasional discounts, during slower periods, to Passport holders, conventioneers, and via radio station promotions. Promotional discounts do not include the seven days of admission to the theme parks. Conventioneers can call (866) 781-1333 for information about special offers just for them; these are typically offered on selected dates during the low season.

Cancellation Policy

Because the number of daily visitors is carefully controlled, a visit to Discovery Cove is more like a tour package or a cruise than a visit to a "regular" theme park. The advance reservation and cancellation policies reflect this fact.

All reservations must be prepaid 45 days prior to your visit, or immediately if your planned visit is less than 30 days away. If you have to cancel your reservation you may incur a penalty. Cancellations made more than 30 days before the reserved date get a full refund; between 15 and 29 days, a 50% refund; between 8 and 4 days, 25%. If you cancel fewer than eight days out, you forfeit the entire amount.

Good Things to Know About . . .

See the *Good Things to Know About ...* section in *Chapter One* for notes that apply to all the parks. These notes apply specifically to Discovery Cove.

Access for the Disabled

Discovery Cove has provided ramps with handrails into many of the water areas. Those who can maneuver themselves into the shallows of the Dolphin Lagoon, will be able to experience the dolphin swim. Special wheelchairs that can negotiate Discovery Cove's sandy beaches are available and work is under way to provide a "platform" that will enable guests to get around in their own wheelchairs. Eventually, Discovery Cove plans to introduce special "flotation chairs." Phone ahead to see what will be available when you visit.

Dolphins

Dolphins have such a wonderful public image as cute and cuddly critters that it's easy to forget that they are, in fact, large, powerful, and unpredictable wild animals. The dolphin PR machine likes to play down the fact that, in their natural state, they vie for dominance by biting, scratching, and fighting. Those scrapes and scars and nicks you'll see on your dolphin friend bear mute testimony to this fact of life in the big bad ocean.

I mention this not to frighten or dissuade you — it's not like you'll be diving into a pool of man-eating sharks — but to encourage you to approach these magnificent creatures with the respect they deserve. Follow your trainer-host's directions and you'll do just fine. Do something stupid and you run the slight but very real risk of injury.

Emergencies

The park is dotted with fully certified lifeguards, but any nearby attendant should be your first stop in an emergency. A first-aid station is located near the Tropical Gifts shop not too far from the front entrance.

Getting Oriented

Discovery Cove does not hand you a paper map as other parks do. Since the park is quite compact, there's really no need. The main axis of the park is a paved walkway, with lockers, changing rooms and restaurant to your right (as you walk from the main entrance) and the beach, lagoons, and river to your left. It's hard to get lost but, just in case, mosaic tile maps called "Points of Discovery" are dotted about on low-slung rocks to help you get your bearings.

Lockers & Changing Rooms

Lockers are free and plentiful. There are two locker locations. There is one near the Dolphin Lagoon and another between the dolphin and stingray pools. You will be directed to a locker location depending on the time of your arrival, but if you have a preference it will most likely be honored. Both locker areas are next to spacious and well-appointed changing rooms complete with showers, extra towels, hair blowers, and toiletries.

Money

The best way to handle money at Discovery Cove is not to. The laminated ID card you receive on arrival bears a bar code that can be linked to your credit card. If you prefer the old-fashioned way, all the shops and refreshment stands accept cash and credit cards.

Sunscreen

Don't bother lathering yourself with sunscreen prior to your visit. You'll just be asked to shower it off. Discovery Cove provides its guests, free of charge, a special "dolphin-friendly" sunscreen. Take care when applying it, because a little goes a long way. It doesn't seem to disappear as readily as most commercial sunscreens, so if you use too much you'll look a bit like you've dipped your face in flour. If you like it, you can pick up more in the gift shops.

Getting Into the Swim: Your Day at Discovery Cove

At first blush, it may seem there are only a few things to "do" at Discovery Cove, but they somehow manage to add up to a very full, relaxing, and rewarding day. Think of your day at Discovery Cove not as a visit to a mere theme park but as a day spent at a very exclusive tropical resort with some highly unusual amenities and you will not only approach the experience with the right attitude but increase your odds of getting the most from your investment.

Even if you are not planning to swim with the dolphins, I recommend arriving early. And if you *are* swimming with the dolphins I strongly advise being among the first to arrive. You can call ahead for specific time requests' otherwise, your dolphin appointment will be made when you arrive. So the earlier you arrive, the more choice you will have.

My personal feeling is that you are better off being in one of the first dolphin swims of the day. The theory is that in the morning the dolphins are more active and curious, because they've had a night to rest and haven't yet spent a day with overexcited tourists. I'm not actually sure how accurate this theory is. After all, the dolphins have been specifically trained for this duty and each dolphin is limited to just six sessions a day. What's more, if a dolphin shows signs of losing interest, the trainers will simply call for a replacement. Still, I find the theory has a certain appeal. Besides, by doing the dolphin swim first thing, you get your day off to a smashing start and you can relax for the rest of the day, without keeping one eye on your watch for fear of missing your appointment with dolphin destiny. And in the summer, a morning swim slot means you will avoid the afternoon thunderstorms that are an Orlando trademark. So, assuming you are arriving early, here's how your day at Discovery Cove might play out.

My first bit of advice is to arrive dressed for the water. This is Orlando, remember, and no one at your hotel will think it odd that you are strolling through the lobby dressed in a swim suit, t-shirt, and sandals. If you like, you can bring along "regular" clothes to change into at the end of the day.

Arriving at the main entrance is a bit like arriving at a nice hotel. The large airy lobby, with its exposed wooden beams and a peaked, thatched roof, is what you might expect at a Polynesian resort. Suspended above you, sculpted blue dolphins frolic amid schools of tiny fish. Arriving guests have their bags inspected and are then directed to one of ten check-in counters, so your wait will be minimal.

Your host will find your reservation and check you in. Your photo will be taken with a digital camera and put on a laminated plastic ID card that you can wear around your neck. The card has a bar code that can be linked to your credit card. That way, you can "pay" for anything in the park with your ID card and settle a single bill on leaving the park. It's a terrific convenience and highly recommended.

If you are booked for a dolphin swim, you will also pick a swim time and be assigned to one of three cabanas. The cabanas are not changing rooms, as the term might suggest, but staging areas where you will be briefed prior to your dolphin encounter. It is your responsibility to arrive at your assigned cabana at the appointed time.

Once checked in, you will join a group of eight or so other guests to be escorted into the park itself. Your guide will tell you a bit about what to expect during your stay and direct you to the lockers and cabanas. During this brief introduction, each family group will pose for a picture, which is included in the cost of admission; you can pick it up later in the day or as you leave the park.

You will be issued a mask, snorkel, towel and dolphin-friendly sun-screen. The snorkel is yours to keep, the mask must be returned. You will also be issued a black and neon-yellow neoprene vest that is a cross between a wet suit and a flotation device. The vest is required wearing in the water. It is actually a clever way to keep you buoyant and visible (and therefore safe) without making you feel dorky. And, like a wet suit, it provides some comfort in the chilly waters of the *Dolphin Lagoon* and *Coral Reef*. If you'd like more wet suit warmth, you can request an actual wet suit, very much like those worn by the trainers. This one comes to mid-thigh and offers more coverage than the vest alone. For non-swimmers and little ones, stiff yellow life vests are also available. If you mislay your towel during the day, replacements are readily issued.

Your next stop will most likely be the lockers. They are simple wooden affairs located in shaded palapas. The doors of unclaimed lockers will be open and inside you will find the key, which is on a lanyard so you can wear it around your neck. (The ID card and key, by the way, tuck neatly inside your vest, so they don't get in your way during the day.) Near each locker area is a changing room, should you need it.

If your dolphin swim is later in the day, now it is time to take advantage of the continental breakfast buffet, scope out the beach area, and choose a lounge chair or two to accommodate your party. Take your time and pick a spot that offers the ideal combination of sun and shade to suit your tastes.

If you have followed my advice and arranged an early dolphin swim, it will now be time to head to your assigned cabana to begin your experience; you can have breakfast after your dolphin encounter, or you might want to head straight for the *Ray Lagoon*. This is because the rays will be hungriest in the morning. Trying to feed a full stingray in the afternoon can be a daunting challenge.

Otherwise, you can pretty much take things easy for the rest of the day, basking in the sun, swimming in the river or saltwater pools, visiting the *Aviary*, or eavesdropping on the later dolphin swims as the spirit moves you.

The 'Twilight Discovery' Option

If you choose the Twilight Discovery option, which is available only during the summer months, your day begins at three o'clock in the afternoon and ends at about nine. Your experience, though shorter, will be much the same as if you had opted for a full day, but with a few important differences. For one thing, there will be fewer of you. This program is limited to just 150 guests.

Most important to my way of thinking, is that the dolphin interaction is a "wade" rather than a "swim." In the evening, all interactions with the dolphins take place in shallow water. That means you will miss out on the thrill of being towed by the dolphin which is one of the great highlights of the daytime experience. Of course, that dolphin ride takes time, so without it you get a little more one-on-one time with your flippered friend. Although the evening interaction is the same 30 minutes as during the day, many people who have done both report that it seems longer.

Obviously lunch is not included in the evening option, but dinner is and it is a decided step up from the midday fare. Chefs personally prepare delicacies like blackened sea scallops or grilled steak and shrimp. They'll even help you create your own pasta dish. Desserts are more lavish as well and include flaming bananas Foster.

Live music is part of the experience, too, and you can expect lively limbo dancing on the Laguna Grill patio. Because the crowds are smaller in the evening, it's possible to slip off somewhere relatively quiet with that special someone and savor the sunset in this very special place.

Attractions at Discovery Cove

Discovery Cove has a limited number of "attractions" but they are some of the best to be found in the Orlando area. They are enjoyable enough that you may be surprised to find a very full day seems all too short.

Swim with the Dolphins

Rating: ★ ★ ★ ★ ★

Type: Animal interaction

Time: About 30 minutes

Kelly says: An unforgettable experience

Your dolphin encounter begins when you arrive at your appointed cabana at the appointed hour for a briefing. This is primarily an exercise in heightening your anticipation with a brief video, but a trainer does put in an appearance to offer some pertinent safety tips, such as keeping your hands away from the dolphin's blow hole. ("It'd be sorta like me sticking my finger in your nose," she points out helpfully.)

Following the briefing you and your "pod" of anywhere from six to nine people will be led to the lagoon. I have heard conflicting reports on the maximum group size for the dolphin encounter. Nine people is said to be the maximum and seven or eight the preferred number. I have been in groups of six and eight. At water's edge you meet the two trainers who will guide your encounter. Your first challenge is getting used to the chilly water, which is kept between 72 and 76 degrees Fahrenheit for the comfort of the dolphins.

The dolphins make a splashy entrance, zipping from their holding pen and leaping into the air in greeting before splitting off to head to their respective human pods. Eagerly, you wade to the edge of a sharp drop-off to meet your new dolphin friend. The dolphin you meet may have been specially trained for duty at Discovery Cove or may be an old pro. I once swam with Capricorn, an aging movie star of sorts who was 36 and had appeared in *Jaws III*.

Here at the edge of deep water you and the other members of the group will get to rub down your dolphin, a tactile interaction the dolphin obviously enjoys. Then you take the plunge into deep water for the main part of the experience. How many people go out at one time is a function of the size and makeup of your group. Our trainers said they usually try take people out as couples, but sometimes they go out in threes.

Exactly what you do with your dolphin will depend to some extent on what behaviors the dolphin has been trained to perform, but you will almost certainly be able to give some hand signals to which the dolphin will respond by chattering excitedly or spinning in a circle. The interaction is carefully planned so that every member of your group gets equal access to the dolphin and no one feels cheated of one-on-one time with their frisky friend. You will also have a chance to feed your new friend several times in the course of the interaction. This tends to keep the dolphin interested, but don't be surprised if your dolphin decides to take an unscheduled break to check out something of greater interest elsewhere in the pool. This is normal apparently and if your dolphin shows sufficient lack of interest in the proceedings the trainers will simply call in an understudy.

For most people, the highlight of the interaction comes at the end when they place an arm over the dolphin's back and cup their other hand over a flipper and get towed back to the shallows. There they pose in a sort of hug with their new-found friend for the still and video photographers who have been carefully documenting the entire dolphin interaction for posterity and profit.

Before you leave, you can stop by the photo pick-up area (to your left, across from Guests Services) and see the photos and videos taken of your dolphin interaction. They're available for purchase, of course, in a variety of formats. The pricing system is complicated and you can quickly run up an enormous tab. Everything is available "a la carte," but if you order one of two packages, the a la carte pricing for other options goes down. To give you an idea, here are some sample prices, which do not include tax.

The Adventure Package ($135) consists of five 6x8 inch prints, a photo on a key ring, and a digital CD with all the photos from your experience. The Basic Package ($50) is three 6x8 prints and a key ring. To these you can add a DVD of your dolphin interaction for $50 ($75 a la carte). The least expensive a la carte offering is a single 6x8 inch print or one 4x6 inch print and four wallet-sized prints for $20. Of all the elements at Discovery Cove, the pricing of the photos and video was the only thing I heard the slightest complaint about.

Tip: Pick your photos up early and stash them in your locker. A line starts forming at around 3:00 p.m. and it gets longer as the day wears on.

Unfortunately, you are not allowed to take those nifty disposable underwater cameras along with you — the dolphins might pinch them and do themselves an injury, I was told. But if a non-swimming member of your party is an accomplished photographer with a telephoto lens, he or she may be able to get some great shots from the shore. The trainers will be more than happy to direct them to the best vantage points.

Tropical River

Rating: ★ ★ +
Type: Circular river
Time: Unlimited
Kelly says: Best for the Aviary

If you've visited a water park, you've probably experienced a variation of this attraction. It's a circular fresh water "river," varying in depth from three to 12 feet, with an artificial current that will bear you lazily along. The river rings the ray pool and the *Coral Reef* and takes about 20 minutes to circumnavigate at an easy pace. This is strictly a one-way river; swimming against the current is discouraged by the lifeguards stationed along the route and it is virtually impossible to be out of sight of a lifeguard. The river is kept several degrees warmer than the saltwater pools. After visiting a saltwater pool like the *Coral Reef*, the river will feel like a warm bath.

Most people bring along their snorkels, although there are no fish in the river and very little to see. An attempt has been made to add visual interest by studding the bottom with chunks of Mayanesque ruins and visitors seem to have created their own decorative touches by arranging stones on the bottom in the form of peace symbols, smiley faces, and hearts.

The high, rocky banks are landscaped with lush, tropical foliage so there are only four places to enter or exit. The main entrance, between the Dolphin Lagoon and the ray pool, broadens out into a large lagoon-like pool backed by a very pretty waterfall behind which is a cool cave-like area.

The best section of the *Tropical River* is the one that passes through the *Aviary*. Heavy waterfalls at either end prevent the birds from escaping. Inside is a tropical paradise and you may be surprised at how closely you can approach birds perched at the water's edge. You can step out of the river here and visit the birds at even closer range.

Aviary

Rating: ★ ★ ★ ★ +
Type: Animal interaction
Time: Continuous viewing
Kelly says: Discovery Cove's best-kept secret

Imagine a jungle paradise where the birds are so tame they'll eat out of your hand and foot-high deer peek about the blossoms as you pet them. This is what you'll find if you step out of the *Tropical River* into the very special world of Discovery Cove's jungle aviary.

The *Aviary* is populated with some 200 exotic birds representing 100 species from the four corners of the world, many of them so intriguingly colored that they look more like products of the vivid imaginations of folk artists than creatures from the natural world. Since many of the birds found here have been hand-raised by Discovery Cove trainers, they are completely tame and will happily eat out of your hand. Food is readily available from some of those same trainers, who can also answer your questions about which bird is which. Typically there are one or two examples of each species, but in some cases, like the gaudily colored conures, you will see a small flock flying through the trees or perching on the branches. There are actually three aviaries here. There is one on each side of the river and the far aviary has a smaller aviary within it housing tiny birds like hummingbirds.

The type of food you choose — grain pellets, fruit, or meal worms — will determine which birds you attract, and unlike the dolphin encounter, your time here is unlimited. You can also feed the tiny muntjac deer, which have their own special diet. If you'd like to develop your bird-watching skills, ask one of the attendants for a laminated chart that identifies the species.

Tip: Most people discover the *Aviary* while cruising down the *Tropical River,* but there are two unmarked land entrances just past the *Ray Lagoon.* They make visiting the *Aviary* several times during the course of the day a very tempting option. Remember, there are three separate areas in the *Aviary.* Don't miss any of them.

Ray Lagoon

Rating:	★ ★ ★
Type:	Animal interaction
Time:	Continuous viewing
Kelly says:	Little kids love it

This shallow saltwater pool seems only slightly larger than the concrete ray pool over at SeaWorld. But instead of hanging over the edge, here you can wade right in and snorkel with these intriguing little critters whose scary look belies their sweet and docile nature. What's more, you don't have to pay a small fortune to feed them here; food is freely available at regular intervals from the attendants, who are extremely knowledgeable sources of information about their charges.

Tip: If you have your heart set on feeding a stingray, come early in the day. Unlike me, stingrays are smart enough to stop eating when they are full.

Coral Reef

Rating:	★ ★ ★ +
Type:	A swim-through aquatic habitat
Time:	Continuous viewing
Kelly says:	A great snorkeling experience guaranteed

Having been disappointed on several snorkeling outings in the real tropics, I was impressed by the variety of multicolored tropical fish on display in this clever re-creation of a coral reef. It's not real coral, of course, but a thin film of algae encourages fish to nibble at the simulated coral outcroppings very much as they do on the real thing.

Here you can snorkel to your heart's content without worrying about visibility being lessened by churning surf. Nor do you have to worry about those nasty little things — jellyfish, fire coral, and moray eels — that frequent real reefs. And the sharks and barracudas are thoughtfully kept behind thick (but virtually invisible) sloping glass walls. You get the illusion of swimming above them without the bone-chilling fear that typically arrives with the realization that you are swimming a few feet from something that might eat you.

The fish are fed periodically, and when the water around you is swirling with bits of food, it will also be alive with a kaleidoscope of fish. Put out your hand and the bolder among them will nibble hopefully at your fingertips as large manta rays cruise the depths below.

Horticulture Tour

Rating:	★ ★ ★ +
Type:	Show and tell from the gardening staff
Time:	About 30 minutes
Kelly says:	How Discovery Cove was created

I have rated this attraction with gardeners and landscaping aficionados in mind. Others might find it less compelling, but I would encourage you not to dismiss this short tour out of hand. It is well worth taking, especially if you are a fan of Discovery Cove and this is your second visit. It will give you a much deeper appreciation of what the landscapers and grounds crew have accomplished.

The tour is simplicity itself. A member of the groundskeeping staff meets you near Guest Services and takes you on a short stroll up the walkway towards the main entrance, pausing as he goes to explain how what looks to most visitors like a jungle — with all the randomness that the term implies — is actually a cleverly designed bit of theatrical stage setting.

I was particularly impressed with the way a wall of bamboo trees was ingeniously placed so as to mask the hum of traffic from a street that lies just a few yards away. You'd never know. You'll also learn the location of "Busch's Window," the favorite vista of the CEO of Anheuser-Busch. It is lovely and offers a nice challenge for the amateur photographer.

Conservation Cabana

Rating:	★ ★
Type:	Fun facts and critters, too

Time: Continuous viewing

Kelly says: Worth a peek

When you reach the beach area of Discovery Cove, look to your left for two square, open-sided, tent-like structures. This is the *Conservation Cabana*, where members of the education staff wait to satisfy your idle curiosity about what you are seeing and provide a deeper understanding of Nature and the importance of protecting it.

The cabana is stocked with a small collection artifacts from the natural world — egg shells, bones, coral, and the like — to pique your interest and encourage discussion. Several times during the day, the conservation staffers bring out animals for show and tell and a brief walk around the park to show them off. You might see a macaw or, my favorite, a two-toed sloth.

Eating at Discovery Cove

Discovery Cove has moved to an all-inclusive model, which means that a continental breakfast and lunch are included in the price of admission. Both are served cafeteria-style at the **Laguna Grill**, another imposing Polynesian-style structure about halfway into the park. Although the service style may bring back memories of your high school lunch room, the food is surprisingly good if somewhat limited in choice.

There is plenty to eat, with a good selection of warm and cold entrees, side salads, soft beverages, and desserts. Anheuser-Busch beers are also available, of course. The entree salads are the fairly standard chef's, chicken or seafood, while the hot entrees tend to be simple pasta combinations or stir fry dishes, the sorts of things that can be served up easily from a steam table. Made-to-order burgers are also available. I found the quality to be quite good although not exceptional. All seating is outdoors, most of it well shaded.

There are two **beach bars** located elsewhere in the park, one near the Dolphin Lagoon and the other near the stingray pool and Aviary. Here you can get soft drinks, iced tea, fruit punch, and lemonade as well as beer and wine coolers. More elaborate fruit smoothies and similar concoctions are also available, as are ice cream floats, sundaes and other "fountain treats."

Shopping at Discovery Cove

The relentless merchandising that characterizes virtually all theme parks is mercifully muted at Discovery Cove. The major shopping venue, **Tropical Gifts**, an airy Polynesian-style building, is strategically located near the main entrance, so you can pick up the bathing suit you desperately need as you enter and the high-priced souvenir you almost certainly do not need as you leave.

The merchandise is as airy and high-class as the surroundings. Here you will find the kind of upscale resort wear for men and women that will tempt you even if you didn't forget to pack your bathing suit or outerwear. For those who want a more tangible souvenir, there is a large variety of dolphin figurines and sculptures in all price ranges; the more elaborate sculptures can range up to $20,000. You will also find some very nice jewelry in dolphin, sea turtle, stingray and other deep sea motifs at moderate prices. On a more practical level, you can find things like film and more of that dolphin-friendly sunscreen you got when you arrived. I would recommend picking up one of the inexpensive disposable underwater cameras. You won't be able to take it with you to meet the dolphins, but you'll find plenty of use for it elsewhere in the park.

Farther into the park is an open air shop artfully located *across* the path, so you pretty much have to walk through it. It specializes in more practical items, like sunglasses and such.

A lavish spread at Discovery Cove's Laguna Grill.

Above: Up a lazy river.
(Loggerhead Lane at Aquatica)

Left: Dolphins above...
(Dolphin Plunge at Aquatica)

Below: ... and dolphins all around.
(Dolphin Plunge at Aquatica)

Above: A day at the beach, next door to SeaWorld. (Aquatica)

Right: Kids meet tortoise. (Aquatica)

Below: A kid's fantasy in water. (Walkabout Waters at Aquatica)

Chapter Four:

Aquatica

ORLANDO IS THE HOME OF THE WATER PARK AS WE KNOW IT TODAY. GEORGE
D. Millay, a former SeaWorld official, started it all in 1977 with the
opening of Wet 'n Wild, still going strong, just a short drive up International
Drive from the SeaWorld parks. Since then, the concept has been copied,
most noticeably by Disney, whose nearby complex has two water-themed
parks. But despite its deep pockets and design talent, Disney hasn't buried
the competition and, with the arrival of Aquatica, Disney has some high-
concept competition of its own.

Aquatica is a spacious and beautifully designed park, with a signature
SeaWorld touch — dolphins! The addition of sea creatures to the water park
formula gives Busch's new entry an edge that's not likely to be matched any
time soon.

An often overlooked selling point of non-Disney water parks like Aquatica is that they all have numerous hotels and motels just a short drive away.
This makes them especially easy to visit. If you are staying near Aquatica,
there is little need, in my opinion, to trek all the way to Disney for a water
park experience.

Like any self-respecting theme park, Aquatica has rides. But the rides
here don't rely on mechanical wonders or ingenious special effects. Indeed
they are the essence of simplicity: You walk up and then, with a little help
from gravity and a stream of water, you come down. The fun comes from the
many variations the designers work on this simple theme.

They say that Aquatica looks to the South Seas for its themes, but the
inspiration seems more geographically specific than that. Most of the names
given to rides and attractions trace back to Australian, New Zealand, and

Maori sources, the Maori being the aboriginal inhabitants of the island nation of New Zealand.

Busch seems to have made a very conscious decision to make this a family park. While there are some rides that qualify as speed slides, none of them are of the extreme-to-terrifying variety you will find at, say, Wet 'n Wild or Disney's Typhoon Lagoon Those more intense rides tend to attract a teenage and young adult crowd, who may find the offerings at Aquatica a bit tame for their tastes.

Before You Come

There really is no pressing need to do much research prior to a visit, but here are the basics. If you want to double-check anything below, you can call (888) 800-5447 or (407) 351-3600 from overseas or in Orlando. The email address is apo-guestrelations@seaworld.com.

You may also want to stop by the park's web site before you visit. There you can find the park's hours of operation during your visit and treat yourself to a multimedia preview of the park. The park's web site is:

www.aquaticabyseaworld.com

When's the Best Time To Come?

Although Aquatica is open year-round and keeps the water on its slides heated to ward off the chill of Orlando's winter, the warmer months are clearly the preferred time for a visit. As I've noted earlier, Orlando in the winter months can be comfortably warm or subject to "killer" frosts. In the summer, Aquatica makes for a refreshing break from the often blistering heat. Just don't forget the sun screen!

If you are visiting during the warmer and, therefore, busier months, you will be well advised to arrive early in the day. Aquatica has proven to be extremely popular; on more than one occasion the park has filled to capacity by 11:30 a.m. with latecomers being turned away.

Getting There

Aquatica is located just across International Drive from the SeaWorld property, conveniently close to Exit 1 of the Bee Line Expressway (Route 528). The official address is 5800 Water Play Way, Orlando, FL 32821. Whether you are traveling east or west on the Bee Line, you will turn left at the bottom of the exit ramp onto I-Drive. Look for the entrance to Aquatica on your left almost immediately. Turn onto Water Play Way, which is the cutesy name given to the driveway to the parking lot.

If you are approaching from the north or south along International Drive, just watch for the signs; it's all very well marked. There is also a free shuttle service from just outside the entrance to SeaWorld.

Arriving at Aquatica

The entrance from International Drive leads you to the far side of the park where the parking lots and main entrance are located. Parking is $10 for cars, $12 for RVs and vans. Preferred parking, which is somewhat closer to the entrance, is $15 ($7 for Passport holders). If you have visited SeaWorld or Discovery Cove the same day, parking is free; just show your parking receipt.

Once you have parked, make your way up the beautifully landscaped walkway, past rocky waterfalls, to the ticket booths. If you have booked on-line, you will find electronic kiosks off to the side where you can print out your tickets.

Opening and Closing Times

For most of the year, Aquatica opens at 10:00 a.m. During busier times, opening is moved to 9:00 a.m. The 9:00 a.m. opening is sometimes reserved for those who have purchased Saturday or Sunday tickets online; this perk allows for first dibs on prized beach locations. The parking lot opens one hour prior to the official opening time and many people will get there early to queue up at the entrance.

Closing time varies with the season; 5:00 or 6:00 p.m. are the most common closing times, but during some holidays periods, the park stays open as late as 10:00 p.m. You can find current hours on the web site or by calling (888) 800-5447 or (407) 351-3600.

One-Day Admission

If you are only visiting Aquatica, here are your options. The following prices include tax:

One-Day Admission:

Adults:	$41.48
Children (3 to 9):	$35.09
Children under 3 **free**.	

If you order your tickets online at www.aquaticabyseaworld.com, at least seven days in advance, you can purchase adult tickets at the child's price. You may also be able to get in an hour early at certain times of the year, although this perk is not always offered.

Information on "Length of Stay" tickets, which combine two or more parks; the Orlando FlexTicket, which includes five or six parks; and "Passports" (annual passes), which also offer access to multiple parks, will be found in *Chapter One: Dive Right In!*

What to Expect

If you've been to a water park before, you will find Aquatica pretty familiar, save for one or two special features that set it apart from the herd. For those who are new to the water park experience, a short introduction to the various types of water park experiences may be in order.

Slides. These are the most basic rides. After climbing a high tower, you slide down a flume on a cushion of running water, either on your back, on a rubber mat, in a one- or two-person inner tube, or in a raft that can carry up to four people. Virtually every slide will have a series of swooping turns and sudden drops. Some are open to the sky, others are completely enclosed tubes. All slides dump you in a pool at the bottom of the run.

Speed slides. Speed slides appeal to the daredevil. They are simple, narrow, flat-bottomed slides; some are pitched at an angle that approaches the vertical, others descend in a series of stair steps. They culminate in a long, flat stretch that allows you to decelerate; a few end in splash pools. They offer a short, intense experience. As noted earlier, the ones at Aquatica are less intense examples of the genre.

Wave pools. These large, fan-shaped swimming pools have a beach-like entrance at the wide end and slope to a depth of about eight feet at the other. A clever hydraulic system sets waves running from the wall to the beach, mimicking the action of the ocean. Most wave pools have several modes, producing a steady flow of varying wave heights or a sort of random choppiness. Aquatica differentiates itself by having two wave pools set side by side, one slightly more sprightly than the other.

Beaches. A large artificial sand beach faces Aquatica's two wave pools. It is filled with lounge chairs and dotted with shade umbrellas. This is where folks come to relax, recuperate, and get a tan. Most people stake out lounge chairs early in the day and make them their HQ during their stay. For those who don't like sand, there are several paved areas filled with lounges.

Lazy river. This is a signature water park attraction. Guests grab an inner tube-like float and drift around a circular water course. Aquatica has two such attractions, one of them considerably zippier than the term "lazy river" would suggest.

Water play areas. These attractions are aimed at the younger set, although older kids and even adults are not immune to their charms. Although they may have a few basic slides, the main draw is the water that spurts and springs and squirts from every imaginable direction. Kids especially like the water cannons that let them squirt unsuspecting friends and strangers. At the top of these often elaborate structures is a huge bucket that fills with water and tips over at regular intervals, sending a wall of water cascading over the kids who have gathered below in eager anticipation.

Good Things to Know About...

See the *Good Things to Know About ...* section in *Chapter One* for notes that apply to all the parks. These notes apply specifically to Aquatica.

Access for the Disabled

All parts of Aquatica are accessible to disabled guests, although no provisions are made for climbing the many stairs to the various slides. Wheelchairs are available for rent at $12 per day. Electric convenience vehicles (ECVs) are $38 per day.

Babies

Little ones under three are admitted free and strollers are available for rent if you don't have your own. Single strollers are $10 for the day, double strollers are $15. Diaper changing and baby nursing areas are also available.

Cabanas

If the forced intimacy of the artificial beach and other lounge chair areas is too declassé for you, you can opt for a private cabana for the day. Just be prepared to pay handsomely for the privilege. The rate is $150 during low season and $175 during high season (Memorial Day to Labor Day) for up to four people. Additional guests cost $30 each, with a maximum cabana capacity of seven. For this you get a small tent-like pavilion, with canvas sides that can be closed for privacy or opened for fresh air. Additional breezes are provided by a ceiling fan.

All cabanas include a mini-refrigerator, soft drinks, water, juice, and sunscreen. Cabana renters also receive a 25% discount on merchandise during their visit. So if you were planning on buying over $600 worth of swimsuits, t-shirts, and souvenirs, your cabana would pay for itself! During the low season at least.

The cabana areas can be found on either side of the two wave pools. On the left-hand side (as you face the pools), you will find the five Narrabeen cabanas and, just a short distance away, closer to *Cutback Cove,* the Uluwatu cabanas. Of the two, the seven Uluwatu cabanas are the nicer and more private ones. They sit in a nicely landscaped cul de sac, with plenty of lounge chairs and a few large umbrella-like shades in the open central space.

At the other end of the wave pools, you will find the six Yallingup cabanas, two of which look directly out onto *Big Surf Shores* pool from a raised bluff. These cabanas are near *Kata's Kookaburra Cove*, handy if you have little ones, and the first aid station. They are also less likely to draw curious visitors than the cabanas at the other end.

Dress Code

Simply put: wear a swimsuit. Aquatica frowns on shorts, cut-off jeans, or anything with zippers, buckles, or metal rivets, as these things can scratch and damage the slides. Those with fair skin can wear t-shirts if they wish. Most people go barefoot, as the parks are designed with your feet's comfort in mind. If you prefer to wear waterproof sandals or other footwear designed for water sports, they are permitted and are sold in shops in the park.

Lockers

Aquatica provides rental lockers and changing areas. Most people wear their swimsuits under their street clothes and disrobe by their locker. At day's end, they take their street clothes to a changing area, shower, towel down, and get dressed, popping their wet suits into a plastic bag. The plastic laundry bag from your hotel room is ideal for this purpose.

Small lockers rent for $8 a day, large ones for $10. For this price, you get unlimited in and out access during the day.

Safety

Water park rides are safe, just as long as you follow the common sense rules posted at the rides and obey the instructions of the ride attendants. There are over 100 of them and all of them are lifeguard certified. Life vest are readily available (for free) and some rides require them.

You are more likely to run into problems with the sun (see below) or with physical exertion if you are out of shape. You will climb more stairs at a visit to a water park than most people climb in a month. If you're not in peak condition, take it slow; pause from time to time and take in the sights.

The Sun

The Central Florida sun can be brutal. If you don't have a good base tan, a day at a water park can result in a painful sunburn, even on a cloudy day. Don't let it happen to you. Use sun block and use it liberally. Most overlooked place to protect: your feet. The sun also saps your body of moisture. Be sure to drink plenty of liquids throughout the day.

Towels

Towels can be rented for $4, $2 of which is refundable when you return them. Of course, you can also buy colorful beach towels (some very nice ones, too) from the shops in the park. It's easy (not to mention cheaper) to bring your own, even if it's one borrowed from your hotel.

Rides and Attractions at Aquatica

Aquatica is laid out in a large, lazy circle, with the zippy Roa's Rapids as its centerpiece. I will describe the attractions in approximately the order you will encounter them on a counterclockwise circumnavigation of the park, starting from the park entrance.

Dolphin Plunge

This ride is far and away the most popular in the park, so expect long lines and be patient. It is a long, but scenic, climb to the top, across a wooden suspension bridge to a staircase that circles a tall, narrow tower. At the top are two flumes, one on either side of the summit platform.

Riders sail down on their backs as they snake through some 250 feet of enclosed tubes which turn transparent as they enter and pass through the Commerson's dolphin habitat (below) before splash down in a small exit pool. It takes some practice to slow yourself down to survey the habitat and its denizens at leisure. Most people ride several times before they glimpse the dolphins that give the attraction its name.

Tip: The translucent tubes are subject to fogging, which can make it difficult to see the dolphins. Regular riders suggest riding in the afternoon, when the sun has had a chance to "burn off" the fog.

Commerson's Dolphin Habitat

As you continue into the park, you have no choice but to pass by the large pool that is home to Aquatica's signature attraction — the pod of Commerson's dolphins that give the *Dolphin Plunge* its name and raison d'être. These adorable critters, native to the waters of Australia, bear black and white markings that give them an unmistakable resemblance to Shamu. Of course, the resemblance is purely coincidental, but it makes for great subliminal marketing.

Chances are a staffer will be posted by the pool, so don't forget to ask him or her when feeding times will be the day of your visit. If you return at the appointed time, you will be treated to a display of enchanting "behaviors" as the frisky dolphins earn their daily bread... er, fish.

At other times, you have a variety of options for checking out these fascinating cousins of Flipper. The surface of the pool is one spot, although the best chance of seeing them break water is during the aforementioned feeding times. The next option is to continue into the park proper, down the stairs, and take a left turn into an underwater viewing area called **Dolphin Lookout** where you can watch them zip about the pool, over, under, and around the clear tubes of *Dolphin Plunge*.

The best option, however, is the underwater window that is part of *Loggerhead Lane,* reviewed below.

Whanau Way

There are four slides at the top of this five-story tower, two on each side. Riders use two-seater tubes to swoosh down 340 feet of curving flumes, through open and closed segments marked by cascading waterfalls, to splashdown. Each flume has a 360-degree corkscrew, either near the top or near the bottom.

The ride is situated in such a way that members of your party who are not riding can get a good view of the entire superstructure and the tubes it supports. It is also just a short stroll away from the left-hand end of the artificial beach and *Cutback Cove* (see below).

Cutback Cove & Big Surf Shores

These twin wave pools are arranged side by side (the only such arrangement in the world, apparently) facing an enormous 80,000 square foot artificial white sand beach filled with beach chairs. Most people will head here soon after arrival to stake their claim to the beach chairs that will form their party's base of operations for the day and I recommend that you do the same. A towel, a t-shirt, a beach bag, or other item is sufficient to mark a lounge chair as "taken." Most of the chairs are in the open sun, although a few offer some shade, yet another reason for getting there early.

Despite the name, *Big Surf Shores* is the calmer of the two wave pools, with gently rolling surf. It is also shallower than *Cutback Cove*, where the depth reaches six and half feet. The waves in *Cutback Cove* reach five feet and are a lot of fun.

The wave action in both pools operates on a 20 minute schedule, 12 minutes off and eight minutes on, although they don't always seem to adhere to that schedule. Electronic signs at the edge of the water variously announce the time, the air temperature, or the remaining minutes left on the current wave cycle.

Back on the beach, you can relax in your lounge chair and look past the twin wave pools to SeaWorld, just across International Drive. You will easily spot the *Sky Tower*, the golden cupola of *Journey to Atlantis*, and the steel spaghetti sprawl of *Kraken*. Be aware that the lounge chairs here are placed quite close together, so there is little opportunity for real privacy. Be prepared to get to know your neighbors.

Roa's Rapids

Just opposite the twin wave pools is one of the main entrances to Roa's Rapids, which occupies the center of the park. There is another entrance opposite *Walkabout Waters* (see below).

This is Aquatica's jazzed-up version of the "lazy river," which is a water park staple. Most lazy rivers gently float folks along on a roughly circular path. But, as the name suggests, Roa's Rapids kicks things up a notch.

Here the water zips along at a brisk four feet per second (or 2.72 miles an hour!) along a twisting, 1,500-foot course, which makes for a very different experience from the usual lazy river.

No inner tubes are available on this one. Brightly-colored neoprene life jackets are required for little ones, but they are highly recommended for all. With a life jacket on, you can simply surrender yourself to the current and float along with little or no effort. Try rolling on to your back with your feet pointed downstream!

Water splashes onto the water course from streamside spouts or waterfalls as you pass under bridges. Periodically, the stream is bisected by small islands, which forces the water into narrower streams with simulated rapids. As noted earlier, there are two spots where you can exit, which can be a bit of a challenge given the strength of the current. But I have noticed that most people are having too much fun to think about exiting after just one circuit.

Roa, by the way, is a Maori word meaning "long time."

Kata's Kookaburra Cove

This delightful area is a self-contained water park designed just for Aquatica's littlest visitors, a fact brought home by a sign announcing a *maximum* height of 48 inches. It is, in effect, a miniature version of the larger park. Its centerpiece is a shallow pool, with depths ranging from six inches to a foot and half, all of it nicely heated, with temperatures ranging up to 104 degrees. There is a raised platform in the middle where the more mischievous will find water cannons they can train on unsuspecting waders.

There are a number of places where little ones can stand under cascading water, including an ingenious station where conical buckets fill with water until their own weight causes them to tip over and splash anyone below.

Around the perimeter are arrayed a number of kiddie-sized slides that mimic the park's grown-up attractions; all of them dump riders into the central pool. **Racer Chaser** is a very mild slide with four flumes. **Slider Rider** is slightly more advanced, with more active water providing a faster ride. **Slippity Dippity** is another zippier slide with a curving "S."

Zippity Zappity is a double innertube ride that forces parents to get involved, with the grown-up sitting in the rear of the tube. There are two side-by-side slides here, with two mild curves on the way down.

All slides here are staffed with lifeguards and the rules require that all little ones under six need a "supervising adult" to ride with them. Should anything go amiss, Aquatica's first aid station is nearby.

Taumata Racer

Taumata is the abbreviated form of the longest place name in the world, Taumatawhakatangihangakoauauotamateaturipukakapikimaungahoronu-kupokaiwhenuakitanatah, a hilltop in New Zealand. Maybe that's Aquatica's way of signaling that it's a long way to splashdown on this combination of corkscrew and speed slide.

There are eight enclosed flumes in a single row at the top of this seven-story tower. Riders travel head first, prone on rubber mats with curved fronts that hide two hand holds. Sped along on an energetic stream of water, they zap through a 360-degree spiral before opening out onto steep speed slides that end in long slow-down lanes. Interestingly, the outside tubes at the top emerge in the middle of the speed slide section, while those at the center open onto the outer lanes of the speed slide.

Walkabout Waters

How to describe this water-soaked extravaganza? Imagine *Shamu's Happy Harbor* at SeaWorld or *Land of the Dragons* at Busch Gardens Africa. Then add water. Lots and lots of water.

This multi-level, multi-component play area seems to have been designed with tweens in mind. That certainly is the major demographic represented. It is decorated in dazzling shades of pink and blue, with Maori designs interspersed throughout and spinnaker-like sails at the top. Water sprays, spritzes, pours, and cascades everywhere. When you get in the middle of the maze-like structure, the noise from falling water is positively deafening.

Topping off this intricate structure are two immense buckets that fill with water and then tip over every several minutes, sending a wall of water to splash off a roof below and onto the excited kids at ground level. You will find rope walks and water cannons on the upper levels. There are a few slides, too. Nothing too extreme, but fun enough for the target audience.

Even though this attraction is obviously aimed at kids from eight into their teens, a lot of adults seem to take guilty pleasure in sampling its attractions.

Walhalla Wave

This is one of two slides that share the same superstructure. *Walhalla Wave* is a "family raft ride," which means that up to four people share a round rubber raft, thoughtfully fitted with hand holds. They zip down a 600-foot series of twists and turns, partly open and partly enclosed and dotted with waterfalls to douse you as you enter or emerge from the tunnels. It's an exhilarating and somewhat disorienting ride to the bottom.

The rafts that this ride uses are brought to the top by a conveyor belt, so you don't have to lug your own. A thoughtful touch.

HooRoo Run

Right next to *Walhalla Wave*, *HooRoo Run* is a broad, straight, open speed slide that zips riders to the bottom in three steps. This requires a minimum of two people per raft (a max of four). Both *HooRoo* and *Walhalla* have a 600 pound maximum load limit, so if you are a "big" family, you may be split up!

Loggerhead Lane

Here is a "lazy river" ride that lives up to the name. The three-foot-deep water course describes a short, meandering circle punctuated with the requisite water spouts and waterfalls. Most people ride in the one- or two-seater inner tubes provided. Most of them are already in the water, so the river is sometimes clogged with unused tubes.

Given its short length, this would be a disappointing lazy river if it were not for a very special feature. At one end, the river passes through a tunnel with a large picture window looking into the *Commerson's Dolphin Habitat*. The effect is spectacular. Not only will you get a great view of the peppy little dolphins as they cavort around the tubes of *Dolphin Plunge*, but you'll see that slide's riders swishing by on their way to splashdown. The current is gentle enough that it's an easy matter to maneuver your tube to water's edge, where you can grab the shore and pause for a longer look. Many people do just that.

A short distance away is a shortcut that links the two sides of the river. Here, under shelter, you will find **Fish Grotto**, a large aquarium filled to bursting with colorful tropical fish.

Note: There are plenty of lawn chairs all along the broad walkway that circles around (but does not completely surround) *Loggerhead Lane*. If you'd prefer not to deal with the sand of the beach in front of the wave pools, this makes an ideal alternative as your base of operations for the day.

Tassie's Twisters

You have to wade across the river of *Loggerhead Lane* to reach this ride. Grab an inner tube as you do. Once you've climbed the tower, you sit in your tube — friends can share a two-holer — and zip down one of two curving water chutes into large bowls where you whirl in a circle until gravity inevitably draws you to the hole in the bottom to splashdown zones right next to the lazy river. From here you can exit the ride or hang on to your tube for a spin along *Loggerhead Lane*. And if you haven't seen the dolphins yet, you'd be foolish not to do just that.

Conservation Cabana

This simple cabana-style tent, just across the way from the Kiwi Traders shop, is home to members of SeaWorld's conservation staff, who have stocked it with various marine artifacts and an aquarium. From time to time, some cute little critter will join them.

There is no formal schedule of shows or presentations, but you can feel free to stop in whenever you're passing by to get an impromptu briefing on the importance of marine conservation, to explore their collection, or to ask any questions that have sprung to mind during your visit.

Eating at Aquatica

Water parks are like a day at the beach. Consequently, dining (if that's the right word) at most water parks is a pretty basic experience. Aquatica sticks fairly close to that model, but adds touches of class. All of the eateries here are cafeteria or convenience-store style. All of them offer a kid's meal served in a souvenir plastic beach bucket, with a little shovel attached. And, of course, this being a Busch park, all of them offer a range of Busch beers on draft or in non-glass containers. No wine or mixed drinks are available anywhere in the park.

If you want to picnic by the beach, you'll have to buy the fixin's at Mango Market (reviewed below). Unlike some other water parks, Aquatica does not allow self-catered picnicking in the park. The only outside food that can be brought into the park is snacks in individual sized containers, bottled water, and baby food. You will be allowed one six-pack-sized cooler if its contents meet the above restrictions. In addition, no straws or plastic cup lids are allowed in the park, this for the safety of the animals.

You *can* picnic with your own food just outside the park, near the bus drop-off area, where picnic tables are provided. Perhaps to make up for this slight inconvenience, Aquatica provides free cooler-sized lockers near Guest Relations at the park entrance.

Waterstone Grill

What:	Upscale cafeteria
Where:	Near the entrance
Price Range:	$ - $$

This is the most elaborate of the eateries at Aquatica. As you enter, you are greeted by an open fire and spits on which various meats are being slow roasted. There is also a large circular cooking surface on which sliced beef for sandwiches is prepared.

To either side are twin cafeteria lines offering simple fare like chicken tender platters and fried fish sandwiches. More elaborate are the Cuban sandwich, the "chef-carved" turkey and ham sandwich, and a cheesesteak sandwich. Cold selections include a few wraps, a Cobb salad, and a grilled breast of chicken salad.

Most of the seating is outdoors and most of it is pleasantly shaded.

Banana Beach Cook-Out

What: Backyard grill fare
Where: Near *Loggerhead Lane*
Price Range: $ - $$

This simple idea is a winner. As the name suggests, all that is served here, in a simple pavilion-like building with twin serving lines, is the sort of fare that mom and dad would whip up themselves at a beach picnic — hot dogs, hamburgers, potato salad, watermelon slices, and the like.

This is an all-you-can eat buffet with an interesting pricing structure. For about $13, you can visit once. Or, for about $20, you can return as many times as you'd like during the day. Because of the pricing plan, entry to the Cook-Out is carefully controlled. There is a large seating area surrounding the serving pavilion.

Mango Market

What: Fast food to go
Where: Near *Kata's Kookaburra Cove*
Price Range: $

Mango Market is designed for "grab and go" eating. Conveniently located at the right end of the park's artificial beach (as you face the wave pools), it is a good place to pick up the fixin's for a beach-side picnic. In fact, they provide plastic shopping baskets just for that purpose.

The first thing you see when you enter is the pizza station and the open "wood fired" oven behind it. There are three varieties of small, individual-sized pizzas to choose from, cheese, pepperoni, and the fairly elaborate vegetable pizza, which features spinach, green and red peppers, and a thick layer of cheese. You can also find chicken tenders here. Chances are, whichever one you choose, there'll be one ready to go, prepackaged in its own paper box.

To either side of this central station are identical deli sections, offering an array of cold selections and beverages that you can collect en route to the cashier stations near the exits. Here you will find sandwiches and wraps, salads, and desserts. Separate coolers and freezers contain beer, soft drinks, and ice cream treats. If you're in the mood to pig out, you can even grab a pint of ice cream. The desserts also include more sensible portions of the very good chocolate-cherry and carrot cakes found over at SeaWorld.

There is plenty of seating just outside, much of it nicely shaded under tent-like coverings, but most people just tote their meals back to their lounge chairs on the beach.

Shopping at Aquatica

There are just a few shops at Aquatica and the merchandise on offer is by and large utilitarian, although often quite nice. **Sunnies n'Such** is a small kiosk just inside the entrance stocking the things you forgot (sunscreen, sun visors) and some things you might want (waterproof disposable cameras, water shoes). A short distance farther in, the much larger **Kiwi Traders** offers a wider selection of the same sort merchandise and adds colorful souvenir beach towels and equally colorful swimwear for men and women. Kiwi Traders also sells some colorful painted metal figures based on the animal symbols found around the park. These renditions of kiwis, kookabura birds, and such make attractive wall-mounted decorative accents.

Near the far end of the park, between Banana Beach Cook-Out and HooRoo Run, is **Adaptations**, an open-sided shop featuring t-shirts, flip-flops, bead necklaces and the kind of sun dresses that you can throw over a wet swim suit. Smaller, mobile kiosks pop up here and there as crowds warrant.

It's all downhill from here. (Taumata Racer at Aquatica)

CHAPTER FIVE:

The Resort Hotels

SEAWORLD AND THE OTHER ORLANDO PARKS DO NOT HAVE THEIR OWN collection of branded, on-site resort hotels, but they have the next best thing. Within a short distance of the parks you will find a number of world-class, luxury resort hotel properties that offer a sort of do-it-yourself option for vacationers who want to combine their theme park fun with a bit of upscale pampering and fine dining when the parks close.

None of the resorts reviewed here offers quite the stroll-to-the-parks convenience of those offered by Universal Orlando (although the Renaissance comes close). You will most likely have to drive from your resort to the park of your choice, but the same is true for many of the hotels at nearby Disney World. And many of these resorts offer shuttle service. In short, I doubt you will feel overly inconvenienced when staying at one of these hotels.

Several of them are home to some of Orlando's finest restaurants, while others offer spacious villa apartments of up to three bedrooms where a large family can spread out and prepare at least some of their meals in their home away from home. All of them offer splendid amenities for pampering and relaxation, including in some cases a golf course right on property. Those who have enjoyed staying at the fine resorts at Disney or Universal Orlando will, I believe, feel right at home when staying at one of these properties.

In this chapter, I cover these Orlando resorts along with some more moderate options for those on a budget. First I will discuss four high-end resort properties that I sampled in depth while writing this book, listed in order of their proximity to SeaWorld. Next I will discuss a number of properties in the Marriott family of resorts and hotels, ranging from the very upscale to the more moderate, that have formed a special relationship with

SeaWorld. Finally, I will briefly touch on other options close to the Orlando parks. For each property reviewed, I provide the approximate driving distance to SeaWorld's vehicle entrance on Central Florida Parkway or walking time to the SeaWorld front gate. Lodging options near Busch Gardens Africa, in Tampa, are discussed in *Chapter Six*.

The Renaissance Orlando Resort seen from SeaWorld (top)
and Mist, the sushi bar in the hotel's atrium.

Renaissance Orlando Resort

6677 Sea Harbor Drive

Orlando, FL 32821

(407) 351-5555; fax: (407) 351-9991

www.marriott.com

Walking time to SeaWorld: 7 minutes

Marriott's Renaissance Orlando Resort at SeaWorld, to use it's formal name, is the closest resort property to SeaWorld, so close in fact that it is clearly visible from within the park. This proximity alone might make it your first choice, but it has much else to recommend it.

A large, ten-story rectangular building, the hotel itself is not architecturally imposing on the outside. It has long been a major destination for conventions, medical symposia, and similar get-togethers and the functional layout of the hotel reflects that mission. As SeaWorld has grown in both stature and popularity, however, the Renaissance has taken on the additional role of playing host to families with nothing but leisure on their minds.

Orientation

You arrive at the Renaissance as you would to any major business hotel. The spacious entrance is all business and efficiency. It is only when you step inside that you begin to experience the full effect of the place, which underwent a $27 million renovation in 2007.

The front desks, accommodating registration, bell stand, and concierge, are backed by large high-definition television screens filled with ever-changing underwater scenes of tropical reefs, which is the resort's signature theme. The immediate effect is both exciting and soothing. Step past the elevator bank and you are in the resort's main attraction, a soaring sun-filled atrium that fills much of the hotel's interior space and rises past the tenth story to a glass roof. Exterior corridors run down the long sides of the rectangular space (this is not a hotel for acrophobes!), while interior rooms on the short sides look out onto the lobby area below.

The blue and white lobby is dominated by eight tall towers that support the skylit roof high above. Four of them in the center of the lobby have been outfitted with blue fabric panels, adding a touch of color and defining the location of a large ovoid structure that serves as the lobby bar. Looming over the bar is a mosaic of sixteen large-screen HD displays that form a single screen on which enormous tropical fish and coral reef creatures appear in a constantly changing show of color and form.

To one side is a casual sports bar, partially hidden behind a waterfall, to the other the hotel's main dining room, and in between plenty of space for well separated seating areas that offer a bit of privacy for meeting friends.

The Renaissance is located on Sea Harbor Drive, just off Interstate 4, and directly across from SeaWorld. It is just a seven-minute stroll across the street and through the SeaWorld parking lot to the front gate. I've timed it! It's even possible to walk from here to Aquatica and Discovery Cove, although those are *much* longer walks.

Rooms and Suites

Despite its proximity to SeaWorld, the 781-room Renaissance is still primarily a meetings venue and the selection of rooms reflects that reality. Most of the higher end suites are designed with business moguls, not traveling families, in mind. Still, there is plenty of room in which to spread out and families can save money by booking connecting rooms rather than a suite.

At 472 square feet, the standard rooms, with either one king-sized bed or two queens, are the largest in the area. High ceilings add to the feeling of spaciousness. They are graciously decorated with high beds and sumptuous bedding, including a riot of pillows in varying sizes. All rooms have 32-inch flat screen high-definition televisions to which you can hook up your laptop. There is also an iPod hookup to the clock radio. Every room has a refrigerator, but no rooms have a microwave.

Executive King rooms are large corner rooms with 685 square feet of elbow room, 42-inch flat screen TVs, and a large table for in-room dining. They have the option of connecting to a standard king room

If you insist on more space, you can book a 780 square-foot "parlor suite," designed for business meetings, with either a king room or a queen room (or both!) connecting.

Room Rates

Here are the quoted rates for Renaissance's standard room configurations, from low to high season:

Standard Room (king or queen)	$129 - $429
Executive King	$259 - $599
Parlor Suite	$259 - $799

Amenities

The Renaissance is a fairly compact property, with much of the available space taken up by meeting rooms and the parking that goes with them. However, they have managed to pack in the kind of recreational activities you'd expect of a well-appointed resort.

Pool

A spacious, heated, Olympic-sized pool is located outside, in a grassy area to the rear of the hotel. A large hot tub is just paces away, as is a fenced-in child's wading pool area. There is plenty of room for sun bathing, on lounge chairs or on the lawn and a poolside bar beckons. There is no lifeguard on duty, so children under 16 must be under adult supervision at all times. Pool hours are 6:00 a.m. to 11:00 p.m.

nèu lotus spa

The nèu (pronounced "new") lotus spa is as low key as the use of lower case letters would suggest. Located on the hotel's second floor, it is a compact and nicely decorated getaway offering a full range of salon services and spa "therapies" with names like "micronized marine algae envelopment." Procedures, or should I say *experiences*, range from $35 to over $200. You can opt for a series of packages ranging from $150 to $405 for a 4-hour 20-minute "Lazy Day Indulgence."

All spa guests have access to the steam rooms and a comfortable "relaxation area," where you can help yourself to a selection of juices, read a magazine, and play with some fun little wooden puzzles. If that's all you'd care to do, it's yours for just $20 a day.

Fitness Center

Just off the main lobby is a sleek health club offering the very latest in pec-pumping paraphernalia. Here you can exhaust yourself on treadmills, recumbent and standing bicycle machines, or stairclimbers. For the die-hard traditionalist, there are also free weights. Access to the fitness center is free, but you will need your room key to unlock the door.

Fitness-minded guests can also stop by the concierge desk for a map of one- to four-mile jogging routes along nearby streets, most of them along paved sidewalks.

Tennis, Basketball, Volleyball

Just past the pool you will find still more options for staying active during your visit to the resort. There are two tennis courts and a full basketball court, both of which are lighted to allow for night time play. During the day, you can take advantage of the nice, sandy volleyball court. Nearby is a recreation area featuring a four-square court, bocce ball, tether ball, and a three-hole putting green.

All are free, as is the equipment needed to play. The hotel staff will even help arrange pick-up volleyball games. This area was scheduled for expansion at press time, so expect more options for active play when you visit.

Good Things To Know About…

Business Center

Like any hotel that caters to the convention trade, the Renaissance has a business center, but it also has an outpost of **FedEx/Kinko's** in one corner of the lobby. It is open Monday through Friday from 7:00 a.m. to 5:00 p.m.

Guest Laundry

The hotel offers dry cleaning services, but has no guest laundry. Guest services will direct you to nearby options.

Internet Access

Internet service is available in all rooms using either USB or Ethernet cables. There is a fee of $14.95 per day, which includes unlimited local and long distance telephone calls. Free wireless Internet access is available in the public areas of the hotel.

Meetings and Conventions

The hotel has 185,000 square feet of meeting space, ranging from cavernous halls suitable for trade shows, to grand ballrooms, to intimate conference rooms. If you'd like to explore holding your next meeting at the Renaissance Orlando, call Conference Management at (407) 351-5555.

Parking

The hotel has ample parking in outdoor lots. The fee for self-parking is $12 per day; valet parking is $16 per day, plus tips, of course.

Pets

Pets are not allowed at the resort.

Smoking

The resort has a totally no-smoking policy and they're serious about it. If you smoke in your room, you will be charged a $250 "room recovery" fee.

Transportation Services

The resort offers complimentary shuttle service to SeaWorld, Aquatica, and Universal Orlando, with three morning departures and three return trips in the late afternoon. There is a paid service to Walt Disney World. You need to make your shuttle arrangements in advance. If you booked a Discovery Cove package through the resort, they will provide a free ride. If you booked elsewhere, you still might be able to get a lift, but it is not guaranteed.

There is also a Hertz rental car counter in the hotel, and taxi and limousine service is readily available.

Dining at Renaissance Orlando Resort

The Renaissance has a limited roster of dining venues, most of them located in or just off the lobby. The exception is the poolside bar out back. There is some overlap in the menus, but enough choice to keep most people happy. And if you don't see anything on the menu you like, ask to see the menus from the other places. You can order from another and have the food delivered to where you are sitting. Guests who just can't get it together to drag themselves to one of these restaurants can take advantage of the hotel's 24-hour room service.

In addition to the restaurants reviewed below, there is a **Starbucks** off the lobby. It is open from 6:00 a.m. to 3:00 p.m.

Tradewinds

What:	Casual American food
Where:	Off the lobby on the ground floor
Price Range:	$$ - $$$$
Hours:	Daily, 6:00 a.m. to 2:30 p.m. and 5:30 p.m. to 10:30 p.m.
Reservations:	Not required, but strongly suggested; extension 2770

This is the resort's most formal dining venue, but it stops well short of the "fine dining" cliches. "Ordinary food done extraordinarily well" is the way they like to put it, and by and large they deliver.

There are no exotic preparations or over the top presentations and there is an emphasis on organic ingredients. The typical entree consists of a few main ingredients straightforwardly presented on a long rectangular plate. The menu is divided into Small, Medium, and Large Plates.

The Small Plates are starters, soups, and salads and include such standards as shrimp toast, onion soup, Caesar salads, and a tomato mozzarella platter with heirloom tomatoes. There are just a few Medium Plates, which are dinner alternatives like burgers and sandwiches. The bulk of the menu consists of the Large Plates.

These entrees are well divided among meat, poultry, and seafood items, with all the beef coming from the organic Harris Ranch in California. There is Florida grouper, and seared yellow tail snapper along with churrasco skirt steak, baby back ribs and a pasta selection. In short, something for everyone. Desserts have their own menu, presented at meal's end. Like the entrees, they are familiar choices done with a certain flair.

The wine list is mercifully short and, if you are picking up the tab, mercifully moderate in price, with most bottles in the $28 to $35 range. The choices are overwhelmingly from California and from familiar mid-market vineyards, with only the occasional interloper from Australia or Italy.

Like the food, the decor is modestly understated — nice enough to be special, yet casual enough to be not in the least intimidating. The entrance decoration suggests a Caribbean beach hideaway.

The Boardwalk Sports Bar

What: Casual bar/restaurant
Where: In the lobby, under a second level
Price Range: $$
Hours: Monday to Friday 2:30 p.m. to 1:00 a.m.; Saturday, Sunday noon to 1:00 a.m.
Reservations: None

Behind a waterfall and a curved staircase that leads to a second-level area used for private functions, this open-sided casual eatery earns its sports bar name by virtue of the flat-screen televisions tuned to sports channels that dot the walls. There is no sign to tell you its name, but it's easy enough to find, as the tables spill out into the lobby on one side.

This is the spot for a quick bite or a long drink. The food is a scaled down version of what you might expect at Tradewinds, served on the same sleek rectangular plates. There is classic bar grub like Buffalo wings and quesadillas (organic ones here). The Main Plates are really appetizer-sized servings of tasty items like baby back ribs, and shrimp with sausage-spiked cheese grits. There are desserts, too.

Despite the sports bar name and ambience, this is a kid-friendly restaurant. It is probably your best bet if you have little ones in tow.

Mist

What: Lobby bar with sushi and designer cocktails
Where: In the middle of the lobby
Price Range: $$ - $$$
Hours: 5:00 p.m. to 10:00 p.m. for sushi; bar to 11:00 p.m.
Reservations: None

This spectacular lobby bar is instantly recognizable by the sixteen-screen video display of gaudily colored tropical fish. It's an ideal place to meet — and impress — guests who might be joining you for dinner. You can have a pre-meal cocktail, a sushi appetizer, or simply stay here and make a meal of the ultra-fresh sushi and sashimi it serves.

The servings are appetizer size and most people seem to use the food as ballast for the fancy (and pricey) martinis and other trendy mixed drinks.

The menu leans heavily to makimono, or rolls of rice and fish wrapped in seaweed. There are just a handful of sashimi (or raw fish) choices. Most dishes are in the $10 to $15 range. Unfortunately, there is only one sampler platter on offer, a sashimi selection. Solution: bring a group, order a selection, and share.

The Palms

What:	Poolside bar with light food
Where:	By the swimming pool
Price Range:	$$
Hours:	5:30 p.m. to 10:00 p.m.
Reservations:	None

Located just steps away from the heated pool, The Palms is a modest bar with a small number of tables under a shaded pavilion. It serves up a good selection of frozen drinks like margaritas and piña coladas as well as "signature drinks" such as a Cruzan Rum Runner and a Pomegranate Margarita. For the less adventurous, there is beer and a selection of non-alcoholic smoothies.

A surprisingly varied menu of light meals is also on offer. The choices range from bar food like chicken wings and nachos to a good selection of sandwiches. The healthier diner can choose from salads like the Tuscan Shrimp or a fresh fruit basket. A small selection of simple desserts rounds out the menu. This is a great place for Mom and Dad to relax while keeping an eye on the kids in the pool.

Shopping at Renaissance Orlando

Put succinctly, there's not much. A **gift shop**, otherwise unnamed, occupies what seems to have been designed originally as two retail spaces. It fulfills all the usual functions of a hotel gift shop, dispensing newspapers (including *The New York Times*), magazines, sundries, and light snacks.

The second room contains a small but quite nice selection of Florida and resort wear. For the women, there are brands like Rafaella and Fresh Produce and for the men, Tommy Bahamas. If you need casual wear or bathing suits, you are likely to find something more than acceptable here. There is also a small selection of jewelry and accessories to fill out your wardrobe.

Above: The Lighthouse Bar on the waterfront. (Grande Vista)

Left: A new take on Bananas Foster. (Nick's Grill at Grande Vista)

Below: The main pool. (Grande Vista)

Marriott's Grande Vista

5925 Avenida Vista

Orlando, FL 32821

(800) 845-5279; (407) 238-7676; fax (407) 238-0900

www.marriott.com

Distance from SeaWorld: 1.6 miles

Welcome to the world of timeshare living! Marriott's Grande Vista is one of nearly 50 properties around the world that are part of the Marriott Vacation Club. Marriott owners have purchased the right to stay here for a week (or more!) each year. Thanks to "flexible usage options," they can swap their week for another week, another resort, or both, all within the Marriott portfolio of properties. Timeshare owners always have the right to skip using their unit in exchange for Marriott Rewards points, which they can use at Marriott hotels. As a result, there is a small number of units available for rent at daily rates to folks like you and me. Because of the limited number of units available at any given time, it's a good idea to book well in advance if this option appeals to you.

And who does it appeal to? Well, families for one, who can prepare many of their meals "at home" and cut down considerably on their vacation expenses. Larger families who find it difficult to find accommodations at some nearby theme park resorts, with their four-people-to-a-room limits, are also good candidates for a Grande Vista stay. To this list, I would add anyone who wants a break from the usual hotel routine; there's something very comforting about returning from a hectic day at the theme parks to a spacious and beautifully decorated apartment where you can spread out and feel like you actually live there — yet still have a maid to make the beds and change the towels.

Orientation

Grande Vista is conveniently located off International Drive, less than a mile south of the trio of SeaWorld parks. Turning off I-Drive onto Avenida Vista, you approach the resort up a broad avenue lined with magnolia trees that are spectacular when they are abloom with white blossoms. Stop at the gatehouse and you will be directed to reception in the **Village Center** building. Once checked in, you will use your room key to open the gates.

There are 900 units in 24 buildings artfully arranged around a long narrow lake that is crossed by a lovely white pedestrian bridge and punctuated with a decorative fountain that sends a spray of water high into the air. The earthy pastels and architectural touches evoke the look and feel of old St. Augustine. The buildings, with their exterior corridors, present a rather anonymous, windowless face to the public streets, but once you step inside your unit, the gracious interior spaces open out onto the lake or the golf course that surrounds the property. All of the units have screened porches that better allow you to savor the view.

All in all, the resort is much like an upscale apartment development, albeit one with hotel services like daily maid service.

Once you have settled in, you are very much at home. You can take a leisurely stroll around the lake to familiarize yourself with the location of pools, dining options, and the golf course. Everything is within easy walking distance, although many guests rent pedal-powered surreys to get around, just for the fun of it.

Villas

No mere rooms here! Everything is a "villa" or, if you prefer, an apartment. Your choices range from studios, to one-, two-, and three-bedroom villas, all of which are lavishly furnished and have fully functioning and well appointed kitchens complete with plates, silverware, and little extras like coffee filters, paper towels and dishwashing detergent. All one-, two-, and three-bedroom villas feature jacuzzi-style tubs, and a washer and dryer.

The villas are lavishly and tastefully decorated, avoiding the pastel Florida vacation home cliches you so often encounter in Orlando-area rental homes. The beds are substantial as is the bedding, with its soft sheets and abundance of pillows. All units have generous seating and dining areas, and some of us will appreciate the televisions in all bedrooms as well as the living area.

Check-in time is 4:00 p.m. and it seems rare that a unit is available earlier. Check-out time is 10:00 a.m., somewhat earlier than you may be used to, so be aware.

Villa Rates

The rates are surprisingly moderate, especially when you consider that a two-bedroom unit can sleep up to eight people. Here are the nightly rates from low to high during the year; they rise and fall in sync with Orlando's tourist traffic (see *Chapter One: Dive Right In*).

Studio	$129 - $259
1 Bedroom	$149 - $299
2 Bedroom	$219 - $399
3 Bedroom	$299 - $499

Amenities

Although it is a resort community, Grande Vista offers many of the same amenities as a resort hotel. In addition to daily maid service, there is daily coffee service, free Internet access, cable television with a wide array of channel choices, and a concierge desk to assist you with finding your way around the resort and Orlando. They'll even give you a wake up call. Here are some other amenities worth noting:

Pools

There are four pools strategically located throughout the property; two are rather elaborate and two others are designated as "satellite" pools. Regardless of where you are staying a pool should be a short stroll away.

The main Village Center Pool, just adjacent to the Village Center is quite elaborate, with plenty of lounging space overlooking the lake. There are several jacuzzi pools. A separate lap pool will appeal to serious swimmers.

A smaller, but no less elaborate pool, called the Vista del Sol, can be found across the lake by the Copa Loca pool bar and grill. It has waterfalls, fountains, a kiddie pool, and a watery play area that makes it especially attractive to kids. There are no lifeguards on duty at any of the pools and resort rules require that all children 12 and under be accompanied by an adult.

Golf

One of the big draws for guests here is the on-property **Faldo Golf Institute** and its nine-hole course that wraps around the resort buildings. You can simply play a single round of golf or choose from a menu of golf instruction that ranges from clinics ($30) to complete two- and three-day golf schools (up to $1,500). Another option is a weekly membership that offers unlimited play (depending on tee time availability) for seven days. More information will be found at:

www.gofaldo.com

Just across International Drive from Marriott's Grande Vista is another golfing option, the 18-hole championship **Grande Pines Golf Club**, which offers "TifEagle greens, rolling fairways, towering pines, sparkling lakes," and GPS-equipped carts to help you navigate it all. More information is available at:

www.grandepines.com

Kids' Activities

Parents will be happy to know that a varied menu of activities for kids of all ages is available daily. Activities range from fingerpainting to model car building to a Kid's Night Out.

Some activities are for specific age groups, while others are open to the entire family, and most require parental supervision. A few are complimentary, but most require a modest fee.

Fitness Center

A small, but perfectly adequate fitness center is located in the Village Center building. It features the usual array of resistance machines, treadmills, stationary bicycles, and stairclimbers. You must be at least 16 years old to use the fitness center. A steam room is located in the adjacent locker room and a sauna is just a short walk away near the Village Center Pool.

Spa

A basic menu of massage treatments and aromatherapy is available in the Village Center Activities Center. If you feel the need for more upscale pampering, the concierge desk will make an appointment for you at the decidedly upscale spa of the Ritz-Carlton Spa Orlando, Grande Lakes, a short drive away.

Tennis, Basketball, Volleyball

In addition to golf, the resort features four clay **tennis** courts. Use is complimentary and you can rent rackets and buy balls for a modest fee. Tennis lessons are available for somewhat more. Near the courts is a half **basketball** court in case you're in the mood for a pickup game. Beach **volleyball** is also available.

Rentals

For laid-back, casual fun right at the resort, stop by the **Harbor Master**, just outside the Village Center building by the lake. There you can rent surrey bikes seating two to four riders ($12.50 to $18 an hour) that you can pedal around the property or paddle boats to take out onto the lake ($10 to $20 a half hour).

If you or the kids would like to try your hand at fishing in the resort lake, you can rent rods ($6 for two hours). And in case you forgot your own worms, they'll sell you some! The Harbor Master opens at 8:30 each morning.

Good Things to Know About ...

Business Center

There is no business center at the Grande Vista. Instead, guests are directed to the Renaissance Resort, a short drive away (see above).

Internet Access

Complimentary wireless Internet access is available in all units. Bridge connectors are available at the front desk. If you didn't bring your laptop, Internet kiosks are located near the front desk.

Laundry

Most units have a washer and dryer. If you are staying in a "guest suite" that doesn't, there are complimentary facilities at several locations around the property. In either cases you will have to supply your own detergent and such, which can be purchased at **The Marketplace** in the Village Center. Dry cleaning can be dropped at the front desk where you checked in; if you drop it off before 8:30 in the morning, it will be back by 7:00 that night.

Parking

There is ample parking around the villa buildings, all of it free.

Pets

Pets are not allowed at the resort.

Smoking

There is no smoking in the villas or balconies. Smoking is restricted to designated smoking areas out of doors.

Transportation Elsewhere

No shuttle service is offered to SeaWorld or any of the other nearby theme parks; the front desk will, however, be happy to get you a taxi.

Dining at Marriott's Grande Vista

Grande Vista is designed as a home away from home for timeshare owners, and since every villa has its own fully-equipped kitchen, on-site dining options are somewhat limited. Still, if you are dead set against doing your own cooking, you needn't go hungry.

In addition to the spots reviewed below, there is **The Marketplace**, a sort of convenience store, open from 7:00 a.m. to 11:00 p.m., that offers grilled panini sandwiches, in addition to kitchen staples, wine, and liquor. Next door is a walk-up window combining a **Pizza Hut** and **Edy's** ice cream. It is open from 11:00 a.m. to 10:00 p.m. and the Pizza Hut delivers on property from 4:00 p.m. to 11:00 p.m. All of these are located in the Village Center building that houses resort reception. In addition, you will no doubt receive several flyers, slipped under your door, advertising local food delivery services.

Located in the lighthouse-like tower that is the resort's centerpiece, the **Lighthouse Bar** is minuscule as bars go, with a limited selection, but it's a great place to meet old Grande Vista hands. The close quarters encourage conversation and new friendships. If you feel the need to spread out, al fresco seating is just steps away.

Copa Loca Pool Bar & Grill

What: Casual bar and poolside fare
Where: Between buildings 84 and 79 on the west side of the lake
Price Range: $ - $$
Hours: Daily, 11:00 a.m. to 10:00 p.m. (kitchen closes at 9)
Reservations: None

The atmosphere is laid back, the servers young and friendly, the view just about perfect, and the food is pretty decent into the bargain. Situated next to one of the resort's nicer pools, the restaurant offers a shortish menu of casual sandwiches and salads. There are pan-seared grouper and Caribbean jerk chicken sandwiches along with turkey wraps, burgers, and hot dogs. The "signature" Copa Club consists of turkey, ham, bacon, swiss and cheddar cheese on toasted sourdough lathered with herbed mayo. Prices are moderate and there's an even cheaper Kids Korner menu.

The bar serves up the usual assortment of poolside beverages, both alcoholic and non, and they make a nice accompaniment to appetizers like coconut shrimp and chicken quesadillas. Desserts, too!

Nick's Grill

What: Casual American food
Where: In the Faldo Golf Institute
Price Range: $$ - $$$
Hours: Daily, 7:00 a.m. to 9:30 p.m.
Reservations: Strongly suggested; extension 4013 or (407) 238-6365

This intimate and classy 60-seat restaurant is the resort's equivalent of a hotel restaurant, serving breakfast, lunch and dinner seven days a week. There is a narrow bar leading to a circular dining room that looks out onto the Faldo Institute's nine-hole golf course; a narrow outside patio offers some outdoor seating during warmer months.

Because the entrance lies just outside the guard house that screens all resort guests, the restaurant is easily accessible to the general public and has a loyal local following that comes for the Tuesday night baby back ribs special or the Wednesday prime rib feast. I'd recommend it, even if you are not staying here. Reservations, then, are vital.

Shopping at Grande Vista

In a word: none. **Marketplace** offers a few clothing items and sundries, but for anything else, you'll have to head off-property. Perhaps the most popular shopping destination is **Publix**, the large supermarket located at the Regency Village shopping center, a bit south of the resort. Turn left at the exit onto International Drive and then right at the second light.

Above: The Peabody Orlando

Left: Duckmaster Dave in full regalia. (Peabody Orlando)

Below: Ducks on duty. (Peabody Orlando)

The Peabody Orlando

9801 International Drive
Orlando, FL 32819
(800) PEABODY; (407) 352-4000; fax: (407) 351-0073
www.peabodyorlando.com
Distance from SeaWorld: 2.2 miles

Everything's just ducky at The Peabody Orlando, starting with the ducks in the lobby. Let me explain.

The Peabody Orlando is an outpost of a Memphis original, which dates back to 1869. In the 1930s, by which time the Peabody had become one of the finest hotels in the South, a mischievous hotel manager snuck some live ducks he had used as hunting decoys (legl back then) into the lobby pool. It was intended as a joke, but it was an instant hit with guests and staff alike and a hotel legend was born. Today, "teams" of ducks grace the lobbies of the three Peabody Hotels (the third is in Little Rock, Arkansas) and have become so identified with the Peabody brand that they are part of its logo. In fact, duck imagery is everywhere in the hotel. There is duck-shaped soap in the rooms, cute little ducklings on the little shampoo bottles, and lots of duck figurines in the gift shop.

The ducks are a lighthearted touch that belies the Peabody's serious commitment to quality and service. For many years, the Peabody was considered Orlando's premier luxury hotel and, while it has some competition now, it consistently wins a four-star rating from the *Mobil Travel Guide*.

Orientation

The Peabody is located on International Drive, eight-tenths of a mile north of the Bee Line Expressway and directly across from the Orlando Convention Center, all three million square feet of it, making it the location of choice if you are combining your Orlando trip with one of the many trade shows that unfold there. It is also just a short drive from SeaWorld. In fact, you can see SeaWorld's *Sky Tower* from the rooms facing the Convention Center. To the north lies the gaudy tourist strip that is International Drive. Within walking distance you will find the Pointe★Orlando shopping center, with a passel of restaurants for every taste and wallet, a posh multiplex cinema with an IMAX screen, and WonderWorks, a science-museum-like interactive attraction.

The hotel's main entrance lies under a massive portico, punctuated with bubbling fountains and tiered waterfalls, a fitting prelude to the stylish lobby inside, where yet more fountains and waterfalls await. As you enter, the reception area, concierge desk, and the hotel's few shops are to your left or the north end of the hotel; dining is to your right at the south end of the building; and the soaring atrium lobby, which is home to the famous Peabody ducks, is straight ahead. The convention and meeting rooms are just past the lobby and down a flight of stairs. The hotel lobby is a popular meeting area that seems to bustle at all times of the day, never more so than when the ducks make their entrance and exit.

Once inside, there's really no reason to leave, except to go to the theme parks or head out to the golf course. All of the hotel amenities are "inside" the hotel. On the Recreation Level, two stories above the lobby, you will find a large pool with generous sunning areas atop the portico in front of the hotel; the tennis courts are over the convention and meeting facilities at the back.

Rooms and Suites

The Peabody Orlando has 891 rooms including 57 suites. At press time, the hotel was undergoing a significant expansion that will add 759 rooms and more meeting space in a separate tower just north of the existing building. The construction is causing remarkably little inconvenience to guests, although you may want to request a room facing the front of the building.

Rooms are designated as superior, deluxe, and executive, each slightly larger than the other and offering enhanced in-room amenities. Rooms facing the front of the hotel have splendid views to the southwest. Orlando often has spectacular sunsets and you'll have a ringside seat. Later at night you can see the fireworks from the Illuminations show at Epcot and the nightly fireworks extravaganza at Magic Kingdom.

The 25th through 27th floors are designated as the Club Level, which offers a certain additional level of privacy in that you can only access those floors with the right room key. Club Level guests are also treated to a complimentary continental breakfast and evening hors d'oeuvres with a cash bar.

Room Rates

The Peabody quotes "standard rates." Just be aware that the price of a room might rise or fall at various times of the year, depending on the tourist and business traffic.

Superior	$395
Deluxe	$425
Executive	$455
Club	$495

Amenities

As noted earlier, all the hotel's amenities are in the hotel. Even when you step outside it is onto spacious terraces on the third floor Recreation Level.

Peabody Ducks

Without a doubt, the hotel's most important amenity is the arrival and departure of its signature ducks to the flower bedecked fountain in the lobby. Each morning at 11:00 a.m. they descend from their "Duck Palace" on the elevators and waddle along a red carpet and up special duck-sized stairs to the fountain, where they splash about merrily and entertain kids of all ages. At 5:00 p.m. sharp the process is reversed as they troop dutifully back upstairs to their off-duty lodgings by the tennis courts on the Recreation Level.

All of this is overseen by Duck Master Dave, resplendent in a scarlet frock coat bedecked with golden epaulets and braid and carrying a cane topped with a golden duck head. He is ably assisted by one or two young guests who, in recognition of their service, are solemnly inducted as "Honorary Duck Masters of the Royal Order" with a gentle tap of the golden duck head on each shoulder. I know it all sounds unbelievably silly, but trust me, you'll love it.

If you want your child to participate (and you do!), call the concierge as soon as you know when you will be staying at the hotel. It's strictly on a first-come, first-served basis. If you find you're too late, you can have your child put on a standby list as cancellations and no-shows do happen.

Pool

A long, narrow pool, almost Olympic-size in length, sits atop the hotel's entrance portico on the Recreation Level. A niche on one side houses two lap lanes for serious swimmers, but there's plenty of room to just loll about, if that's more your speed. To one side is a comfortably sized kiddie pool, complete with waterfall.

There's plenty of lounging space as well as a jacuzzi spa that can accommodate a fair sized group. A terrace a few steps above the pool offers still more lounging chairs as well as tables that surround a pool bar. Light meals are offered in addition to the usual range of alcoholic and non-alcoholic refreshments. You can eat by the bar, or be served by wandering waiters anywhere in the pool area.

At either end of the pool are cabanas which can be rented by the half or full day; a twilight special is also offered. The pool is open from 7:00 a.m. to 11:00 p.m.

Fitness Center

The fitness center, or the Peabody Athletic Club as they like to call it, is on the Recreation Level, near the pool. It is a compact facility with a full range of Nautilus machines and a small selection of treadmills, stairclimbers, and stationary bikes. Free weights and dumbells are available for traditionalists. The men's and women's locker rooms contain steam rooms and saunas, with a shared coed jacuzzi.

Tennis Courts

Four hard surface tennis courts sit side by side on a terrace at the rear of the Recreation Level. Hours are 8:00 a.m. to 10:00 p.m.; there is no charge, but reservations are required. Racquets can be rented for a modest fee and balls are available for sale. Lessons are also available. The Peabody Athletic Club can handle all arrangements.

Golf Pro Shop

Just by the tennis courts is a golf shop operated by Captain's Choice Golf Services. The Peabody doesn't have its own golf course, but here you can gain access to 20 different area courses, many of them at a discount. Part of the service provided by Captain's Choice is matching players of varying levels of ability to the right course for them. Transportation is $50 for a two-some or a foursome and clubs can be rented for another $50. Greens fees range from $75 to $125 in the torrid summertime to $125 to $280 in the peak season, during the winter. For more information, call (407) 352-1102 or extension 4491 within the hotel. Captain's Choice web site is:

www.oflgolf.com

Salon and Spa

The Shala Salon & Spa is also located on the Recreation Level and although it looks very much like a standard-issue hair salon, they offer an extensive menu of services beyond the usual hair design and hair coloring, including bikini waxes and something called a Chocolate Latte Manicure. Various packages that combine a number of treatments are available at suitably astronomical prices. The telephone is 407-248-8009 or on the Internet at:

www.shalasalon.com

Good Things To Know About . . .

Hotel Services Fee

A $10 per day "Hotel Fee" is added to your room rate. This covers your Internet access, a daily pass to the I-Ride Trolley (both discussed below), two bottles of water in your room each day, and overnight shoe shine service. It also includes lobby coffee in the morning from 5:30 to 7:00 a.m. Since there are no coffee makers in the rooms, this perk is worth noting.

Hotel Expansion

As you read this, the Peabody is undergoing a major expansion in the form of an adjoining tower building that will add 759 rooms, a 17,000 square foot spa area, a "grotto-like" swimming pool, a restaurant with a Napa Valley wine theme, and yet more parking and meeting space. Because the new addition, scheduled to open in 2010, is somewhat separate from the existing hotel, guests will experience little inconvenience during construction. The biggest effect that I've noticed is that self-parking is temporarily not available, so you will have to use the hotel's valet parking service (see below).

I-Ride Trolley

The I-Ride Trolley (buses dolled up to look like trolleys, actually) is a shuttle service that runs along the International Drive corridor, linking the outlet malls to the north of the Peabody with SeaWorld and Aquatica to the south. The Hotel Services Fee covers two chits per room for the length of your stay. If you want additional passes, you will have to purchase them, but the cost is moderate (a five-day pass is just $7). The pass offers unlimited hop-on-hop-off privileges and allows you not only to get to SeaWorld but to explore the upper reaches of I-Drive, with its many restaurants (some of them quite good), lesser tourist attractions, dinner shows, and shopping. For more information, visit:

www.iridetrolley.com

Internet Access

Thanks to the Hotel Services Fee, wireless Internet access is available throughout the hotel. The connection is nice and zippy and there are no cumbersome log-in or terms of service screens to negotiate.

Parking

Parking comes in two flavors, valet ($18 a day, plus tips) or self ($6 a day). While the hotel expansion is under way, self parking has been discontinued, so you will have to use the hotel's valet parking service. Once the new wing is complete, it will be business as usual.

Pets

Pets are not allowed at the Peabody. The ducks wouldn't approve.

Smoking

The fourteenth floor has been set aside for smokers. All other rooms and public areas are strictly non-smoking.

Dining at The Peabody

The Peabody has two restaurants with price points that put them very much in the splurge or special occasion category. There is one moderately priced restaurant that has the advantage of being open 24 hours and offering some excellent cuisine. Beyond that, there are few offerings other than the very nice (if brief) **afternoon tea** served in the lobby from 4:00 to 5:00 p.m. and light poolside dining. Perhaps in deference to the denizens of the lobby fountain, duck is not served at any of the Peabody's eateries.

There are two bars in and just off the lobby that never seem to lack for customers, especially when a convention's in town. The **Lobby Bar** opens at 11:00 a.m. and stays open late. The nearby **Mallards** opens at 5:00 p.m. during the week and stays open to 2:00 a.m. It has extended hours on weekends. Finally, the hotel offers 24 hour room service; menus will be found in your room.

Dux

What:	Award-winning gourmet cuisine
Where:	Off the lobby on the ground floor
Price Range:	$$$$+
Hours:	Tuesday to Saturday, 6:00 p.m. to 10:00 p.m.
Reservations:	Strongly suggested; (407) 345-4550

Fine dining served in a self-consciously luxurious setting is getting harder to find in touristy Orlando, but it is alive and well at Dux. This is the Peabody's top of the line restaurant and perhaps the best in Orlando; the AAA has seen fit to award it the prestigious four-diamond rating year after year. Jackets and tie are no longer *de rigeur*, but you will want to dress up.

Perhaps the best way to experience Dux is to opt for the Chef's Tasting Menu with wine pairings, which will set you back something north of $100 a head. A vegetarian version of the Tasting Menu is slightly less and foregoing the wine brings the tab down considerably. This is a three- or four-course extravaganza featuring a selection of two from the appetizer portion of the menu, your choice of an entree, and an over the top dessert creation.

You can save a bit of money, but not much, by ordering a la carte. The menu changes to match the best the seasons have to offer, so predictions are somewhat iffy. Appetizers can range from delicate soups and salads to Maine lobster pasta, and cost from $12 to over $20. Entrees might include such delicacies as black grouper cheeks or Kobe beef rib eye at prices that can flirt with $50. Interestingly, prices are more moderate during the summer months, which is a slow period for the convention trade and the big expense accounts that accompany it.

The wine list is shorter than you might expect at such a high-end restaurant, which for many of us will prove a blessing. The selections seem very well thought out as well. Yes, you can spend several hundred dollars for a so-called "super Tuscan" wine, but some moderately priced bottles offer good value for the price. A glassed-in, temperature controlled wine cellar sits between Dux and the adjacent Capriccio Grill. You can pop in and browse the selection if you wish.

Capriccio Grill

What:	Italian steakhouse
Where:	Off the lobby on the ground floor
Price Range:	$$$ - $$$$+
Hours:	Daily, 6:00 a.m. to 11:00 p.m.; bar opens at 5:00 p.m.
Reservations:	Not required, but strongly suggested; (407) 345-4450

This is a handsome restaurant with black and white marble squares on the floor, black and white tiles in the open kitchen, and brass accents throughout. The service is suave, attentive, and thoroughly Continental. The spacious but not overwhelming bar that greets you when you enter is a great place to wait for your table or to have an aperitif before dining.

Yes, it's Italian, but the accent is most definitely on the steakhouse. You would be remiss if you ate here and didn't try one of their superbly tender steak or chop offerings. In addition to the expected filet mignon (12 and 8 ounce servings), rib eye, and New York Strip, you will find lamb and pork chops and a veal loin steak. In true steakhouse fashion, they are accompanied by side dishes of perfectly prepared vegetables at prices that would get you an appetizer at other restaurants.

You will find Italian specialties among the appetizers, including fried calamari and mussels alla diavola. Italian entrees include such staples as chicken parmigiana, veal marsala, pizzas, and a variety of pasta creations. There is seafood as well, including lobster tail and giant prawns, served with the same sides as the meat. The dessert menu includes the now trendy dessert-in-a-shot-glass concept, but you might be better off throwing caution to the winds and getting the chocolate bread pudding souffle with Jack Daniels sauce.

Capriccio Grill shares its wine list with Dux and offers some very thoughtful selections by the glass.

B-Line Diner

What:	Casual American food
Where:	Past the main lobby and to the right
Price Range:	$$ - $$$
Hours:	24 hours
Reservations:	None

This smart take on a traditional diner evokes the Art Deco era in black and white with stainless steel accents. It occupies a long narrow space at the back of the lobby level. There are cozy grey upholstered booths, four-top tables, and a lunch counter to choose from.

The place is open 24 hours a day with the menu changing with the advancing clock. Breakfast is served from 6:00 a.m. to 11:00 a.m., lunch from 11:00 a.m. to 5:00 p.m., and dinner from 5:00 p.m. to 11:00 p.m. At 11:00, a limited late night menu, featuring burgers, sandwiches, and breakfast fare kicks in until 6:00.

While the decor says diner, the cuisine says something more, with the daily lunch and dinner specials offering some very good eating for the price. The lunch menu features primarily salads, burgers, and sandwiches, while the dinner menu adds more substantial entrees like roasted lemon-thyme chicken and a New York Strip Steak. Some items, such as the Florida Shrimp Rosa, Portabella Carbonara, and chicken pot pie are available at both lunch and dinner. Desserts are mammoth and are displayed near the entrance to tempt you. As for the breakfasts, the corned beef hash comes highly recommended. A Sunday brunch is offered from 11:00 a.m. to 4:00 p.m.

The **B-Line Express**, a walk up window near the entrance, is open from 6:00 a.m. to 11:00 p.m. and offers refugees from the hotel's nearby convention and meeting area a chance to grab a quick bite to take away. Signs framing this window offer an abbreviated selection of fast food, but you can order anything that's on the regular menu, including the daily specials.

Shopping at The Peabody

Shopping is muted here. There is a **Gift Shop** (7:00 a.m. to 11:00 p.m.) at the north end of the lobby offering the usual assortment of newspapers, magazines, and sundries. Here you will find a surprising variety of duck-themed souvenirs and pricey Peabody robes. The other major theme is men's casual wear. There is little for the ladies, perhaps because just across the way is **Feathers** (9:00 a.m. to 7:00 p.m.), which specializes in women's clothing that seems to have been selected with the more conservative older woman in mind.

And that's about it, except for a few items in the Peabody Athletic Club and the Golf Pro Shop on the Recreation Level. More shopping is a short stroll from the hotel in the Pointe★Orlando shopping center just to the north.

Above: The Rosen Shingle Creek.

Right: Eighteen holes of golf, just outside. (Rosen Shingle Creek)

Below: The posh concierge lounge is open to all — for a fee. (Rosen Shingle Creek)

Rosen Shingle Creek

9939 Universal Boulevard
Orlando, FL 32819
(866) 996-9939
www.rosenshinglecreek.com
Distance from SeaWorld: 3.4 miles

Harris Rosen is something of a legend in central Florida tourism circles. In fact, the College of Hospitality Management at the University of Central Florida is named after him. His Rosen Hotels is the largest independent hotel company in Florida, with over 6,300 rooms. Shingle Creek, which opened in 2006, is his crowning achievement. It is quite obviously a labor of love and bits and pieces of Rosen family lore are sprinkled about the property. The family feel extends to such touches as the nature photography by Garritt Toohey, a Rosen vice-president, that hangs in the guest rooms.

Shingle Creek, it turns out, was one of Florida's original settlements, so named for the cypress roof shingles the area once produced in abundance on this very spot. It is also designated as the headwaters of the Everglades, a fact in which the hotel takes great pride. Indeed, Shingle Creek displays a deep respect and affection for the history and ecology of New York native Harris Rosen's adopted state. In fact, as he was designing his hotel, Rosen was inspired by a historical novel, *A Land Remembered*, about three generations of a Florida pioneer family. I picked up a copy while I was there and found it to be a ripping yarn. You will find echoes of the novel throughout the hotel. Rooms and restaurant menu items are named for ancient Florida tribes and historical personalities and the novel lends its name to one of the hotel's poshest restaurants.

Orientation

Rosen Shingle Creek is massive. There are 1,500 rooms and suites in the hotel and 445,000 square feet of meeting and event space in the vast convention center next door, all of it nestled with an 18-hole golf course on 230 acres just a stone's throw from the even more massive Orlando Convention Center.

The hotel's design might be described as 1900s Spanish Revival on steroids. You arrive at a large portico on the so-called Lobby Level, the hotel's second floor. Inside the doors is a lobby that seems to go on forever. Towards the rear of the hotel, past a Victorian bird cage filled with zebra finches, the lobby soars to wooden beams overhead and overlooks the Cafe Osceola below with views through ceiling-high windows to the expansive pool area.

On the Lobby Level you will find the posh Cala Bella restaurant and a wide corridor to the right heading to the convention center, along which are more dining and shopping options. Still more dining is on the Lower Lobby level, along with the fitness center. The golf clubhouse and another upscale restaurant are reached via a covered walkway that begins at the entrance portico. Upstairs, the corridors stretch far from the elevator banks, so if you are averse to long walks to and from your room, ask for a room near the elevators.

Rooms and Suites

With 1,500 guestrooms and 139 suites, Rosen Shingle Creek gives you lots to choose from. Their "standard" rooms, either single or double, have the sort of amenities you'd expect of a "deluxe" room elsewhere. They are configured with either two queen beds or one king and boast luxurious bedding, 32-inch flat-screen TVs, a mini-refrigerator and a small seating area.

Suites come in a variety of flavors. The Petite Suite is much like a compact studio apartment, while the one- and two-bedroom Executive Suites let you spread out in style. Hospitality Suites, although designed for corporate entertaining can do double duty as family accommodations. At the top, there are three 1,700 square foot Presidential Suites that are equivalent to four or five regular hotel rooms.

Oh, and if you take a fancy to the robe in your room, it's yours for $75.

Room Rates

Rosen Shingle Creek's rates are what you might expect of an ultra luxury hotel, but they are competitive with other properties in the Orlando market. Be aware that the rates below are "typical" and that they can spike sharply upward at times of peak demand as the hotel begins to sell out.

Standard room	$375 – $425
Petite Suites	$500 – $600
Hospitality Suites	$900 – $1,050
One-Bedroom Executive	$1,200
Two Bedroom Executive	$1,500
Grande Suites	$1,500 – $1,750
Presidential Suites	$2,700 – $3,000

Amenities

Concierge Lounge

Many hotels set aside one or more floors as the "concierge level," with restricted access and a string of perks. Shingle Creek takes a more democratic approach. Here, *anyone* can have access to the Concierge Lounge on the 14th floor — for a mere $50 a day extra, tacked on to the room rate.

The silver key card that $50 gets you grants access to a long narrow lounge decorated in dark wood and muted earth tones. Comfortably upholstered chairs and sofas divide the space into more intimate conversation areas. Here you can get breakfast from 6:30 to 10:00 a.m., hors d'oeuvres from 6:00 to 7:30 p.m., desserts from 9:00 to 10:30 p.m., and coffee all day long. In the evening there is also an "honor bar," which means you keep track of your consumption and the charge ($4.75 for beer and wine) is added to your room bill. Paying for concierge lounge access brings other privileges such as free Internet access, free admission to the Fitness Center, and free valet parking.

Golf

An 18 hole, 7,228-yard golf course designed by David Harman wraps around the hotel. Five sets of tees are said to allow players to set their own level of difficulty and yet the course was named one of the most difficult in Orlando by a local publication. It was also awarded four stars from *Golf Digest's* "Best Places To Play" feature.

The golf carts have GPS capability and a delivery cart catches up with players every four holes or so to offer liquid refreshment. While here, you can also arrange for lessons with the **Brad Brewer Golf Academy**; Brewer is considered one of the nation's best instructors. Greens fees range from $60 to $130, depending on the time of year and day of the week. Arrange a tee time by calling (866) 996-9933 or (407) 996-9933.

Pools

At the rear of the hotel, Shingle Creek has three large sun-soaked pools and a smaller kiddie pool all within hailing distance of one another and all overlooking the golf course. The lap pool is designed for the serious exerciser, while the free-form, zero-entry family pool lets families play together. A short distance away is the adult pool, with the **Cat-Tails Pool Bar & Grille** close at hand. Between the adult and family pools is a small circular kiddie pool. All of these pool areas offer plenty of space in which to lounge about and the lounge chairs in which to do it.

Spa

The Spa at Shingle Creek, to use its full name, offers a dizzying array of pampering treatments that include various forms of massage, aromatherapy, facials, nail and foot treatments, the list goes on. "Body Treatments" include such intriguing choices as the Calusa Cocoon and the Muskogean Body Shine. A six-hour regimen that includes a spa lunch is $650. All spa guests receive all-day access to the steam room, sauna, and whirlpool.

Fitness Center

The fitness center, which is conveniently located close to the lap pool, has a spartan feel to it, but it gets the job done with a good selection of treadmills and weight machines. The fee of $10 per day or $20 for your entire stay includes access to steam room, sauna, and whirlpool bath. The men's and women's locker room contain separate facilities.

Sports Activities

The resort has two tennis courts, one of which doubles as a basketball half court. To one side is a sand volleyball court and nearby is a fishing dock, where a strict catch and release protocol is in place. Nature trails and jogging trails round out the menu of activities. All this is complimentary; more information can be obtained through the fitness center.

Good Things To Know About . . .

Business Center

A business center offering photocopying, faxing, printers and the like is located along the long corridor that leads from the Lobby level to the convention center.

Getting To The Theme Parks

The hotel participates in the Super Star Shuttle offering bus service to SeaWorld, Aquatica, Universal Orlando and Wet 'n Wild. There are several departures in the morning with fewer return trips in the evening. A schedule can be obtained from the Concierge on the Lobby Level.

Internet Access

Shingle Creek offers wired high speed access in all rooms and wireless in a few "hot spots" on the first floor. There is a menu of charges: You can pay $4.95 per hour, $9.95 a day for in-room access, or $12.95 a day for access both in your room and at wireless hotspots elsewhere in the hotel.

Parking

Valet parking is available to guests at a charge of $18 a day. Self parking in an open lot next to the hotel is $8 a day.

Guest Laundry

A self-service laundry is provided on the Lower Lobby level, near the fitness center. Washers are $3.25 and dryers are $1.75 in quarters. Detergent is a veritable steal at just $.75. Needless to say, a change machine is provided.

Pets

No pets are accepted at the resort.

Smoking

Shingle Creek is a totally non-smoking facility.

Dining at the Rosen Shingle Creek

Shingle Creek has two extremely good restaurants at price points that will deter all but the well heeled and the expense account crowd. For those whose ship has yet to come in, there are more moderate choices close at hand. In addition to the eateries reviewed here, the hotel offers the **Häagen-Dazs Creek Ice Creamery**, located near 18 Monroe Street (reviewed below) and the pool area. Also by the pool is **Cat-Tails Pool Bar & Grille**, an outdoor bar offering light meals and pizzas in addition to the usual poolside beverages. An alternative for a quick breakfast is offered by **Smoooth Java**, a Starbucks lookalike on the way to the convention center. Needless to say, there is also 24-hour room service.

Finally, by the first tee of the golf course is a snack operation called **Par Take**. As the name suggests, you can get snacks to take with you on the course, but if you get caught short on the 12th tee, you can place an order from your golf cart and, thanks to your cart's GPS system, they'll find you and deliver. The delivery cart comes complete with a bar!

A Land Remembered - Steakhouse

What:	Fine American cuisine
Where:	In the golf clubhouse
Price Range:	$$$$+
Hours:	Daily 5:30 p.m. to 10:00 p.m.
Reservations:	Recommended; (407) 996-3663 or extension 17025
Web:	www.landrememberedrestaurant.com

A Land Remembered, located in the golf course clubhouse a short stroll from the main building, takes its name from a historical novel by Patrick Smith about three generations of Florida pioneers. It's for sale at the Golf Shop nearby and is a favorite of hotelier Harris Rosen.

The restaurant is on the intimate side, seating 120 at comfortably separated tables and booths, the lighting provided by quaint lampposts topped with metal palm fronds. The noise level is wonderfully muted and there is a small section of outdoor seating. The adjoining bar is nice place to meet or wait for a seat; from 2:30 to 5:30 p.m., it serves some tasty appetizers.

The food has gained the place a very good reputation as you might expect of a steakhouse that serves five diamond prime steak from the famed organic Harris Ranch prepared by chef James Slattery, who trained under Emeril Legasse at the Universal Emeril's and Tchoup Chop restaurants. But be forewarned, if you're not careful, you can wind up paying more than $100 a head here — before wine!

Steaks and other cuts of beef are the order of the day and include a mammoth 24 ounce prime rib with horseradish sauce. A "surf and turf" option features South African lobster tail. Sauces for your steak cost extra, as do simply but expertly prepared vegetable sides.

A separate, slightly less expensive section of the menu offers fish dishes, at market prices, and non-beef specialties like chicken and "lamb tequesta." Appetizers and soups and salads may be a tempting alternative if you want a lighter meal. The desserts are architectural wonders, especially the chef's unique take on key lime pie.

You can spend $500 for a bottle of wine here, but there are more moderate choices, as well as a good selection of wines by the glass. Your server will be happy to suggest a good pairing. There is a private dining room seating 22 for small groups and celebrations.

Clubhouse Grille

What: Casual luncheon fare
Where: In the golf clubhouse
Price Range: $$
Hours: Daily 11:00 a.m. to 2:30 p.m.
Reservations: None

The A Land Remembered dining room does double duty during the day as the casual Clubhouse Grille. In fact, you may see it referred to as A Land Remembered Grille, but the staff seems to favor the Clubhouse designation. The food comes from the same kitchen and the same chef as A Land Remembered, but the menu is far simpler (not to mention less expensive). There are appetizers like Buffalo wings and chicken quesadillas, soups, salads, and sandwiches (including a blackened prime rib). There is also a small selection of heartier entrees like grilled salmon and skirt steak.

Cala Bella

What: Fine Italian cuisine
Where: Off the main lobby
Price Range: $$$$+
Hours: Daily 5:30 p.m. to 10:00 p.m.
Reservations: Recommended; (407) 996-3663 or extension 17640
Web: www.calabellarestaurant.com

Like A Land Remembered, Cala Bella is not the sort of place to visit if you're on a tight budget, but if $40 pasta dishes don't make you faint, you will no doubt find the food to your taste.

Bella's Bar serves as something of an antechamber to the restaurant proper. It's a nice place to sip a fine wine or perhaps share an appetizer platter with a group of friends. Once inside the restaurant, you will receive the kind of attentive service that the prices should lead you to expect.

Pizzas are among the least expensive items on the menu, which is surprising since they are rather exotic as pizzas go, featuring ingredients like Florida goat cheese and lobster with smoked mozzarella. Among starters, Cala Bella's version of ribollita, a Tuscan bean and bread soup, is worth sampling.

Entrees include the fearsomely expensive Seafood Pescatore and baked scallops with focaccia bread crumbs and truffle butter. The somewhat more extensive selection of meat dishes includes Asiago Chicken with fried wild mushrooms, a Pork Porterhouse, and a 14-ounce veal chop. Contorni, or side dishes, are extra. Desserts are as elaborate as the entrees. The restaurant adds an automatic 18% service charge for groups of six or more.

Cafe Osceola

What:	Buffet restaurant
Where:	On the Lower Lobby level, open to the floor above
Price Range:	$$ - $$$
Hours:	Breakfast 6:30 a.m. to 10:30 a.m.; lunch 11:00 a.m. to 2:30 p.m.; dinner 5:30 p.m. to 10:00 p.m.
Reservations:	None

This is Shingle Creek's moderately priced, casual dining option. It is a light and airy space, open to the floor above with a great view out to the pool area. The Cafe takes its name from a Seminole chieftain who once controlled much of the surrounding area and many of the menu items reflect this theme. Hot fudge brownie sundaes become "Indian Peace Offerings," for example.

There is one menu for breakfast and another for lunch and dinner. Each meal has its own buffet, with prices rising as the clock advances. Evening buffets have different themes (Caribbean, Asian, Italian, Southern BBQ, and seafood) throughout the week, with weekends reserved for prime rib. The buffets are bounteous and the quality above average. All-you-can-eat aficionados take note.

The a la carte lunch and dinner menu offers salads, sandwiches, and burgers. A short list of "specialties" includes heartier entrees ranging from pastas, to fish, to filet mignon, which at $25 is the most expensive item on the menu.

18 Monroe Street Market

What: Fast food and mini market with beer and wine
Where: On the Lower Lobby Level
Price Range: $$
Hours: 24 hours
Reservations: None

Here's an interesting idea — a fast food counter-style operation combined with a compact mini mart and open 24 hours a day.

To one side a curving counter offers a number of stations offering a variety of specialties. The Bakery serves up fresh baked goods ideal for that quick breakfast; line up for Sandwiches and get just that, thick stacks of cold cuts with names evoking Old New York; the "Monroe Diner" serves up freshly carved warm meats; and, finally, the Pizzeria offers individual-sized pizzas.

The market carries a variety of nuts, candies, cookies, chips, dips, and other snacks — in short, the sort of thing that will go nicely with drinks in your room. The most substantial offerings are the dried cereal for breakfast, and a small selection of pre-packed fruit platters, sandwiches, and salads.

And speaking of drinks in your room, there is also a good selection of beer and wine, many of which have odd names. Alligator Drool beer anyone? No alcohol sales from 2:00 a.m. to 9:00 a.m., though.

The 18 Monroe Street name, by the way, is a nod to hotelier Harris Rosen's boyhood home on Manhattan's Lower East Side.

Headwaters Lounge

What: Bar with light meals
Where: Between the hotel and the convention center
Price Range: $$
Hours: Daily 11:00 a.m. to 1:00 a.m.
Reservations: None

Stroll along the broad corridor that links the hotel with the vast convention center next door and you will see this spacious bar with a generous seating area set off by a low wall. It can be mobbed when trade shows and meetings are in session, but in its off hours it is a quiet place to grab a cooling drink and a light meal.

An abbreviated menu offers appetizers like nachos and fried calamari, and a small selection of salads. Somewhat more substantial are a pecan chicken salad wrap, burgers, a Cuban sandwich, and a fish taco with grouper and remoulade sauce. While not extensive, the menu offers a very reasonable alternative for a more than adequate lunch or dinner.

Shopping at the Rosen Shingle Creek

Most shopping is concentrated along the corridor leading to the convention center. **Alta Moda** concentrates on upscale women's clothing with a continental flair. This, by the way, is the same Alta Moda that has an outpost at Universal Orlando's Portofino Bay Hotel. The **Eagle's Nest** is the hotel's gift and sundries shop. Most of it is given over to inexpensive t-shirts, polos, and sweats for men, women, and especially kids. There are plenty of kids' toys and beach gear as well. In addition to a small selection of magazines and trashy novels, there is an eclectic selection of gifts and bric a brac.

John Craig Fine Menswear offers resort styles for today's metrosexual. In addition to Craig's own brand, the shop offers clothing from other upscale boutique designers like Ike Beha and Robert Graham. It's mostly shirts and slacks, but if you find yourself in need of a chic sports jacket, this shop can fix you up. **The Gallery** is a vest-pocket art emporium specializing in bright, gaudy paintings, many with a tropical theme, colorful figurines, and jewelry.

Over at the golf course clubhouse, the 1,600 square foot **Pro Shop** is an extremely well stocked emporium of upscale golf togs for men and women, including golf shoes. They also offer club sales and rentals as well as other golfing necessities. Here, too, you can pick up a copy of the historical novel, *A Land Remembered*, which inspired the restaurant of the same name and which has many other echoes throughout the resort. The **Spa** has a small selection of fancy cosmetics, mostly for women, along with some cute t-shirts and gift items, also mostly for women.

The Marriott Connection

SeaWorld has entered into a strategic alliance with Marriott International to offer packages at twelve nearby Marriott properties that combine a hotel stay with length-of-stay theme park tickets and a suite of additional perks, making them especially attractive choices for those looking for an all-in-one option.

You can build your own package on the SeaWorld web site, but I find the choices a bit confusing, so I'll try to unravel them for you. If you are traveling with kids nine or under, the Kids Free packages offer two adult length-of-stay tickets and a free child's ticket for each paying adult, up to two. You also get one day at Aquatica. The regular "Build Your Own Vacation" option does not include the free kids' tickets, but does include a free plush toy at check in if you have kids in tow. A third option gives you length-of-stay admission to both SeaWorld and Aquatica (Discovery Cove is not included in any of these packages).

The problem is, it's not easy to comparison shop on the web site to compare one option to another and, computers being what they are, you may not always get the best pricing available. For that reason, you may want to call SeaWorld at (800) 55-SHAMU and go over your options with a reservationist to make sure you're getting the best deal. Or you may just want to have your travel agent take care of the details.

Every package comes with a **Guest Value Book**, a booklet of coupons that cover up to four guests. The perks currently provided by these coupons are a free upgrade to preferred parking, ride again privileges on *Kraken, Wild Arctic* and *Journey to Atlantis,* a free *Sky Tower* ride, $10 off admission to the *Makahiki Luau* and the *Sharks Deep Dive*, 50% off a child's meal at *Dine With Shamu*, and $1 off the *Saving A Species* tour. All subject to change, of course.

The twelve Marriott properties are all relatively near to the parks, ranging from walking distance to six miles away. They also cover a fairly wide range of configurations and amenities. For convenience, I group them into three categories.

Resort Properties

These hotels are big and splashy, with the full range of services and amenities that you would expect in a first-class resort.

Renaissance Orlando Resort

This property, the closest you can get to SeaWorld, was reviewed earlier in this chapter.

J.W. Marriott Resort

4040 Central Florida Parkway
Orlando, FL 32837
(800) 576-5750
(407) 206-2300
(407) 206-2301 fax

This ultra-luxurious 1,000-room hotel on 500 lushly landscaped acres is the grandest of the Marriott properties included in the Marriott/Sea-World packages. It has received four diamonds from AAA and three stars from Mobil and is home to a pair of gourmet restaurants. There are 518 double rooms, 418 king rooms, and 64 expansive suites, all with luxurious bedding. And if this isn't grand enough for you, you can move next door to the Ritz-Carlton.

Price Range: $$$ - $$$$+

Amenities: Golf course designed by Greg Norman, smoke-free policy, business center, paid high-speed Internet access, spa and pool, concierge desk.

Distance to SeaWorld: 3.1 miles

Marriott World Center

8701 World Center Drive
Orlando, FL 32821
(800) 621-0638
(407) 239-4200
(407) 238-8777 fax
www.marriottworldcenter.com

This is a splashy, sprawling 2,000-room convention meeting hotel at the southern end of International Drive. Its proximity to Walt Disney World makes it an attractive choice to families who will be visiting Mickey as well. You might also want to consider the two timeshare properties, Royal and Sabal Palms (see below) next to the hotel.

It's a strikingly modern tower, featuring a soaring atrium lobby and exterior elevators that zip up 27 stories, offering expansive views to the south. The hotel also features what may be the nicest looking pool of all the properties reviewed in this chapter. It is, however, the most distant from the parks and is frequently booked solid with meetings and conventions.

Price Range: $$ - $$$$

Amenities: Several fine restaurants, many rooms with balconies, paid Internet access, golf course on property, large swimming area with many waterfalls, fitness center, fast food court, some shopping on property, spa and fitness center, golf school, concierge desk.

Distance to SeaWorld: 6 miles

Timeshare Resorts

These properties were designed for the vacation ownership market and many of the units in them are occupied by owners. However, a number of units are always available for vacation rentals. These resorts work best for families, who can take advantage of the extra space and fully equipped kitchens to cook at least some of their meals "at home" during their vacation. Even better, the rates are very comparable to those at nicer hotels in the area.

Marriott's Grande Vista

This property, which is arguably the best of the timeshare properties near SeaWorld, was reviewed earlier in this chapter.

Marriott's Cypress Harbour

11251 Harbour Villa Road
Orlando, FL 32821
(407) 238-1300
(407) 238-1083 fax

All of the "villas" at this property are two-bedroom units, with a screened porch or balcony and interior decor on a par with that found at the Grande Vista. The three- and four-story buildings are set in beautifully manicured grounds dotted with ponds and surrounding the Grande Pines golf course. There are two large adult pools and a smaller children's pool.

Price Range: $$$$

Amenities: Full kitchens with granite countertops, all utensils, business center, high-speed Internet, on-site dining including Starbucks and Edy's, barbecue facilities, game room, sauna, biking and jogging trails, sauna, smoke-free policy, concierge desk.

Distance to SeaWorld: .9 miles

Horizons by Marriott Vacation Club

7102 Grand Horizons Boulevard
Orlando, FL 32821
(407) 465-6000
(407) 465-6267 fax

Horizons is a separate brand within the Marriott family — its official name is Horizons at Orlando by Marriott Vacation Club — and it represents the "quality tier" of vacation ownership as opposed to the "moderate tier" represented by Cypress Harbour and Grande Vista. Translated from brand-speak, that means it costs a bit less. Even so, its pirate ship themed kids' pool is one of the coolest amenities at any of the resorts reviewed here and makes this an obvious choice for families with younger kids.

Just across the street from Cypress Harbour, it features hotel-like guest rooms as well as one- and two-bedroom villas.

Price Range: $$ - $$$$

Amenities: Full kitchens with utensils, DVD players, screened balcony, on-property restaurant, the HarborSide Bar & Grill, pirate-themed activity program for kids, smoke-free policy.

Distance to SeaWorld: .9 miles

Marriott's Royal Palms

8404 Vacation Way
Orlando, FL 32821
(407) 238-6200
(407) 238-6247 fax

This is one of two timeshare properties that flank the Marriott World Center hotel; Sabal Palms, below, is the other. Both of them offer only two-bedroom units that sleep up to six people. Thanks to their proximity to the Marriott World Center Hotel, both resorts have access to some very nice dining options. And given their proximity to Disney World, they make a good choice for families who plan to visit there.

Price Range: $$$$

Amenities: High speed Internet, one large swimming pool, tennis and volleyball, hiking and biking, fitness center, concierge desk, access to various amenities at the adjacent World Center Hotel including their spa and fitness center.

Distance to SeaWorld: 6 miles

Marriott's Sabal Palms

8805 World Center Drive
Orlando, FL 32821
(407) 238-6200
(407) 238-6219 fax

Sabal Palms is somewhat smaller than Royal Palms and the buildings here are four floors instead of two, but otherwise there is little to distinguish the two resorts.

Price Range: $$$$

Amenities: Amenities are similar, if not precisely the same, as those at Royal Palms.

Distance to SeaWorld: 6 miles

Moderate and Budget Choices

These properties may not offer all the bells and whistles of the larger resorts, but they have some nice amenities and are easier on the pocketbook. They are, in very approximate order of cost:

Fairfield Inn on International Drive

7495 Canada Avenue
Orlando, FL 32819
(407) 351-7000
(407) 351-0052 fax

This is the most "hotel-like" of the Marriott properties. It is near the busy intersection of I-Drive and Sand Lake Road, with Orlando's "Restaurant Row" a short drive to the west. Also close by are the Pirates Adventure dinner show, Magical Midway, a favorite teen hangout on I-Drive, and a bowling alley. A few king suites with separate sleep areas are available.

Price Range: $$

Amenities: Heated pool with whirlpool, breakfast buffet, 100% smoke free, free high-speed Internet access, fitness room, microwave and fridge in all rooms.

Distance to SeaWorld: 4.2 miles

Residence Inn, International Drive

7975 Canada Avenue
Orlando, FL 32819
(800) 380-6761
(407) 345-0117
(407) 352-2689 fax

Designed for the longer stay, this property features apartment-like units and looks much like a small condo development with the units scattered among separate two-story buildings. There are studios, double studios (with two queen beds), and a few "penthouses," which feature a loft bedroom on an upper level. All of them have kitchen facilities complete with utensils.

It is just a short way down the street from Fairfield Inn, so the notes about what's nearby apply to this property as well.

Price Range: $$ - $$$

Amenities: Outdoor pool, small exercise room, plenty of guest laundries, full basketball court, fireplaces in some units, hot breakfast buffet, free high-speed Internet access.

Distance to SeaWorld: 4.0 miles

Courtyard, International Drive

8600 Austrian Court
Orlando, FL 32819
(407) 351-2244
(407) 351-3306 fax

The Courtyard formula is similar to Residence Inn, but is aimed at the shorter stay business traveler. The price points are also somewhat lower. This one is located in one of the many U-shaped streets off I-Drive. Other than a few restaurants, there are no attractions within comfortable walking distance. Because of its proximity to the Convention Center, it draws a considerable business trade.

Price Range: $ - $$

Amenities: Well-equipped business center, breakfast buffet, heated outdoor pool and whirlpool, lobby convenience store, free high-speed Internet access, fitness center, newspaper Monday through Friday.

Distance to SeaWorld: 3.4 miles

Residence Inn, SeaWorld

11000 Westwood Boulevard
Orlando, FL 32821
(800) 889-9728
(407) 313-3600
(407) 313-3611 fax

This is the closest of the moderate Marriotts to the parks, so it commands a premium price. Unlike the Residence Inn on Canada Avenue, described above, all the units here are in a single hotel-like building. You could conceivably walk to SeaWorld from here, but it's a long walk.

Price Range: $$ - $$$

Amenities: Breakfast buffet, exercise room, large pool with zero-entry kids' section, children's playground, picnic tables with grills, basketball and volleyball, small convenience store, bar and grill, smoke-free policy, pets allowed with additional fee, free high-speed Internet access.

Distance to SeaWorld: .8 miles

Other Choices Near the Parks

If the resort hotels covered so far are a little rich for your blood (and they frequently are for mine!), you will be pleased to know that a number of more moderate choices are available quite close to SeaWorld and its sister parks. An added benefit is that all of the choices here are within walking distance of SeaWorld and I have listed them in order of proximity.

Hilton Garden Inn

6850 Westwood Boulevard
Orlando, FL 32821
(877) 782-9444; (407) 354-1500; fax (407) 354-1528

A mid-scale hotel with an accent on the business traveler, this 223-room property features seven suites and walk-to-the-park convenience. One of its neatest features is the ability to print from your laptop in the room and pick up your pages at the business center.

Price Range: $$ - $$$
Amenities: Heated pool, jacuzzi, kids' play area, fitness room, restaurant, lounge, evening room service, on-site convenience store, complimentary 24-hour business center, free high-speed Internet access
Walk to Park: 10 minutes

International Plaza Resort and Spa

10100 International Drive
Orlando, FL 32821-8095
(800) 327-0363; (407) 352-1100
www.intlplazaresort.com

This refurbished hotel is the only one in this section that falls into the "resort" category. A 17-story tower is surrounded by 19 two-story buildings spread out over 28 acres. There is a "SeaWorld Gate" at the rear of the property. It opens at 8:00 a.m. and closes an hour after the park does. This is also the closest hotel to Aquatica and walking there is very doable. Despite the address, the main entrance is on Westwood Boulevard.

Price Range: $$ - $$$$
Amenities: Three heated pools, two kiddie pools, putting green, fitness center, spa, restaurant, lounge, poolside bar
Walk to Park: 10 minutes

Note: Walking distance to SeaWorld from the following hotels was calculated using an unnamed service road that runs alongside the International Plaza Resort property and connects Westwood Boulevard and Sea Harbor Drive. From Sea Harbor Drive, the route then cuts diagonally across the SeaWorld parking lot.

Sleep Inn

6301 Westwood Boulevard
Orlando, FL 32821
(877) 424-6423; (407) 313-4100; fax (407) 313-4101
www.orlandosleepinn.com
www.sleepinn.com

This is a clean, four-story, budget motel with a glacially slow elevator. It has a 100% non-smoking policy. The Village Inn is on one side and the "undiscovered" Persian restaurant, Shiraz Grill, is on the other.

Price Range: $ - $$
Amenities: Small pool, breakfast buffet, 3 channels of HBO plus Showtime, tiny guest laundry.
Walk to Park: 12 to 15 minutes

Hawthorn Suites Orlando SeaWorld

6435 Westwood Boulevard
Orlando, FL 32821
(800) 527-1133; (407) 351-6600; fax (407) 351-1977
www.hawthorn.com

Hawthorn follows an all-suite format with one- and two-bedroom suites and kitchenettes in every unit. Good prices, too. The Shiraz Grill Persian restaurant is next door.

Price Range: $ - $$
Amenities: Free buffet breakfast, large heated pool, kiddie pool, poolside BBQ grills, children's play area, game room, convenience store, Nintendo and video cassette players in rooms, free shuttle to WDW.
Walk to Park: 13 to 16 minutes

Extended Stay America & Extended Stay Deluxe

6443 Westwood Boulevard
Orlando, FL 32821
(888) 788-3467 for both; (407) 351-1982, fax (407) 351-1719 for Extended Stay Deluxe; (407) 352-3454, fax (407) 352-1708 for Extended Stay

This basic (only the Deluxe brand has a breakfast buffet) all-suite chain featuring studios with kitchenettes comes in two flavors, both of which are represented here, one behind the other. The deluxe version is only slightly enhanced. Daily and weekly rates are available. You have to pay for Internet access here, but it costs just $5 for your entire stay.

> *Price Range:* $$ - $$$ ExtStay Deluxe; $ - $$ ExtStay
>
> *Amenities:*   Seasonal pool and exercise room, barbecue facilities (Deluxe only)
>
> *Walk to Park:* 15 to 18 minutes

Wynfield Inn

6263 Westwood Boulevard
Orlando, FL 32821
(800) 346-1551; (407) 345-8000
www.wynfieldinn.com

This independent, three-story, ultra-budget motel is a blast from the past. Its 299 functional rooms are laid out in an "L" on eight acres. There are two pools each with a large hot tub and a bar between them that offers a regular menu of things to do (karaoke, poker) to keep people engaged. It caters to the European holiday trade. Ask for an interior room to avoid the traffic noise from the busy Bee Line Expressway. The Village Inn is on property, features a kids-eat-free policy, and serves a great key lime pie. Just a short stroll away is a strip mall with more restaurants.

> *Price Range:* $
>
> *Amenities:*   Pools and poolside bar, breakfast buffet, free shuttle to Universal, SeaWorld, and Epcot.
>
> *Walk to Park:* 15 to 18 minutes

Above: Hangin' out.
(Lemur in Edge of Africa, Busch Gardens Africa)

Left: King Tut.
(Egypt, Busch Gardens Africa)

Below: On safari.
(Serengeti Plain, Busch Gardens Africa)

Above: Diving Hippopotamus.
(Edge of Africa, Busch Gardens
Africa)

Right: Tiger peekaboo.
(Jungala, Busch Gardens Africa)

Below: A window on a wild world.
(Jungala, Busch Gardens Africa)

Chapter Six:

Busch Gardens Africa

BUSCH GARDENS AFRICA IS A SOMEWHAT SCHIZOPHRENIC MIXTURE OF zoological park and amusement park, with a dash of variety show thrown in. Given the seemingly disparate demands of these elements, the designers have done an admirable job of creating an attractive whole. Aesthetically, a stroll through Busch Gardens is one of the most pleasing in Central Florida.

Like any good theme park, Busch Gardens has one. In this case it's Africa, the mysterious continent so linked in the popular imagination with wild animals and adventure. Borrowing a page from the Disney manual, the park is divided into "lands," or as Busch calls them, "themed areas." With few exceptions, they take their names from countries or regions in Africa. The metaphor works wonderfully for the zoo side of things, although it results in the occasional oddity (Clydesdales in Egypt?). It is largely extraneous to the park's other elements. A roller coaster is a roller coaster, whether it's named after an Egyptian god (*Montu*) or in a Congolese dialect (*Kumba*).

So why schlep to Tampa for another theme park? There are two main answers: the animals and the roller coasters. Disney's Animal Kingdom has created some competition to Busch's great apes and white Bengal tigers, but it has just one roller coaster. SeaWorld has animals and thrill rides, too, but it is short on land-based mammals.

There are other reasons, as well. For early risers at least, Busch Gardens is a very doable day trip from Orlando. And Busch even provides shuttle service from SeaWorld, to spare you the hassle of driving. The inclusion of Busch Gardens in SeaWorld's reasonably priced Passports and its participation in the Orlando FlexTicket program (see *Chapter One: Dive Right In!*) adds another incentive to make the trip.

Finally, Busch Gardens Africa has an allure all its own. The innovative animal habitats temper the frenzy of the rides, and the rides give you something to do when just sitting and watching begins to pale. The park is beautifully designed with some absolutely enchanting nooks and crannies. While it's a great place to do things, Busch Gardens is also a delightful place simply to be.

My only caution would be that the amusement park side of the equation can tend to overshadow the zoo. Many of the animal exhibits reward quiet, patient observation, but the excitement generated by the smorgasbord of giant roller coasters and splashy water rides will make it hard to cultivate a contemplative state of mind, especially for the younger members of your party. Perhaps the best strategy is to use exhibits like the *Myombe Reserve* (great apes), *Edge of Africa* (lions and hippos), and the walk-through aviary to chill out and cool down between bouts of manic activity. Another strategy is to devote one visit to the amusement park rides, another to the zoo exhibits.

Before You Come

You can hear some recorded information and, if you're lucky, reach a real live person by calling (888) 800-5447. In Tampa, you can call the Guest Relations number, (813) 987-5888, during park hours.

For the latest on Busch Gardens' zoo animals, you can check out the park's animal information site at www.buschgardens.org.

Another web site provides information for the amusement park side of Busch Gardens Africa. The address is www.buschgardens.com. An unofficial fan web site, www.bgtguide.com, is a good source of late-breaking news.

When's the Best Time to Come?

Plotting the best time of year at which to visit is less of a consideration than with the other major theme parks of Central Florida. As we saw in *Chapter One*, Busch Gardens gets the fewest visitors of the major theme parks in central Florida. On the other hand, attendance continues to grow and on several recent visits large groups of foreign tourists and American high school kids were much in evidence.

Getting There

Busch Gardens is roughly 75 miles from Universal Orlando, about 65 miles from the intersection of I-4 and US 192 in Kissimmee. You can drive there in about one and a quarter to one and a half hours depending on where you start and how closely you observe the posted speed limit. Drive west on I-4 to Exit 7 (US 92 West, Hillsborough Avenue). Go about 1.5 miles and turn right on 56th Street (SR 583); go another two miles and turn right on

Busch Boulevard. Busch Gardens is about two miles ahead on your right.

Shuttle Bus Service

If you'd rather not drive from Orlando, you can take advantage of the shuttle bus service that Busch (in association with Mears Transportation) operates from a lengthy list of hotels in the Orlando area. The roundtrip fare is $10 per person, but if you have a five-park FlexTicket the service is free. Buses depart between roughly 8:30 a.m. and 10:00 a.m. with return journeys at 6:00 or 7:00 p.m., depending on the current closing hours at Busch Gardens Africa, which vary seasonally (see below). Be aware that there may be as many as three stops en route and that arrival time at Busch Gardens can be as late as 11:30 a.m.; so if you'd like to arrive bright and early, driving is your best option. Reservations are required. To make one, or to check the latest schedule and pick-up points, call (800) 221-1339.

Parking at Busch Gardens Africa

You know you're almost at Busch Gardens when you see the giant roller coaster *Montu* looming overhead. You'll probably also hear the screams as you pull into the parking lot. Actually, there are a series of parking lots with room for 5,000 vehicles. Lots A and B are near the park entrance and are reserved for handicapped and preferred parking, respectively. There is much more parking across the street, which is where you will most likely be stowing your car. Trams snake their way back and forth to the entrance, but if you're in A or B it's just as easy to walk.

Motorcycles and cars park for $9, campers and trailers for $10, tax included. If you have any Busch Gardens annual pass, parking is free. Preferred Parking, in Lot B, costs $14 ($7 for most Passport members, free for Platinum Passport holders). Valet parking is $20 ($18 for Passport members).

Opening and Closing Times

The park is usually open from 10:00 a.m. to 6:00 p.m. every day of the year. However, during the summer months and at holiday times the hours are extended, with opening at 9:00 a.m. and closing pushed back until 7:00, 8:00, 9:00, or 10:00 p.m. The Morocco section stays open a half-hour or so later than the rest of the park to accommodate last-minute shoppers. Call Guest Relations at (813) 987-5888 for the exact current operating hours.

One-Day Admission

Busch Gardens sells only one-day admissions, but adults can get a discount if they purchase their tickets seven days in advance on the Internet. The following prices include tax. The discounted price is given in parentheses.

One Day Admission:

    Adults: $62 ($51.30)

    Children (3 to 9): $51.30

    Children under age 3 are admitted **free**.

Two-Park Ticket:

(One day each at Busch Gardens and SeaWorld)

    Adults: $106.95 ($96.25)

    Children: $96.25

Two-Day Two-Park Ticket:

(One day each at Busch Gardens and Adventure Island)

    Adults: $78.05

    Children: $67.35

Information on "Length of Stay" tickets, which combine two or more parks; the Orlando FlexTicket, which includes five or six parks; and "Passports" (annual passes), which also offer access to multiple parks, will be found in *Chapter One: Dive Right In!*

Staying Near the Park

If you'd like to spend a few days at Busch Gardens or just want to avoid doing the roundtrip from Orlando in one day, you may want to consider staying at one of the motels within walking distance of the park, none of which is particularly fancy. Other, more upscale hotel choices are available just a short drive away.

Rodeway Inn

4139 East Busch Boulevard

Tampa, FL 33612

(813) 386-1000; fax (813) 386-1011

    A standard budget motel.

    Price Range: $$ - $$$

    Amenities: Pool

    Walk to Park: 20 minutes

Days Inn

2901 East Busch Boulevard

Tampa, FL 33612

(813) 933-6471

    A standard mid-range motel.

    Price Range: $$ - $$$

    Amenities: Pool, restaurant

    Walk to Park: 30 minutes

La Quinta Inn & Suites

9202 North 30th Street

Tampa, FL 33612

(813) 930–6900; fax (813) 930–0563

Standard mid-range hotel, probably the best of the three options listed.

Price Range: $$ - $$$

Amenities: Pool

Walk to Park: 30 minutes

Special Events

Busch Gardens Africa hosts a growing number of razzle-dazzle themed events timed to the calendar. The oldest of these is an alcohol-free New Year's Eve celebration for young people and families. Halloween shenanigans are in evidence during October. These are typically after-hours affairs that require a hefty separate admission (a recent Howl-O-Scream event was $58). However, if you purchase your tickets in advance or have an annual pass, discounts are substantial.

From early June to mid-August (the exact dates differ each year), when the park is open to 9:00 or 10:00 p.m., Busch Gardens presents **Summer Nights**, a varied menu of outdoor entertainment at venues throughout the park. You might see a comic ventriloquist, an aerial act, juggling acts, or a DJ.

During the Christmas season there are nightly tree lighting ceremonies and in the fall the park hosts a series of big band concerts. A patriotic July Fourth celebration was in the planning stages at press time. To learn more about what events may be planned during your visit and to get the latest on ticket prices, call toll-free (888) 800-5447.

Eating at Busch Gardens Africa

On the whole, the dining experience at Busch Gardens is a step down from that at its sister park, SeaWorld, in Orlando. While **Crown Colony House**, the sole full-service restaurant in the park (in the Crown Colony section, 'natch) can't hold a candle to Sharks Underwater grill at SeaWorld, it has a few tasty dishes. The main draw here is the great view of the *Serengeti Plain*.

For more casual dining, I recommend the **Desert Grill** in Timbuktu, where you can be entertained in air-conditioned comfort while you dine, the **Zambia Smokehouse** for better than average barbecue amid the roars and screams of *SheiKra* in Stanleyville, and the outdoor **Zagora Cafe** in Morocco. And speaking of Morocco, I find it disappointing that Busch Gardens has not chosen to extend its African theme to its restaurant menus. I found myself wishing for something akin to the first-rate Moroccan restaurant at Epcot in Walt Disney World Resort. All the restaurants mentioned here are reviewed later in this chapter.

(An interesting note: No straws are provided at any of the park's restaurants or fast-food outlets in deference to the safety of the animals.)

Shopping at Busch Gardens Africa

The souvenir hunter will not leave disappointed. There are plenty of logo-bearing gadgets, gizmos, and wearables from which to choose. The t-shirts with tigers and gorillas are especially attractive. Tiger fanciers will also be drawn to the beach towels with the large white Bengal tiger portrait.

Best of all are the genuine African crafts to be found here and there around the park. Look for them in Morocco and Crown Colony, but they sometimes show up elsewhere. The prices can be steep for some of the nicer pieces, but there are some very attractive (and attractively priced) smaller items to be found. Clothing is another good buy at Busch, with some of the better shops located in Morocco and Crown Colony.

Most of the shops offer a free package pick-up service that lets you collect your purchases near the front entrance on your way out, so you needn't worry about lugging things about for half the day. You can avail yourself of Busch Gardens' mail order services by dialing (800) 410-9453 or (813) 987-5060.

Good Things to Know About ...

See the *Good Things to Know About ...* section in *Chapter One* for notes that apply to all the parks. These notes apply specifically to Busch Gardens Africa.

Access for the Disabled

Handicapped parking spaces are provided directly in front of the park's main entrance for those with a valid permit. Otherwise, physically challenged guests may be dropped off at the main entrance. The entire park is wheelchair accessible and companion bathrooms are dotted about the park. Some physically challenged guests may not be able to experience certain rides due to safety considerations. An "Access Guide" is available at Guest Relations near the main entrance.

Wheelchair and ECV rentals are handled out of a concession next to the Jeepers and Creepers shop in Morocco. Wheelchairs are $10 a day. Motorized carts are $35. ECVs are popular, so get there early to be sure you get one.

Animal Observation

Busch Gardens does an excellent job of displaying its animals in natural settings. One consequence of that is that they can sometimes be hard to see.

So if spying out elands or catching a glimpse of a rare rhino baby is important to you, consider bringing along a pair of binoculars. They will come in handy on the *Skyride*, the *Trans-Veldt Railroad*, and even at lunch in the Crown Colony House restaurant.

Babies

Diaper changing tables are located in restrooms throughout the park. A nursing area is located in Land of the Dragons.

If you don't have your own, you can rent strollers at the concession next to Jeepers and Creepers in Morocco. Nifty looking Jeep Strollers are $10 for the full day, double strollers are $15.

First Aid

First aid stations are located in Timbuktu behind the Desert Grill restaurant and in Crown Colony in the *Skyride* building. If emergency aid is needed, contact the nearest employee.

Getting Wet

The signs say, "This is a water attraction. Riders will get wet and possibly soaked." This is not marketing hyperbole but a simple statement of fact. The water rides at Busch Gardens are one of its best kept secrets (the mammoth roller coasters get most of the publicity), but they pose some problems for the unprepared. Kids probably won't care, but adults can get positively cranky when wandering around sopping wet.

The three major water rides, in increasing order of wetness, are *Stanley Falls Log Flume*, *Congo River Rapids*, and the absolutely soaking *Tanganyika Tidal Wave*. (The *Mizzly Marsh* section of Land of the Dragons can also get tykes very wet.) Fortunately, these three rides are within a short distance of each other, in the Congo and Stanleyville, allowing you to implement the following strategy:

First, dress appropriately. Wear a bathing suit and t-shirt under a dressier outer layer. Wear shoes you don't mind getting wet; sports sandals are ideal. Bring a tote bag in which you can put things, like cameras, that shouldn't get wet. You can also pack a towel and it's probably a good idea to bring along the plastic laundry bag from your motel room.

Plan to do the water rides in sequence. When you're ready to start, strip off your outer layer, put it in the tote bag along with your other belongings, and stash everything in a convenient locker. There are lockers dotted throughout the Congo and Stanleyville. A helpful locker symbol on the map of the park will help you locate the nearest one. Now you're ready to enjoy the rides without worry.

Once you've completed the circuit, and especially if you rode the *Tidal Wave*, you will be soaked to the skin. You now have a choice. If it's a hot summer day, you may want to let your clothes dry as you see the rest of the park. Don't worry about feeling foolish; you'll see of plenty of other folks in the same boat, and your damp clothes will feel just great in the Florida heat. In cooler weather, however, it's a good idea to return to the locker, grab your stuff, head to a nearby restroom, and change into dry clothes. Use the plastic laundry bag for the wet stuff.

The alternative is to buy a Busch Gardens poncho (they make nice souvenirs and are readily available at shops near the water rides) and hope for the best. This is far less fun and you'll probably get pretty wet anyway.

Kids' ID System

Stop by Guest Services to pick up wristbands for your young children. Guest Services will label them with your name and cell phone number so staff members can easily get hold of you if they encounter your child on the loose. Wristbands are available free of charge, and are uniquely numbered, so that even if the writing on the wristband smears, they can still use this number to look up your information back at Guest Services, should the need arise. If you become separated from your child, contact the nearest employee. Found children are returned to the Security Office next door to the Marrakesh Theater in Morocco.

Rain Checks

Busch Gardens Africa offers a "rain guarantee." If you feel your visit has been ruined by the rain, they will issue a complimentary ticket valid for another day's admission within the next seven days.

On Safari:
Your Day at Busch Gardens

The bad news is that it's difficult — probably impossible — to see all of Busch Gardens in a day. The good news is that most people will be happy to forego some of the attractions. The more sedate will happily pass up the roller coasters to spend time observing the great apes, while the speed demons will be far happier being flung about on *Montu* or challenging their fear limit on *SheiKra* than sitting still for a show in The Desert Grill.

In many respects, Busch Gardens is a "typical" theme park. Each area of the park is decorated and landscaped to reflect its particular "theme," which is also reflected in the decor of the shops and restaurants (although not nec-essarily in the merchandise and food being offered). The attendants wear appropriate uniforms and a variety of rides, exhibits, attractions, and "street-mosphere" compete for your attention. If you've been to any of the other big theme parks in Central Florida, it's unlikely you'll find anything radically different about Busch Gardens.

As I noted earlier, Busch Gardens combines a number of seemingly dis-parate elements into an eclectic whole. Here, then, are some of the elements in the Busch Gardens mix:

The Zoo. Home to 2,700 animals, representing hundreds of species (the numbers will probably have risen by the time you visit), Busch Gardens is one of the major zoological parks in the nation. It is also a highly enlightened zoo, embodying the latest thinking about how animals should be housed and displayed to the public. You will receive an understated but persistent message about the importance of conserving and protecting the planet's animal heri-tage. Like SeaWorld, Busch Gardens boasts a zoological staff that is friendly, visible, approachable, and more than happy to answer questions.

Meet The Keepers. One way in which the staff helps spread the conser-vation message is through regular "Meet The Keepers" shows built around feeding and caring for the animals. The presence of food means that the ani-mals are usually at their most active during these shows; the attendants also attempt to coax their charges into appropriate poses for those with cameras. You can pick up a schedule of Meet The Keepers sessions when you enter the park.

Roller Coasters. Busch Gardens boasts one of the largest concentrations of roller coasters in the nation. They range from the relatively modest *Scor-pion* to the truly awesome *SheiKra*. Even the smallest of these rides features elements, like loops, that are not to be found on just any roller coaster. You will be well advised to take advantage of the coin-operated lockers located near every roller coaster to store your loose gear. Anyone who is serious about their roller coasters will definitely want to put Busch Gardens on their must-see list for their Central Florida vacation.

Water Rides. Busch Gardens is also home to a group of water rides that are designed to get you very, very, very wet. They are great fun, but require some planning and strategizing. Unless, of course, you're a young boy, in which case you simply won't mind walking through the park sopping wet from the top of your head to the toes of your $100 sneakers. See *Good Things to Know About ... Getting Wet*, above.

Live Shows. There is a regular schedule of entertainment throughout the day in open-air amphitheaters and indoor, air-conditioned theaters. A few are animal-oriented, but most are pure variety entertainment shows that change periodically. Most shows don't gear up until 11:00 a.m. or noon. Thereafter, they run pretty regularly until closing time. A show schedule is available near the main entrance.

Orientation to Busch Gardens

Your very first step on any visit to Busch Gardens Africa is to pause near the main entrance and pick up a copy of the park map along with a separate sheet of paper listing the times of the various shows and the schedule of Meet the Keepers sessions. As you will see by perusing the map, Busch Gardens is divided into eight "themed areas" (nine if, like me, you count Land of the Dragons as a separate area), most of them named after a country or region of Africa. Each area is relatively compact but the entire park is quite large (335 acres), making covering the entire place a bit of a challenge.

In describing the nine areas, I will start with Morocco, the first area you encounter as you enter the park, and proceed clockwise around the park, ending with Egypt. I am not suggesting that you tour Busch Gardens in this order (although it would be the most direct route if you were to walk the entire park). Use the descriptions that follow, along with the suggestions given above, to pick and choose the attractions that best suit your tastes and that you can comfortably fit into the time available. Remember that you can use the *Skyride* between Stanleyville and Crown Colony to cut down on the walking.

In addition to the attractions listed below, Busch Gardens features a number of strolling musical groups playing peppy music designed to put a bit of bounce back in your step as you stroll the grounds. The **Mystic Sheiks of Morocco** are a brass marching band outfitted in snappy red and black uniforms that make them look like a military band from a very hip African nation. They are most frequently sighted in Morocco and Crown Colony. The **Men of Note** offer up the kind of close harmony, a capella doo-wop music more associated with the streets of Philadelphia than the souks of Morocco. Still, they can often be found entertaining departing guests there or holding forth at the Marrakesh Theater.

Photographing Animals at Busch Gardens Africa

(The following section is adapted from *America's Best Zoos: A Travel Guide for Fans and Families* by Allen W. Nyhuis and Jon Wassner.)

The most important thing to understand is that anyone can take great animal pictures, even without spending a fortune on expensive photography equipment. But getting a great picture means taking into account a number of factors that can change on a daily basis. Specifically, dream shots require timing, patience, and often a little research. Here are a few tips that should prove helpful in almost any situation:

Timing. By timing, we mean time of day, and specifically the lighting. Early morning light is usually the softest of the day; it almost lights the subject from within. On the other hand, midday light can be bright and harsh, and in the late afternoon, the setting sun creates problematic shadows. Cloud cover can be a bonus when it comes to lighting; the diffuse light illuminates evenly without creating harsh shadows. Be aware of these factors when composing a shot. But timing also can include attending planned zoo events like Busch Gardens Africa's Meet the Keeper series. These informative interactive presentations also present excellent picture-taking opportunities.

Patience. Patience may be the most important factor in getting a good photo. Finding an animal in a zoo isn't always tough, but finding one in the right position can be quite difficult. If a gorilla is hiding behind a bush, spend a few minutes waiting to see if it will move. Trying to find an animal in the right context, however, **does not** mean tapping on the glass to get its attention. Glass-tapping is a clear violation of zoo manners and rules. Repeatedly tapping on their glass tanks can even harm some animals, such as reptiles. Even though it will take longer, waiting for the right shot, instead of artificially creating it, is much more satisfying.

Angles and equipment. Modern zoo exhibits bring animals closer and closer to visitors, so even a disposable point-and-shoot camera can produce some nice shots. Quite often, these close encounters with animals are achieved through creative use of glass barriers. Unfortunately, the downside of glass is the potential for glare. The best way to eliminate glare is to take the picture from a forty-five-degree angle. For those willing to purchase more advanced equipment, a glare-reducing filter can significantly improve photos of animals taken through glass. If you are fortunate enough to have an SLR camera with detachable lenses, bring along a wide-angle lens to the zoo.

Zoos are in the business of recreating natural habitats. While close-up pictures of animals are certainly impressive, don't forget to include a few pictures that showcase their surroundings – you might even be able to convince someone you actually went on an African safari!

For more information about *America's Best Zoos*, visit . . .

www.americasbestzoos.com

Big Game

For those with limited time or who want to skim the cream of this multifaceted park, here are my selections for the trophy-winning attractions at Busch Gardens:

For coaster fans, **SheiKra**, **Montu** and **Kumba** are musts and you'll want to ride **Gwazi** just to be complete. Of the water rides, **Congo River Rapids** is my favorite and the **Tanganyika Tidal Wave** is highly recommended for those who want to get totally drenched. The best theater show by far is **KaTonga**.

Animal lovers will not want to miss the chimps and gorillas in **Myombe Reserve** or the tigers in **Jungala**. **Edge of Africa** is another must-see animal habitat, but the **Serengeti Safari Tour** (for an extra charge) is the best way to get close to the animals. **Rhino Rally** is a fun way to get an all-too brief glimpse of some other veldt dwellers combined with a mild thrill ride on a raging river. And finally, if you have preschoolers in tow, you will not want to miss the spectacular **Land of the Dragons**.

The One-Day Stay for Ride Fans

1. Plan to arrive at the opening bell. As soon as the park opens, grab a map just inside the turnstiles and proceed directly to *SheiKra* in Stanleyville (bear left), bypassing *Gwazi* for now. If crowds are sparse, and if you dare, ride *SheiKra* more than once. (If *Rhino Rally* is on your list, try to get there first thing in the morning, before you ride anything else; lines form quickly and the ride handles many fewer riders per hour than the coasters.)

2. After *SheiKra*, continue to the Congo and ride *Kumba*. If the *Skyride* is operating, you can use it to head to *Montu* in Egypt; otherwise just walk. Then, walk back through Egypt, Crown Colony and Morocco to *Gwazi*.

3. Once you've done the coasters, head back to Stanleyville and ride *Stanley Falls* and the *Tanganyika Tidal Wave*, finishing up with a ride on *Congo River Rapids*. Now head south, pausing to admire the tigers in Jungala as you check the map and Entertainment Guide. If the timing's right, catch the *Skyride* again and head back to the Moroccan Palace Theater to catch *KaTonga*.

4. After lunch, you have several choices. You can hit your favorite rides again, try the lesser rides, or (my personal suggestion) visit the various zoo attractions, perhaps catching another show at some point in the afternoon. Don't forget to check the schedule of Meet The Keeper shows.

The One-Day Stay for the More Sedate

1. If you are not a ride fanatic you don't have to kill yourself to get there at the minute the park opens, although a full day at Busch Gardens, taken at a moderate pace, is a full day well-spent. For now, I'll assume you are arriving early. Grab a park map and the Entertainment Guide and bear to the right as you stroll towards Crown Colony. En route, peruse the times for the variety shows and the Meet The Keeper sessions.

2. If you plan to take the *Serengeti Safari Tour*, sign up now. Take a leisurely tour of *Edge of Africa*, and if you're interested and the lines aren't too long, you might want to walk to Egypt and pop into *King Tut's Tomb*. Otherwise, stroll to Nairobi for a visit to *Myombe Reserve* and *Jambo Junction*. Don't dismiss

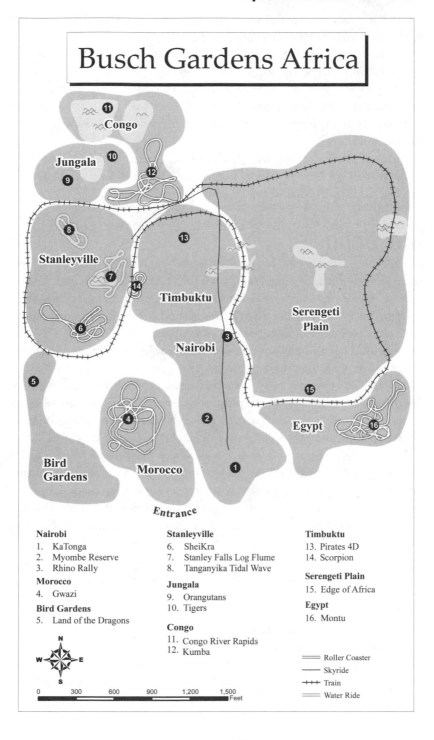

Busch Gardens Africa

Nairobi
1. KaTonga
2. Myombe Reserve
3. Rhino Rally

Morocco
4. Gwazi

Bird Gardens
5. Land of the Dragons

Stanleyville
6. SheiKra
7. Stanley Falls Log Flume
8. Tanganyika Tidal Wave

Jungala
9. Orangutans
10. Tigers

Congo
11. Congo River Rapids
12. Kumba

Timbuktu
13. Pirates 4D
14. Scorpion

Serengeti Plain
15. Edge of Africa

Egypt
16. Montu

0   300   600   900   1,200   1,500
Feet

Roller Coaster
Skyride
Train
Water Ride

Rhino Rally out of hand. Although it is touted as a "thrill ride," the thrills are very muted and the wildlife worth a look.

3. Now board the *Trans-Veldt Railroad* at the Nairobi Station for the journey around the Serengeti.

4. Now you're ready to see some shows. You can walk to Timbuktu for the musical variety show at the Desert Grill (and have lunch if you haven't grabbed a bite yet) or you can stroll the other way to catch *Ka Tonga* at the Moroccan Palace.

5. Round out your day with a visit to Bird Gardens and the *Critter Castaways* show. If you have little ones in tow, don't forget to let them have their own special time in Land of the Dragons.

Morocco

Morocco is your first stop in the park, so some of the available space is given over to housekeeping. Here you'll find Guest Relations and the Adventure Tour Center, where you can make arrangements for the special tours described at the end of this chapter. Just around the corner to your right is the stroller and wheelchair rental concession. Since Morocco is also the exit to the park, a fair amount of space is given to souvenir and other shops, the better to lure those on the way out.

Note: On especially busy days, they open the Nairobi Gate, which is directly to the right of where the parking lot tram drops off new arrivals. This entrance lets visitors into the park at a point about equidistant from Nairobi, Crown Colony, and Morocco.

Otherwise, the main business of Morocco is stage shows of one sort or another. There are two theaters (reviewed below) and an **alligator pond**, where several times a day a Meet The Keepers show takes place. It's a zoologically correct version of the more popularized shows you get at Gatorland and other gator-themed attractions. A raised platform called the **Sultan's Tent** hosts **photo ops** with animals during busier times.

Rock A Doo Wop (Marrakesh Theater)

Rating: ★ ★ ★ +
Type: Live stage show
Time: 25 minutes
Kelly says: Rock down memory lane

On a thrust stage with Moorish arches and purple curtains, this peppy revue pays homage to the early days of rock and roll, when simple melodies and a snappy beat swept across the nation and transformed a generation, not to mention the generations that followed.

A four-man combo, some of whom look old enough to remember the era first-hand, provide solid backing for a troupe of eight youngsters, four men, four women, who run through a repertoire that seems oh-so familiar to the mostly grey-haired crowd this show attracts. There are solos, duets, ensembles, and a number of energetic dance routines. Despite the title, just one number is in true a capella doo-wop style, but it is "In The Still of the Night" and it is a smashing success. After the show, some of the performers mingle with the audience for **photo ops**.

Note: This show changes from time to time, but the theme remains the same — pop rock standards with an accent on oldies.

KaTonga (Moroccan Palace Theater)

Rating: ★ ★ ★ ★ ★
Type: Indoor theater show
Time: About 40 minutes
Kelly says: Simply marvelous and not to be missed

The 1,200-seat Moroccan Palace Theater is an extremely well-appointed performance space capable of Broadway-quality spectacle. Busch Gardens has risen to the challenge with *KaTonga*, a dazzling musical extravaganza that sets a new (and very high) standard for theme park entertainment. "Ka-Tonga" is apparently an African word for "a special place where tales are told," or something along those lines. A quartet of master storytellers from across Africa are gathered for a sort of competition and the tales they tell are brought magically to life by a troupe of multi talented dancers, puppeteers, and acrobats from around the world. The morals to these stories teach timeless truths: strive to be the best, know yourself, seek out love, and above all, celebrate life.

Too often, in shows of this type, everything's a mishmash of clashing motifs and styles. But here, the music, singing, costumes, lighting, puppets, choreography, and special effects come together beautifully to create a unified artistic vision. All in all, this is the best theatrical theme park show in all of Central Florida and I include the shows at Walt Disney World in that reckoning. Don't miss it.

Eating in Morocco

One of Busch Gardens' largest eateries, in terms of seating capacity, is located in Morocco and they haven't forgotten to include a place to pop in as you arrive for a sugar-fueled breakfast and to return to at the end of the day for a well deserved treat. Another dessert option is the **Moroccan Delights** ice cream parlor nearby.

Zagora Cafe

What: Cafeteria with outdoor seating
Where: In the central plaza as you enter the park
Price Range: $

This cafeteria has a number of lines and plenty of outdoor seating, about a third of it shaded under an overarching roof. Tables in the open air afford a great vantage point for people watching; everyone entering or leaving the park must pass by here.

Given the overall African theme, fajita wraps may be a somewhat inappropriate centerpiece for the menu, but I've heard no complaints. The chicken and steak version is recommended. There are sandwiches like grilled cheese and chicken strips and a "Classic Italian" with provalone cheese and salamis on foccacia bread.

Slightly more elaborate are burgers, including a bacon cheeseburger platter. Beer is on offer along with the usual soft drinks. The Safari Kids Meal here consists of a hot dog or chicken strips, with a choice of fries or fresh carrots. Desserts are good, too, although you might prefer the larger selection across the way at Sultan's Sweets.

Sultan's Sweets

What: Pastries and desserts
Where: En route to *KaTonga*
Price Range: $

Every theme park needs a place near the entrance where those who forgot to have a healthy breakfast can opt for an unhealthy one. And this is the place in Busch Gardens. Load up on oversized croissants and muffins or keep telling yourself "I'm on vacation" and head straight for the large selection of gooey desserts. Wash it all down with coffee, which comes in a number of designer versions.

One section of this emporium serves as a more or less standard candy shop with a goodly selection of chocolates and fudge. Later in the day, this is a good place to stop for tea or coffee and a treat. A small number of outdoor tables allow you to survey the passing scene.

Shopping in Morocco

Some of the best shopping to be found at Busch Gardens Africa is thoughtfully provided here and I recommend lingering on the way out of the park to browse. This area stays open a little later than official closing time to accommodate you.

I especially like the **Marrakesh Market**, where you will find some very nice clothing for women (and a lesser selection for men). Here, too, are some very nice crafts and decorative objects from Morocco and elsewhere.

Across the plaza, **Outfitters** is stocked with casual clothing, geared to the season, for both men and women. It's a good place to look for a broad-brimmed hat to protect yourself from the Florida sun. In the opposite direction, just past Sultan's Sweets, **Nature's Kingdom** offers some fun gift items and bric-a-brac with a nature or eco theme.

Bird Gardens

As the name suggests, Bird Gardens houses most of the birds in the Busch Gardens zoo collection. In addition to the few larger bird displays mentioned below, the area is dotted with flamingos and other exotic water fowl, their wings obviously clipped, in beautifully landscaped open settings with ponds and streams. They are joined by a rotating group of visiting Florida species. Some of the walkways are lined with gaudy parrots in free-hanging cages. Over all, the effect is enchanting, rather like the private gardens of a rich and tasteful eccentric.

Bird Gardens is also home to *Gwazi*, a mammoth twin-track wooden roller coaster that greets you as you enter. Near *Gwazi*, you will find **River Rumble**, a water game, and **Xtreme Zone**, where you can climb a simulated cliff or bounce on a trampoline. There is an additional charge for these activities. A short stroll away and often overlooked is **Eagle Canyon**, a quiet corner devoted to these magnificent raptors.

Gwazi

Rating:	★ ★ ★ ★ +
Type:	Dueling wooden coasters
Time:	About two and a half minutes
Kelly says:	Up-to-date nostalgia

For those who remember the days when all roller coasters were made of wood, *Gwazi* will be like a stroll down memory lane — until the first drop reminds you that this isn't your father's coaster.

The "gimmick" here, of course, is that there are two separate coasters, each holding 24 passengers, one representing a tiger, the other a lion. As you snake your way to the departure platforms, you get to choose which one you'll take on and each route has its own theming — the lion territory evokes an African desert environment, while the tiger territory is reminiscent of the jungles and streams of Asia. The dueling trains depart simultaneously and "race" to the finish with six "fly-bys" along the way. The close encounters may not be quite as scary as on some of the dueling steel coasters — the realities of wooden coasters mandate a decent amount of space between the rail and the edge of the superstructure — but they are pretty scary nonetheless. Likewise, the ride itself may seem tamer. After all, it's hard to do an inversion on a wooden coaster. But the rumble and rattle of wood makes *Gwazi* seem faster than its 50 miles per hour and on some of the turns the cars seem to be at right angles to the ground. Wooden coasters also have a liveliness that steel coasters don't. Coaster enthusiasts would say, "it's alive!" which is another way of saying that the give in the wood makes each ride seem different from the last.

Tip: Any serious coaster buff will want to ride at least twice, once on each track. After many rides, coaster mavens seem to agree: the lion coaster has the steeper first drop, but the tiger coaster is, over all, the more intense experience.

There are some other good things to be said about *Gwazi*. It lasts longer than some of its zippier competitors and because the height restriction here is only 48 inches, more members of the family will get a chance to ride. *Gwazi* is also quite beautiful, in a way in which the more modern steel coasters aren't. The wood is weathered rather than the more traditional white and blends in nicely with the African conical thatched roof motif of the entrance. And from the top you get a fascinating (but brief) glimpse of one of the park's "backstage" areas, as well as the surrounding terrain.

Even if you don't choose to ride, *Gwazi* is worth checking out if only to marvel at the way a million board feet of lumber have been put together to create this behemoth. It has a delightfully scary way of looking rather flimsy in spite of its massive size. One good vantage point is to be had just inside the exit, where riders can purchase pictures to commemorate the experience. Another place to get a fairly good look is further into Bird Gardens, near the eagle display and the Clydesdale statue.

Critter Castaways (in Bird Theater)

Rating: ★ ★ ★ +
Type: Live amphitheater show
Time: About 20 minutes
Kelly says: A potpourri of pettable performers

The creators of this show seem to have borrowed heavily from *Pets Ahoy* over at SeaWorld and the kiddie show next door in Land of the Dragons. The result is a harmless bit of fluff that should appeal to most, especially the littler ones in your party.

The backdrop is a fairly elaborate set depicting the wreck of the Amazon Queen, an old tug boat by the looks of her. Our singing hostess, Jane, lives here in harmony with a few shipwrecked friends and a passel of animals from around the world. Jane is one of those annoying, sugar-sweet types you see on early morning TV shows aimed at tots. She sings a saccharine song about "living in harmony" until you want to go up on stage and throttle her.

But to give Jane and her fellow cast members their due, this is not about musical theater. This is about the animals. They range from humble cats and dogs (all alumni of local rescue centers, apparently) to emus and kangaroos, and a variety of multicolored birds of all shapes and sizes. For good measure, there are cameos by a mouse, a skunk, and two pigs.

There is less "edutainment" in this show than there was in previous incarnations, although we do learn that the maribou stork can fly almost as high as an airplane and we get to see how a lesser anteater uses its long tongue to slurp jelly out of a tube. The joy and the fun of the show derives quite simply from our age-old fascination with animals of all types. Just watching them walk across the stage — which is all most of them do — qualifies as entertainment. Some of the dogs and cats do considerably more, performing some nifty tricks. And a beautifully plumed parrot flies around the auditorium, neatly zipping through a series of hoops. It's enough to make you forget that annoying song.

Note: This show seems to change more than most, but given the elaborate set I suspect this edition will be around for a while. Although I have liked some versions of this show better than others, it has always been worth seeing.

Hospitality House Stage

Rating: ★ ★ +
Type: Live music
Time: About 20 minutes
Kelly says: Diverting with lunch

On a small outdoor stage near the Hospitality House (see Eating in Bird Gardens, below), a small, cheerful combo holds forth on a regular schedule. The selections are all likely to be familiar and they are all certified toe-tappers put over with a great deal of good-humored élan. If you find yourself near here at show time, why not grab a free beer and a pizza slice inside and give a listen?

Brewmaster's Club

Rating: ★ ★ ★ ★
Type: Free beer!
Time: 30 to 40 minutes
Kelly says: For beer buffs

This is pretty much a carbon copy of the Brewmaster's Club at SeaWorld and I will refer you to *Chapter Two* for a more complete description.

Suffice it to say that, if you like beer, you should truly enjoy this experience. And even if you don't, it's still pretty interesting.

It's easy to miss this location. The Club is behind Hospitality House, near the Eagle Canyon area. A small pathway next to Hospitality House Stage will take you right to the entrance.

Aviary

Rating: ★ ★ ★ +
Type: Walk-through animal exhibit
Time: Continuous viewing
Kelly says: A lovely place to pause

This is a smallish habitat compared to others in the park, but its size belies its enchantment. Essentially a large tent made of a dark mesh fabric, the aviary lets you visit a wide variety of tropical birds in a remarkably realistic setting, instead of peering at them through the bars of a cage. Benches allow for long and leisurely viewing. Some, like the roseate spoonbill, may look familiar but others, like the odd Abdim's Stork and a beautiful blue Victoria Crowned Pigeon that thinks it's a peacock, will probably be new to you.

I have discovered that the longer you sit and relax here, the more the mesh tent fades from your consciousness. What remains is a charming encounter with some very lovely birds.

Eating in Bird Gardens

Perhaps the most noteworthy feature of the dining scene in Bird Gardens is the **free beer** that is dispensed in the beautifully designed and sited Hospitality House. Yup, free beer. The cups are on the small size (about 10 ounces) and there's a limit (one sample at a time, two per day), but it's still a gracious gesture. Many of Anheuser-Busch's brands are available, including the nonalcoholic O'Doul's. Besides Hospitality House, you will find a few modest refreshment stands.

Hospitality House Pizza

What: Pizza and fries
Where: In Hospitality House
Price Range: $

This is a vest-pocket walk-up stand serving a limited menu of club sandwiches and pizza and fries combos. Most of the real estate in Hospitality House is given over to the several serving lines dispensing free beer. There's no indoor seating, but the outdoor seating area overlooks one of the nicest views in the park.

Shopping in Bird Gardens

Xcursions, near the entrance to Bird Gardens, is perhaps the handsomest shop in the park. The emphasis is on nature and earth sciences, with toys and books aimed at a younger audience who will also appreciate the plush toys. There is some nice casual clothing for adults, costume jewelry for women, and a good selection of figurines, with the eagle statuettes and the Wyland sculptures the standouts. At the other end of this land is **Garden Gate,** a gift shop for the serious gardener featuring everything from seeds to small potted plants to decorations and whirligigs and other decorations for the garden.

Land of the Dragons

Although officially part of Bird Gardens, this play area for the preschool set is different and special enough to warrant separate treatment. Other theme parks in Central Florida have similar kiddie areas but nowhere will you find the concept pulled off with as much wit and verve as the Land of the Dragons. Here, the clever design of *Fievel's Playland* at Universal and the size of *Shamu's Happy Harbor* at SeaWorld come together to create the only five-star kiddie attraction in this book.

There are animals to be seen here, too, of course. At one end are iguanas, monitor lizards, and komodo dragons, the **Living Dragons** that give the area its name. At the other, in a separate circular area, is *Lory Landing,* described below. But the emphasis is on fun in the Land of the Dragons and the little ones will not be disappointed.

Interactive Play Areas

Rating: ★ ★ ★ ★ ★
Type: Hands-on activity
Time: As long as you want
Kelly says: The best of its kind in Central Florida

Most of the Land of the Dragons is given over to a series of loosely connected climb-up, crawl-through, slide-down play areas that can keep little ones occupied for hours. I have given them the rather cumbersome name of "interactive play areas," but each has its own identity and special attractions, as we shall see.

Dominating the north end of the area is the **Dragon's Nest**, an elaborate two-story structure colorfully painted and shaded by a large tarp covering and towering live oak trees. On the lower level, it features a net climb, an "air bounce" (a large inflated floor on which kids can jump to their hearts' content), and a "ball crawl" (a pit filled with colored plastic balls into which kids can literally dive). The upper level is reached either via the net climb or, for less agile adults, a stairway. There you will find a two-level, kid-sized, climb-through, maze-like environment forming a delightful obstacle course. No one higher than 56 inches is allowed in this one, so Mom and Dad are excused.

From this upper level extend two rope bridges. Both go to the **Tree House**, one directly and the other via an intermediate tower, from which kids can zip down a corkscrew slide to ground level. The Tree House itself is a kid's fantasy of a humongous old tree girdled by a spiral wooden staircase leading to a "secret" room at the top. Along the way, climbers can detour into jungle gym-like environments that snake off through the Land of the Dragons. Kids will love it; nervous parents may find it hard to keep track of their little ones.

At the foot of the Tree House lies **Mizzly Marsh**, a watery play area where kids can really get soaked. The marsh leads through and around the old tree and comes complete with a friendly dragon whose snake-like body appears and disappears beneath the water. Set apart and surrounded by a fence is the **Dragon Diggery**, a large and ingeniously designed sandbox with adorable playhouses, one in the shape of a giant mushroom.

The overall effect of these interlocking entertainments is pure delight. Not only is virtually every activity conceived by the preschool mind represented here, but the design and attention to detail are wonderfully imaginative.

Tip: If your kids are old enough to be turned loose in the Land of the Dragons, you can draw some comfort in the knowledge that there is only one way out, at the southern end. There is no exit at the north end, near *Lory Landing*.

Kiddie Rides

> *Rating:* ★ ★ ★
> *Type:* Mechanical rides for toddlers
> *Time:* A few minutes each
> *Kelly says:* Variations on a single theme

Sprinkled around Land of the Dragons are small kiddie rides. You know the kind of thing: tiny vehicles that go round and round in a tiny circle with tiny little people sitting in them. The ones here are better designed and executed than most, with cutesy names like *Eggery Deggery*, *Chug-A-Tug*, and *Dapper Flappers*. If your kids are the right age (under three) they'll have a ball.

Friends Forever (Dragon's Tale Theater)

> *Rating:* ★ ★ ★ +
> *Type:* Live outdoor show
> *Time:* About 15 minutes

Kelly says: Entertainment for tots

This is a delightful little sing-a-long and audience participation show for the kids. Adults should check their sophistication at the door. Dumphrey, the Fire-Breathing Dragon who is sort of the mascot for Land of the Dragons, and a beautiful princess help a dashing knight search for his lost dog, Percy, and the kids in the audience get to help. Along the way they learn lessons about diversity and tolerance. Dumphrey is a costumed character, of course, but Percy is played by a real live dog and he just may be the best actor of the bunch. It's all good fun and the little tots at whom this show is aimed seem to love every minute of it.

Lory Landing

Rating: ★ ★ ★ +
Type: Walk-through animal exhibit
Time: As long as you like
Kelly says: Close encounters with inquisitive charmers

Lorys and lorikeets are the main attraction in this aviary within an aviary. About halfway between parakeets and parrots in size, lorys are as curious as they are colorful. As you walk through their jungle-themed aviary, they are likely to land on your head, shoulder, or arm to check out your shiny jewelry or angle for a handout. Busch Gardens encourages this by selling "lory nectar" ($3) just in case you forgot to bring your own.

This is great fun for kids (grown-ups, too!) and well worth a visit. In the antechamber to the lorys' digs are large cages displaying their larger cousins — cockatoos, macaws, and the like.

Eating and Shopping in Land of the Dragons

There's not much to eat here, except for pretty basic refreshments, and the shopping is equally muted, focusing as you might expect on inexpensive toys for wee ones. Head north to *Zambia Smokehouse* or south to *Hospitality House Pizza* for a real meal (and don't forget the free beer!).

Stanleyville

Stanleyville is a compact, cleverly designed area that quite literally has something for everyone. At the southern end is what is arguably the best roller coaster in all of central Florida, the first stop we encounter on the park-circling *Trans-Veldt Railroad,* as well as a quite nice barbecue restaurant. At the other end are two delightful water rides and in the middle is a spacious theater that serves up some first-rate live entertainment on a somewhat erratic schedule. The *Skyride* (described in the Crown Colony section, below) offers a shortcut to Crown Colony and Egypt. The only downside is that there are very few animals to be seen here, but I seriously doubt you'll care.

SheiKra

Rating:	★ ★ ★ ★ ★
Type:	Floorless vertical dive coaster
Time:	3 minutes
Kelly says:	Gulp!

SheiKra (pronounced SHEEK-rah) is America's first "vertical dive roller coaster" and its presence cements Busch Gardens' reputation as *the* central Florida destination for coaster freaks. And just to add to the fun, they removed the floor, adding an extra layer of terror to the experience. If pushing yourself to the limit is your idea of having a good time, then you will not want to miss this fall-filled fear-fest.

Although *SheiKra* officially lasts a full three minutes, the first 70 seconds or so are taken up by the slow crawl to a height of 200 feet where, after a tight U-turn, you reach the first drop. There you pause just over the lip for several hours (okay, three or four seconds) as you contemplate your fate. Then you drop straight down at a 90 degree angle before swooping upwards to do it all again. The second drop takes you straight through the mist-filled center of a ruined tower, underground, up again for another tight turn, and down for a watery splashdown that slows you for a quick return to safety.

The best seats in the house. The ride vehicles are broad and compact, with three eight-seat rows. On top of that, they feature "stadium-style seating," meaning that each row is a little higher than the one in front of it. The result is that virtually every seat gives you a great view of the terrors that face you. Still, the true believers will want to ride until they get into the first row for the unobstructed view of the first drop during that eternal pause.

One of the best touches in this ride is a simple engineering trick used in that final splashdown. Twin tubes mounted on the outside rear edges of the ride vehicle dip into the water on either side of the track, sending up two towering plumes that crash down on the kids who have eagerly gathered at pool's edge. And thanks to the clever siting of the ride, you will have plenty of time to figure out exactly how it's done.

In fact, *SheiKra* offers the best views for non-riders of any Busch Gardens coaster, so you can walk under and around it and get an excellent idea of exactly what you are missing. That is almost as much fun as riding. Almost.

Trans-Veldt Railroad

Rating:	★ ★ ★
Type:	Steam railroad journey

Time:　　　　30 – 35 minutes for a complete circuit
Kelly says:　　Shuttle with a view

Right under *SheiKra*, you can board a reconstruction of the type of steam railroad that served as mass transit in turn-of-the-century Africa, rest your weary feet, and get some great views of the animals of the *Serengeti Plain*. This is one of two vehicular viewing venues for the Serengeti (the *Skyride*, described in the Crown Colony section below, is the other).

It makes a leisurely circuit of the park in a generally counterclockwise direction with stops in Nairobi (the closest stop to the main entrance) and the Congo (near Timbuktu). Since you can board or exit at any of the three stops, the *Trans-Veldt* is a great way to cut down on your walking time, and it provides glimpses of animals you probably wouldn't see otherwise.

As you travel from Stanleyville to Nairobi you will get a tantalizing preview glimpse of *Rhino Rally* (described below), which might help you decide if you want to brave its long lines. Continuing through Egypt on your way to the Congo, you will pass right through the superstructure of *Montu* and enter the Serengeti where you will see giraffes and a variety of veldt antelopes. Too bad you can't stop for a longer look. A narrator on the train helps make sure you don't miss any of the animals and offers interesting facts about the ones you do see.

After the Congo stop, the train loops around the Congo and back to Stanleyville. This portion is the least scenic, although it does provide some fun, "backstage" glimpses of the park, including a close-up look at some portions of *Kumba*. In fact, the route of the *Trans-Veldt* takes you past every roller coaster in the park.

Tip: The left-hand side of the train offers the most interesting views of the Serengeti.

Stanleyville Theater

Rating:　　　★ ★ ★ to ★ ★ ★ ★ ★
Type:　　　　Live entertainment
Time:　　　　Varies
Kelly says:　　Keep your fingers crossed

It's hard to predict what, if anything, you'll be able to see here when you visit. The schedule is erratic and anything but predictable. But if you're lucky, you may be able to catch your favorite stars of yesteryear in live performance, making this the hottest show in town.

Past acts that have played here include Gary Lewis and the Playboys, Herman's Hermits, and Juice Newton. There have been Big Bands, too, like the Tommy Dorsey, Glenn Miller, and Les Brown Orchestras. Performances tend to be from Thursday through Sunday only, so plan accordingly if this sort of thing interests you. Usually, there are three shows a day and tickets, which are free, are required. You can get them near the theater.

Stanley Falls Log Flume

Rating: ★ ★ ★ +
Type: Water ride
Time: About 2 minutes
Kelly says: The last drop is a doozy

This is a fairly ordinary log flume ride, especially when compared to more recent variations on the theme. On the other hand, it is one of the longest in the nation, they say. The car in which you ride is a log-shaped contraption with two seating areas scooped out of it. Each car holds four people, adults or children. However, when the lines aren't too long you can ride two to a car.

Your log rumbles along at a moderate pace in a water-filled flume, takes a few turns, and then climbs slowly to a modest height. The first small drop is merely preparation for the finale, a slow ride up yet another steep grade and an exhilarating drop to the bottom in full view of the passing crowds. Like all water rides, this one has a warning about getting wet, but the cars, with their scooped out fronts, seem designed to direct the wave generated by the final splashdown away from the passengers. It's unlikely that you'll get seriously soaked on this one.

As you exit, pause for a moment to commune with the black and white ruffed lemurs with their beautiful coats and long, bushy tails.

Tanganyika Tidal Wave

Rating: ★ ★ ★ ★
Type: Water ride
Time: About 2 minutes
Kelly says: A first-class soaking

If the nearby *Stanley Falls Log Flume* lulled you into a false sense of security about staying dry, this one will dispel any such notions. Like the log flume ride, this is all about the final drop. In fact, until then, this ride is far tamer. It snakes lazily through a narrow waterway past stilt houses, whose porches are piled high with Central African trade goods, before taking a slow climb to the top.

Then, all bets are off as the 25-passenger car on which you're riding plunges wildly down a sharp incline into a shallow pool of water, sending a drenching wave over not just the passengers but the spectators who have eagerly gathered on a bridge overhead. No two ways about it. This one really soaks you. Even with a poncho you'll still be pretty darned damp. Since you're probably soaked to the skin anyway, why not top the ride off by standing on the bridge and waiting for the next car to come by? For those who don't want to take the ride or get soaked on the bridge, there is a glassed in viewing section that offers the thrill of a wall of water rushing at you, without the soaking effects.

See *Good Things to Know About . . . Getting Wet*, earlier in this chapter, for some tips on negotiating Busch Gardens' water rides.

Eating in Stanleyville

There are limited dining options in Stanleyville, but barbecue lovers will want to make a beeline for the he-man platters served up at the Zambia Smokehouse. If you have room left after that, you can toddle over to **Shei-Kra Sweets** for dessert.

Zambia Smokehouse

What: Barbecue, cafeteria-style
Where: Under *SheiKra*
Price Range: $ - $$

This cafeteria-style eatery serves up some of the best casual food in the park. Barbecue is the order of the day and the platters are sumptuous. Choose between baby back ribs (in whole or half racks), regular ribs, beef brisket, and smoked chicken. A Sampler Platter lets you try three of them. All platters come with fries and a dinner roll.

There's a Latin entree, too, chicken with black beans and yellow rice. Sandwiches and wraps include smoked turkey and beef brisket. The kids meal here is barbecue chicken or ribs in a souvenir lunchbox. And what barbecue meal would be complete without a tall frosty beer, which is served here on tap, along with the usual soft drinks.

Another great reason to eat here is the location, right under *SheiKra*. Yes, you can eat inside in cool cave-like comfort, but a better choice is on the patio, which offers a terrific view of the coaster's watery splashdown. And since *SheiKra* is almost eerily quiet you won't be bothered by loud noises — except for the screams of the riders, of course, but that's more fun than frightening.

Shopping in Stanleyville

The main shopping venue here is **Kariba Marketplace**, near *ShieKra*, offering a range of t-shirts, flip-flops and foot gear, and some swim suits, none of it particularly distinguished. For the rest, there is the usual assortment of inexpensive souvenirs. Over by *Tanganyika Tidal Wave*, is a small hut called **Tropical Wave** where you can pick up some of those very nice beach towels (which you might actually need if you've just ridden) and a selection of Panama Jack merchandise ranging from sun tan oil to some very nice straw hats.

Jungala

The newest "themed area" at Busch Gardens Africa ditches the geographic metaphors used in most of the park. Jungala is a made-up word designed, I suspect, to suggest this section's blend of spectacular animal habitats and fun activities for kids. Besides, it is home to animals that are not native to Africa but to India and Southeast Asia. And what animals they are! Tigers and orangutans are some of the most fascinating animals on display at the park. Of course, they are also some of the least active, so what you actually get to see is somewhat "luck of the draw." If you have the luxury of time, repeat visits will be rewarded.

If Land of the Dragons is for preschoolers, Jungala is for tweens, that "awkward" age, roughly eight to thirteen, between child and teenager. Some of the non-animal attractions here have been specifically designed for that age group, with others thoughtfully excluded.

Orangutan Habitat

Rating: ★ ★ ★ ★
Type: Animal habitat
Time: Unlimited
Kelly says: Another winner

This is the first habitat you encounter, to your left, as you enter the bridge to Jungala from Stanleyville. A shaded portion of the bridge allows a good view of the entire enclosure, which is a sort of raised island surrounded by steep cliffs and water. Don't overlook the ingenious video binoculars here that allow for a closer look at the inhabitants.

Orangutans are powerful and agile climbers and the habitat has been designed to let them show off their skills. There are three large metal towers topped with platforms (no attempt at jungle verisimilitude here); the towers are linked by vine-like ropes that allow the orangs to shuttle between them.

Step into Jungala and to your left you will find **Orangutan Outpost,** an indoor (but not air conditioned) viewing area with glass walls looking into the enclosure. A sort of shelf made of logs rims the viewing area and the orangs, seemingly as curious about us as we are about them, often come up for a closer look at the odd creatures in the theme park habitat. A great touch here is a plexiglass section of the floor that looks down on a square rope hammock where the orangs like to come and chill out. There are Meet the Keepers sessions a few times a day here. At other times, signs around the room and interactive video screens provide information about this fascinating species.

Tiger Enclosure

Rating:	★ ★ ★ ★ ★
Type:	Animal habitat
Time:	Unlimited
Kelly says:	Ingenious and enchanting

This sprawling habitat has been cleverly designed to provide the tigers plenty of variety while allowing the visitor many options for viewing. The space is divided in two separate enclosures, with a rocky tunnel, punctuated with windows, running between them.

Tiger Lodge is an indoor, air conditioned viewing area with floor to ceiling windows that allows for comfortable long term viewing of one of the enclosures. Outside, **Tiger Trail** runs through the tunnel separating the enclosures allowing you to peer into both. Overhead is a glass paneled walkway that lets the keepers move tigers from one enclosure to the other. Usually it is closed off, but sometimes you will see tigers lolling in this passageway, apparently drawn by the warmth of the small enclosure (hey, they're cats). The trail then curves around the outside of the second enclosure offering a number of views, including an underwater view of one of the tigers' pools. (Alone among the big cats, tigers tolerate, even enjoy, water.) There's also a great view from a wooden bridge into a sort of canyon, with waterfalls and large dead trees that let the tigers climb from one level to another.

Best of all is the **Tiger Pop-Up Viewing** hole. Reached via a cramped tunnel, it allows you to stick your head up inside the tiger enclosure offering a chance for a truly up close and personal view. When a tiger is lying near this observation post, lines form quickly.

There are more Meet the Keepers sessions here than at the orangutan habitat and Tiger Lodge provides much the same sort of signage found at Orangutan Outpost. Of course, tigers are cats, so most of the time they are napping. As with the orangs, repeat visits will eventually be rewarded.

Treetop Trails

Rating:	★ ★ ★ +
Type:	Interactive play area
Time:	Unlimited
Kelly says:	Adults follow kids at their peril

This is Jungala's version of Land of the Dragons and like that larger space it is a sprawling interactive play area that encompasses a number of other attractions. At ground level, there are two water play areas, one set aside for toddlers. Above rises the **Canopy Walk**, a maze of climb-through mesh tunnels, rope bridges, and walkways that wind past several small animal habitats showing off gibbons, gharials, and flying foxes. The gharial habitat (they are needle-nosed crocodilians) has a kid-sized tunnel with glass sides that give an underwater view of the denizens within.

Adults are allowed here, but no concessions have been made for aging bones. Many parts of this maze are designed for tween-sized explorers, so proceed at your own risk.

Wild Surge

Rating:	★ ★ ★ +
Type:	Mini thrill ride
Time:	About 2 minutes
Kelly says:	Strictly for kids

This is a scaled down version of a standard amusement park ride. Two rows of seven seats are positioned back to back around a central tower. The seats are raised to a height of 35 feet, offering a view of the Treetop Trails area, and then dropped for a sequence of three bounces, then raised and dropped again. A final drop falls all the way to the bottom of the shaft and a return to terra firma. The ride sits in a sort of cave and raised viewing areas let nonriders share the fun vicariously.

Jungle Flyers

Rating:	★ ★ ★ ★
Type:	Zipline ride for youngsters
Time:	20 seconds (that's not a typo!)
Kelly says:	I wanna ride, too!

This is far and away the most popular ride at Jungala and waits of 90 minutes are not uncommon. To reach it, you must climb a set of stairs from the Canopy Walk, but not so fast! The ride is for those 48 inches tall and 6 to 13 years of age. Anyone older must be accompanied by a kid who meets the requirements and cannot weigh more than 220 pounds. How do they know? They weigh you!

From the launch platform, three twin zip lines head off in different directions. Riders are seated in a sling chair, hoisted to a height of 63 feet above ground level and let free to slide over the *Treetop Trails* area to a distant post and back again. It all takes just 20 seconds!

Because of the long wait times, unless your kid absolutely needs mommy or daddy nearby to summon the courage to ride, I would suggest adults sit this one out and give the kids a chance.

— and then reduce

Eating in Jungala

In addition to a few snack options, there are two cafeteria style eateries in the Jungala section. Both of them are perfectly adequate, but nothing more.

Orang Cafe

What: Chicken and ice cream, cafeteria style
Where: Next to the orang habitat
Price Range: $

Chicken is the featured food here. You will find a Chicken Stripes Platter and a spicy chicken wrap, as well as chef's salad. But for my money, the real attraction here is the soft serve ice cream. Only soft beverages are served here.

The Dirt Sundae is sprinkled with crumbled Oreo cookies and the waffle-cone sundae comes with a choice of strawberries or hot fudge. Regular soft serve ice cream comes with a selection of toppings.

There are twin cafeteria lines with seating on either side. The obvious choice is the side looking out onto the orangutan habitat. Here you can linger over lunch while you watch the charming primates across the way. After a while you start to wonder who's watching whom.

Bengal Bistro

What: A bit of everything, with an accent on fish
Where: Across from the tiger habitat
Price Range: $

This is not an Indian restaurant as the name might suggest (too bad!), but a fairly standard cafeteria style eatery with an accent on fried fish of all things. One of the menu items is the Jungala Catch of the Day. There's also a fish wrap. For the rest, there's something to appeal to most tastes, from smoked turkey leg platters, to hot dogs, to chicken Caesar salad, to Italian meatballs, and taco salad.

Shopping in Jungala

The main attraction is **Tiger Treasures,** which is filled with nearly irresistible tiger plush toys and some classy looking tiger-themed t-shirts. More expensive are the tiger figurines, some of them fairly large, depicting playful tiger cubs. There are orang plush toys, too, but, to mix a metaphor, tigers get the lion's share of the space. Worth noting, too, is the shop's semi-private view into the tiger habitat, secluded in an old tree trunk. In the *Treetop Trails* area, **Cub's Closet** is a small open sided hut offering a small selection of kids' merchandise.

The Congo

The Congo is even more compact than it used to be, having ceded much of its land to Jungala. It remains a cleverly designed area with twisting tree-shaded walks and a number of spectator bridges over rides offering vicarious fun for non-riders. All of the space — there is no dining and very little shopping here — is given over to some of Busch Gardens' best thrill rides, so expect lots of excited kids and teenagers jostling for space. The predominant architectural motif is round buildings with conical wooden stick roofs.

In addition to the two major attractions profiled below, the Congo contains a bumper car ride (**Ubanga-Banga Bumper Cars**) and remote control trucks and boats. There is also a stop for the *Trans-Veldt Railroad* (described in the Stanleyville section, above).

Kumba

> *Rating:*   ★ ★ ★ ★ ★
> *Type:*   Steel roller coaster
> *Time:*   Just under 3 minutes
> *Kelly says:* Yet another superb roller coaster

Once, *Kumba* was Busch Gardens' blockbuster ride. It's since been overshadowed by *Montu* and *SheiKra*, but it's still pretty amazing and is the largest of its kind in the southeastern United States. *Kumba* means "roar" in a Congolese dialect, the P.R. people say, and it's well named. Riders are braced with shoulder restraints into 32-seat vehicles (eight rows, four abreast) that roar along almost 4,000 feet of blue steel track that winds up, around, over, and through the surrounding scenery. There are loops, camelbacks, and corkscrews to terrify or thrill you, as the case may be. One of the more disorienting maneuvers takes you on a "cobra roll" around a spectator bridge, which is a great place for the faint of heart to get an idea of what they're missing. Remember to wave to Aunt Martha as you whiz by.

Congo River Rapids

> *Rating:*   ★ ★ ★ ★ ★
> *Type:*   Water ride
> *Time:*   About 3 minutes
> *Kelly says:* The best of the water rides

It doesn't have the steep drops of the flume rides in Stanleyville, but for me *Congo River Rapids* provides the most enjoyable overall water ride experience in Busch Gardens. Here you climb aboard 12-seater circular rafts that are then set adrift to float freely along a rapids-filled stretch of river. The raft twists, turns, and spins as it bumps off the sides and various cunningly placed obstacles in the stream. In addition to the raging waters, which periodically slosh into the raft, the course is punctuated with waterfalls and waterspouts, all of which have the potential to drench you to the skin. The most insidious threat of all comes from your fellow park visitors, who are encouraged to spray you with water cannons (at 25 cents a shot) from the pedestrian walkway that skirts the ride.

Despite all the white water, the raft proceeds at a relatively stately pace and the "river" drops only several feet over its quarter-mile course. The real excitement is generated by the ever-present threat of a soaking. How wet you get is only somewhat a matter of chance. It seems that the wetness quotient has been increased since the ride first opened. Time was that some people emerged virtually unscathed, while others got soaked. Now it seems that almost everyone get thoroughly doused. On a hot Florida afternoon, that seems to be just the ticket, which makes this my favorite water ride and explains the five-star rating.

Eating and Shopping in Congo

You can grab some light refreshments in Congo, but that's about it. On the shopping front, the **Congo River Rapids** gift shop has some nice souvenirs, including large beach towels, which you just might need.

Timbuktu

Timbuktu is, of course, the legendary sub-Saharan trade crossroads that figures prominently in the popular imagination of adventure and exploration. Here at Busch Gardens, Timbuktu is an open, sun-drenched plaza dotted with palm trees and featuring architecture that mimics the mud towers of its namesake. There is precious little shade here unless you venture indoors. The attractions in Timbuktu are a mismatched assortment, having little to do with either Timbuktu or even Africa. But then, Timbuktu is emblematic of far-flung trade, so perhaps it's not so farfetched that it contains an eclectic grab bag of themed attractions from around the world.

There are no zoo animals here. In their place are a variety of typical **amusement park rides**, including Busch Gardens' only **carousel** and several other **kiddie rides**. Also at hand are a collection of **midway games**, cleverly disguised as a sub-Saharan marketplace, and a **video arcade**.

The Scorpion

Rating:	★ ★ ★ +
Type:	A beginner's roller coaster

Time: About a minute
Kelly says: Roller coasters 101

This is the place to come to decide if you have what it takes to tackle the bigger coasters in the park. *The Scorpion* is far and away the tamest of the lot, although it does have one up-and-over loop. So if you've never been "inverted," this is as good a place to start as any. Otherwise, it's no more terrifying than, say, Disney's *Thunder Mountain*.

Cheetah Chase

Rating: ★ ★ ★
Type: A "baby" roller coaster
Time: About a minute and a half
Kelly says: Take the kiddies

If the *Scorpion* is too much for you, head here. It's what's known in the amusement park trade as a "wild mouse" ride. Little four-seater cars zip along a sinuous elevated track with sharp turns and a few mild drops. Kids love it but adults sit high in the little cars and may feel exposed, which can be fun (or not) depending on your taste. The ride does give you a nicely elevated view of the surrounding Timbuktu area.

One downside to the ride is that only two widely-spaced cars are on the track at any given time. This is for safety reasons, but it does lead to slow loading times, which can translate into long waits in line.

Pirates 4-D (Timbuktu Theater)

Rating: ★ ★ ★
Type: 3-D film
Time: About 25 minutes
Kelly says: A 3-D show that makes a splash

With this show, Busch Gardens takes on Disney and Universal in the 3-D movie sweepstakes and comes in a solid third. Starring Leslie Nielsen as Captain Lucky and Eric Idle as his sidekick Pierre, *Pirates 4-D* tells the tale of an evil pirate — that would be Captain Lucky — who returns to Dead Man's Cave to reclaim his buried treasure. What the crew doesn't know is that Captain Lucky buried his former crew along with the treasure and plans to do likewise with his current collection of scalawags.

What Captain Lucky doesn't know is that one member of his old crew — the cabin boy — survived and has rigged the entire island with devilishly clever booby traps.

Much of the fun of the film comes from setting off those traps, which involve crabs and spiders and bats and bees, along with an array of seat-side special effects that place the creepy crawlies in our midst. It's all great fun and not really very scary, although very young tots don't seem to know that.

An additional attraction is the air-conditioned Timbuktu Theater, making this a great show to catch during the hottest part of the afternoon. The flick unspools regularly throughout the day.

Best seats in the house. The seats in the front half of the house get the best of the water effects.

The Phoenix

Rating:	★ ★ ★
Type:	Amusement park ride
Time:	5 minutes
Kelly says:	Only if you haven't done it before

This is a very familiar amusement park ride. A curved boat-like car seating 50 people swings back and forth, gaining height. At the apex of its swing, it pauses and the passengers hang briefly upside down, screaming merrily. Then on the next swing it goes completely up and over.

Chances are, there's a ride like this at an amusement park somewhere near your home, which leads to the question: Ride this one or spend the time doing things you can't do near home? I'd recommend the latter.

Musical Variety Show at the Desert Grill Restaurant

Rating:	★ ★ ★ ★
Type:	Musical variety show
Time:	About 20 minutes
Kelly says:	Best with a meal

What you see here during your visit to Busch Gardens is hard to predict. That's because the stage at the spacious and blessedly cool Desert Grill plays host to a constantly changing roster of musical and dance variety troupes. What's easy to predict is the quality of the shows, which in my experience have been uniformly excellent.

Typically, you will be entertained by a young, energetic, and talented cast. Some shows I've seen have involved intricate percussion and acrobatics. Others have featured championship ballroom dancers, strutting their stuff in a variety of dancing styles. Many times the show will spill out into the audience and they always seem to be looking for a way to get the kids involved. It's all bright and cheerful and makes for a pleasant way to end a meal.

The Desert Grill Restaurant is a cafeteria-style eatery to the side of the main auditorium. All seating in the theater is at long trestle tables, set perpendicular to the stage. It's best to arrive a half an hour or so before the posted show time. That should give you time to get your meal and eat most of it before the show starts, so you can enjoy the musical entertainment over dessert.

Eating in Timbuktu

Two refreshment stands, **The Oasis** and **Sahara Snacks** serve thirst slakers and tummy expanders, but the preferred dining destination is the Desert Grill.

Desert Grill Restaurant

What: Cafeteria-style sandwiches and platters
Where: In the Desert Grill theater
Price Range: $

A variety of hearty fare is on offer at this eatery in the cavernous Desert Grill theater. Three cafeteria lines serve up sandwich platters like the Das Alpine, featuring "mile-high" corned beef and Swiss cheese, and the Italian sausage sandwich. There is also grilled chicken served over alfredo noodles and occasional specials like baby back ribs. Desserts are on offer as well along with beer to wash it all down. The lines are cleverly designed so that if all you want is a beverage, you can easily grab one without having to go through the entire line.

Shopping in Timbuktu

Most of the shopping is concentrated at the southern end of Timbuktu, just before you depart for Nairobi. **Airbrush Arts** lets you choose which design you'd like airbrushed on a t-shirt. The **Crafts Bazaar** is an outdoor shaded area that, despite the name, offers a grab bag of souvenirs and costume jewelry, none of it particularly crafty. The most elaborate shopping venue is the blissfully air conditioned **Sahara Traders** offering mostly clothing, most of it fairly tasteful, including some nice casual wear and handbags for women. Also here is a section selling cigars hand-crafted in nearby Tampa, which has a very vibrant cigar manufacturing culture.

Nairobi

This is Busch Gardens' most zoo-like themed area. To the east, the plains of the Serengeti stretch as far as the eye can see. On the other side are a string of animal exhibits ranging from the merely interesting to the truly wondrous. In addition to those described below, there are displays of **rhinos** and **Asian elephants**, with occasional Meet The Keeper and Animal Encounter sessions. The *Trans-Veldt Railroad* (described in the Stanleyville section, above) stops right in the middle. The showpiece of Nairobi, however, is the *Rhino Rally* attraction, which is part African animal encounter and part thrill ride.

Rhino Rally

Rating: ★ ★ ★ +

Type: Drive-through animal tour and water ride

Time: 7 minutes

Kelly says: Nifty idea that's more clever than thrilling

Rhino Rally artfully blends safari-style animal encounters with a tame water ride. The ride is carved out of a 22-acre patch of the *Serengeti Plain* near the border between Nairobi and Timbuktu. But, unlike rides at other parks that use animated robotic figures, *Rhino Rally* calls on its cast of exotic African water buffalo, zebras, antelope, elephants, and rhinos to play themselves in a real-life action adventure.

The adventure begins as you board a 17-passenger converted Land Rover with your guide and driver to take part in the 34th annual running of Rhino Rally, an off-road race along the Zambezi River across the rugged and dangerous terrain of the African veldt. One adult in the group is chosen to ride next to the driver (a great seat, by the way) and serve as the navigator who, in off-road rally tradition, will be blamed if anything goes wrong. Along the way, your sturdy vehicle splashes through crocodile-infested waters and comes almost face to face with elephants, rhinos, and other wild critters. The course has been cleverly designed to allow the Land Rovers to nosedive into streams and water holes and cross narrow bridges over deep ravines.

The trip provides close-up, although brief, encounters with elephants, Grant's zebras, cape buffalo and scimitar-horned oryx. The ancient Egyptians, we learn, domesticated these beasts and forced their long curving horns to grow together into a single horn, creating the myth of the unicorn. After driving past two rare white rhinos (they are actually gray), the vehicle fords a stream filled with real crocodiles cruising just a few feet away.

Then, as often happens in theme park thrill rides, things go awry and, of course, it's all the navigator's fault. A fateful wrong turn takes your vehicle into a tree-shaded gulch just as a cloudburst hits, obscuring the view out the front window. As your driver nervously tries to cross a rickety pontoon bridge, a freak flash flood comes roaring over a cliff on the left. Before you can say "Dr. Livingstone, I presume," the bridge breaks apart, carrying you and your vehicle on an unscheduled ride down a meandering river.

After drifting through a narrow canyon and under a drenching waterfall, the bridge fragment on which your vehicle is riding crashes against yet another washed out bridge and comes to a bumpy halt. Fortunately, your intrepid guide is able to drive out of this predicament and up the side of the river, bringing everyone safely to the finish line.

A great deal of the fun of this ride is supplied by the driver/guide. The best ones really get into the spirit of things, teaching you a few handy Swahili phrases and getting everyone involved in the action. So you'll probably want to ride more than once. The problem with that is the line quickly grows to daunting lengths. Figure on an hour's wait unless you arrive at opening time.

Tip: If you are alone or if there are just two of you, you may be able to get in a vehicle a bit sooner by following the sign for the single riders line. If you are waiting in the main line, you can accomplish much the same thing by holding one or two fingers aloft during the boarding process. Ride attendants sometimes look for singles or couples to fill in empty spots on the Land Rover that's about to depart.

The best seats in the house. The seats on the left hand side of the vehicle offer not only the best views of the wildlife but a front row seat to the spectacular flash flood. You will, however, get wet.

Myombe Reserve: The Great Ape Domain

Rating: ★ ★ ★ ★ ★
Type: Ape habitat
Time: Continuous viewing
Kelly says: The zoo's crown jewel

Of all the animal habitats at Busch Gardens, this is the hands-down winner. The beautifully imagined setting here would be almost worth the visit without the chimps and gorillas. But it is these fascinating primates that we come to see, and the scenic designers and landscape architects have given them a home that provides plenty of variety for the animals while making it easy for us to spy on them. The achievement is remarkable and ranks right up there with the spectacular habitats at SeaWorld.

The habitat is divided in two, with the first area given over to a band of nine chimpanzees in a rocky, multi-leveled environment complete with spectacular waterfalls, calm pools, and a grassy forest clearing with plenty of climbing space. Best of all is a glassed-in viewing area that allows us to spy on the chimps' private behavior.

Passing through a tunnel, we reach the lowland gorilla habitat. There's a wonderful theatricality to this entrance as we pass through a simulated jungle fog to "discover" the gorillas grazing on our left. Talk about gorillas in the mist! In addition to a glassed viewing area, this habitat features a small amphitheater for extended observation and video cameras that allow us to observe individuals in the far reaches of the habitat.

There's plenty of explanatory information provided via blackboards (the conceit here is that we are visiting a jungle outpost of a scientific expedition), photos and "field notes" containing tidbits of animal lore posted on signs, and voice-over narration in the hidden viewing area. If you only have time for one zoo exhibit between roller coaster rides, make it this one. The entrance to Myombe Reserve is opposite the Moroccan Palace Theater; the exit leads you into the rest of the Nairobi section.

Jambo Junction

Rating: ★ ★ ★
Type: Animal exhibit
Time: Continuous viewing
Kelly says: Lifestyles of the cutest and cuddliest

Busch Gardens Africa maintains a cadre of "Animal Ambassadors," a team of smaller critters who make public appearances around the park, at nearby schools, and even on television. The senior ambassador, Harry, a two-toed sloth has appeared on the major late-night talk shows. The ambassadors' job is to foster greater awareness of the animal kingdom and mankind's responsibility for protecting it. This is where they live between gigs. A visit here is most entertaining when there is a member of the education staff on hand to answer questions and maybe even help you pet a flamingo.

Curiosity Caverns

Rating: ★ ★ +
Type: Walk-through exhibit
Time: Continuous viewing
Kelly says: A real "Bat Cave"

Decorated to evoke a prehistoric cave, complete with wall paintings, this darkened walk-through tunnel displays, behind plate glass windows, a variety of critters that most people think of as "creepy," although the nocturnal marmoset is positively cuddly. Aside from the snakes and reptiles, the main attractions here are the bats. Fruit bats cavort in a large enclosure decorated with bare trees artfully draped with bananas, apples, and other yummy treats. Nearby, in a smaller display, are the vampire bats (yes, they really exist!), the animal blood on which they thrive served up on dainty trays hanging in their cages.

Eating and Shopping in Nairobi

Other than the **Kenya Kanteen**, a walk up stand that offers turkey legs, hot dogs, cheese fries, and funnel cakes, there's no dining here. Shopping's another matter.

The **Gorilla Gallery,** an outdoor stand near one of the entrances to the Myombe Reserve, has some of the nicest t-shirts in the park — gorilla-themed, of course. A short stroll away, **Caravan Crossing** offers more animal themed t-shirts and plush toys.

Crown Colony and Egypt

This area, officially known as Egypt, actually combines two distinctly themed environments. Crown Colony takes its theme from the great British colonial enclaves of East Africa, where the well-heeled lived the good life and played cricket and polo while being waited on by the unshod. A real British Colonial would probably not recognize the place, but for the rest of us it'll do just fine. The overall impression is one of casual elegance and good taste. Crown Colony serves as a comfortable home to several attractions (like the Clydesdale stables, and the **Show Jumping Hall of Fame**) that stretch the African metaphor a bit. It is also the home of the Crown Colony House, a very nice full-service sit-down restaurant.

Egypt is one of Busch Gardens' smallest lands, at least in terms of strolling space and amenities. Its primary purpose is to give the mega-coaster *Montu* a home. The *King Tut* attraction seems a bit of an afterthought, and the only eatery here is a kiosk dispensing snacks. The shopping is a bit more elaborate but not much.

The design evokes upper Egypt as it might have looked about the time Howard Carter was unearthing King Tut's treasure. The scale is appropriately grandiose but the statuary and wall carvings fall well short of the originals. Still, it's pleasant enough. There's a clever "archaeological dig," called **Sifting Sands**, that is, in fact, a shaded sand box in which little ones can uncover the past. A small selection of **midway games** is also offered.

For most people, however, Egypt will be glimpsed briefly en route to the massive temple gates at the end, beyond which lurks the terrifying *Montu*.

Edge of Africa

Rating: ★ ★ ★ ★ ★
Type: Brilliant animal habitat
Time: Continuous viewing
Kelly says: Up close and personal with lions and hippos

Edge of Africa is an animal habitat to rival *Myombe*. Here, on a looping trail that evokes a number of African themes, are displayed a compact colony of adorable meerkats, a pride of lions, a pack of hyenas, a few hippos, and a troop of ring-tailed lemurs. The genius of the design is in the glass walls that allow you, literally, to come nose to nose with some of these animals.

The best display is built around the metaphor of a scientific encampment on the Serengeti that has been invaded by lions or hyenas (the zoo operation alternates these species in the exhibit). Two Land Rovers are built into the glass wall that separates you from the beasts, allowing you to climb into the vehicles and re-create an actual safari experience. At feeding time, the handlers drop meat morsels into the enclosure from above the Land Rovers, encouraging the animals to climb into the backs and onto the hoods of the vehicles. The effect is breathtaking as you sit a hand's breadth away from these snarling carnivores.

The hippo exhibit evokes an African river village with the huts raised over the water on stilts. The viewing area is nicely shaded by the huts and the extensive glass wall allows a terrific underwater perspective on these beasts. While they may seem lumbering on land, under water they are surprisingly graceful as they lope past swarms of freshwater tropical fish. One visitor compared them to flying pigs.

The key to really enjoying *Edge of Africa* is to come at feeding time when the animals will be at their most active and most visible. At other times they will most likely be off relaxing in the shade somewhere. The attendants doing the feeding are all experienced animal handlers who are more than happy to share their extensive knowledge with you, so don't be shy about asking questions. Unfortunately, there is no regular feeding schedule. Feeding times are varied to mimic, to some small extent, life in the wild, where animals can never predict when — or even if — their next meal is coming.

The solution is to ask the attendants at the attraction when feeding time will be. You may have to be persistent and you must also be willing to drop whatever you're doing elsewhere in the park to return at the appointed time. Take it from me, it's worth it.

Note: The main entrance to *Edge of Africa* is in Crown Colony but you can also reach the attraction from Egypt.

Serengeti Safari Tour

Rating: ★ ★ ★ ★ ★
Type: Guided tour
Time: 30 minutes
Kelly says: A safari for those who can't get to Africa

First the bad news: There is a hefty extra charge for this attraction of $34 for everyone five and older (Passport holders get a $2 discount). That will probably be a budget-buster for many families; but if the cost doesn't scare you off, this one will provide experiences you'll remember for a good long time. If it's any consolation, it's a heck of a lot cheaper than going to Africa.

The tour begins when about 20 people are loaded on to the standing-room-only back of a flatbed truck. A small awning provides some shade at the front, but since it is lowered for the animal feedings much of the time you will be in the searing sun; a hat, not to mention water, is not a bad idea. Your friendly tour guide, a Busch Gardens' education staffer, lays down a few simple safety instructions and then it's off to the interior of the Plain for the real highlight of the tour — a chance to hand feed the giraffes and elands. Along the way, you will see ostriches and maribou storks, but the giraffes are the stars of the show.

The adult giraffes tower over you, while the youngsters just get their heads over the edge of the truck. They are remarkably tame and will let you pet their stiff, tawny necks and soft muzzles. You may also get a demonstration of how they use their long black tongues to pluck the dainty leaves off thorny acacia bushes. For most people, this is the highlight of the tour. To have two or three of these gentle giants leaning into the back of the truck as you feed them and stroke their powerful necks is a very special experience indeed.

The best seats in the house. The back of the truck where you stand has a padded rail around the rim. I suggest positioning yourself at one of the back corners since giraffes will often trail after the slow-moving vehicle looking for another handout.

Tip: The trucks have a maximum capacity of 20 people and on a typical day there are just five tours. While the high price keeps the crowds down, tours do fill up quickly. You can reserve ahead for the first tour of each day only, which departs at 11:15 a.m. and is the only morning tour. The morning tour also offers the advantage of beating the heat of midday. Call (813) 984-4043 to make your reservation. When you arrive at the park, look for the Adventure Tour Center in Morocco (on your left), where you can pay for your tour with cash or credit card. If you don't reserve ahead, you must sign up in advance for one of the afternoon tours when you get to the park; it is wise to do so early.

Serengeti Plain

Rating: ★ ★ ★
Type: Extensive animal habitat
Time: Continuous viewing but access is limited
Kelly says: Takes persistence to see it all

This is one of Busch Gardens' major zoological achievements, a 50-acre preserve that evokes the vast grasslands of Eastern Africa. (Serengeti is a Masai word meaning "plain without end.") Here, Busch displays a representative cross-section of African plains dwellers, from charming curiosities like giraffes and the endangered black rhinoceros, to the herd animals — lithe gazelles and lumbering wildebeest (or gnus). There are some African birds here, too, like the maribou stork, but most of the birds you will see are what Busch Gardens calls "fly-ins," Florida species that recognize a good deal when they see one. The rule of thumb is that if it's a bird and white, it's a Tampa Bay local.

It's a brilliant idea and, by and large, well executed, although it still looks far more like Florida scrub land than the real Serengeti. The concept and the design involve a number of tradeoffs. By mimicking nature, the designers have made the animals hard to see — just like in the wild. Although you can see into the Serengeti from Nairobi or the terrace of the Crown Colony House, the only way to get a good look is to go inside. Unless you are willing to pay the stiff extra fee for the *Serengeti Safari Tour*, that can be accomplished only by the *Skyride* (see below) and by the *Trans-Veldt Railroad* (see the Stanleyville section, above) that circles the perimeter. So your routes through the Serengeti are predetermined as are the lengths of your visits. This creates a number of minor problems. There's no guarantee that the animals will be in prime viewing position (or even visible) when you pass by, although it's unlikely that you will miss much. And, if an animal catches your fancy or is doing something particularly interesting, your vehicle simply keeps on going; you don't have the luxury of stopping. You also have no control over how close you can get to the animals (with the notable exception of the *Serengeti Safari Tour*). The nature of the park experience, however, suggests that most people will glimpse the animals briefly on the short rides. And that's too bad.

That being said, the *Serengeti Plain* remains a major feather in Busch Gardens' zoological cap. The animals enjoy a much more spacious and natural environment than they would have in a more "traditional" zoo and we probably shouldn't complain too much about the compromises we must make for their comfort.

The Skyride

Rating: ★ ★ ★
Type: Suspended gondola ride
Time: 5 minutes
Kelly says: Shortcut with a view

If you've been on the sky ride at Disney World, you know what this one's all about. This isn't intended as a tour of the *Serengeti Plain*, although it does pass over *Edge of Africa* and *Rhino Rally* and offers a glimpse of the plains animals in the distance. Rather, this is a one-way shortcut from Crown Colony to Stanleyville, or vice versa. Your vehicle is a small four-seat gondola suspended from an overhead cable. You can board at either end, but you cannot stay aboard for a roundtrip. The ride dips down for a dog-leg left turn at a checkpoint on the northern end of the *Serengeti*. This is not a disembarkation point but is used primarily to adjust the spacing between gondolas to assure a smooth arrival.

You can get good views of the Serengeti on this ride, although most people will take the opportunity to check out the action on *Montu* and

Kumba or perhaps to spot the towers of Adventure Island, Busch Gardens' water park, down the road.

Clydesdale Hamlet

Rating:	★ ★ +
Type:	Horse stables
Time:	Continuous viewing
Kelly says:	For horse lovers and Bud fans

This is a smaller version of the Clydesdale Hamlet at SeaWorld. The horses are magnificent; there may be a foal on view during your visit. Even if you aren't a horse lover, the stroll through the stables makes a pleasant detour en route to Egypt. The Clydesdales also pose for **photo ops** several times a day. Check the Meet The Keepers schedule you picked up at the main entrance when you arrived.

Montu

Rating:	★ ★ ★ ★ ★
Type:	Inverted roller coaster
Time:	About 3 minutes
Kelly says:	The next best (i.e. scariest) thing to *SheiKra*

This one is truly terrifying. It is also, for those who care about such things, the tallest and longest inverted steel roller coaster in the southeastern United States.

Montu (named for a hawk-headed Egyptian god of war) takes the formula of *Kumba* and quite literally turns it on its head. Instead of sitting in a car with the track under your feet, you sit (or should I say "hang") in a car with the track overhead. Once you leave the station, your feet hang free as you climb to a dizzying 150 feet above the ground before being dropped 13 stories, shot through a 360 degree "camelback loop" that produces an eternity of weightlessness (actually a mere three seconds), and zipped, zoomed, and zapped along nearly 4,000 feet of track that twists over, above, and even into the ground. Fortunately, when you dip below ground level you do so in archaeological "excavation trenches," in keeping with the Egyptian theme. There's not much to see in these trenches, but then you don't spend much time in them and you'll probably have your eyes jammed shut anyway.

Each car holds 32 passengers. At maximum capacity, 1,700 guests can be pumped through this attraction each hour. Nonetheless, lines can be formidable. If this is your kind of ride, plan on arriving early during busy seasons.

The best seats in the house. The best (and scariest) seats are in the front row. Otherwise, the outside seats are the ones to hope for. Given the overhead design of this ride, the interior seats offer a very obstructed view, which may not be a problem if you tend to ride with your eyes shut most of the time. Getting the front seats is pretty much the luck of the draw, although every once in a while you may be able to step in when the faint of heart opt out of the front row.

Even if you can't or don't ride roller coasters, *Montu* is worth a visit for a close-up view of the crazy people who are riding. Position yourself at the black iron fence that you see as you pass through the massive temple gates that lead to the ride. Here you'll get an exhilarating close-up look of 32 pairs of feet as they come zipping out of the first trench. If you do ride, don't forget to look for your terrified or giddy face on the instant photos they sell.

King Tut's Tomb

Rating: ★ ★ +
Type: Walk-through attraction
Time: About 10 minutes
Kelly says: A "spirited" guide to an ancient tomb

Here's your chance to walk in the footsteps of Howard Carter, the legendary archaeologist who discovered King Tut's tomb in the 1920s. As you wait in the darkened entrance to the tomb, old newspaper headlines and period newsreels re-create the excitement and wonder of the discovery. Then, the projector jams, the film melts and, as you enter the tomb proper, the spirit of Tut himself takes over as tour guide.

What you see is a re-creation of the tomb as it looked at the time of discovery, the many treasures and priceless artifacts piled in jumbled disarray. As lights illuminate specific artifacts, Tut tells us about his gilded throne, his golden chariot, and his teenage bride. Moving to the burial chamber, we see his solid gold sarcophagus and the golden goddesses who guarded the cabinet containing alabaster urns filled with his internal organs.

For newcomers to Egyptology, this attraction will serve as an intriguing introduction. The marvelously air-conditioned tomb also makes for a pleasant break from the burning Florida sun. Those who are familiar with Tut may want to skip this one.

Eating in Crown Colony and Egypt

Nothing but refreshments are available in the compact Egypt area, so for something more substantial you'll have to head for Crown Colony. Fortunately, the park's best dining option is found here and a comfy bar serving a range of draft beers is nearby.

Crown Colony House Restaurant

What: Pleasant full-service restaurant

Where: In Crown Colony House, overlooking the Serengeti Plain

Price Range: $$ – $$$

This spacious restaurant is the only full-service, sit down restaurant in the park. It offers moderately priced "family style dinners" that consist of platters of chicken or fried fish served with a variety of side dishes. There is also a section of "Healthy Choices" on the menu, consisting of salads with grilled chicken, fruit platters, and a vegetable platter that mixes grilled and steamed veggies to good effect. Heartier entrees include a seafood medley, broiled mahi-mahi, and chicken or shrimp alfredo over fettuccine. The desserts are good, but I can't recommend the wine list. Stick to beer.

Tip: No reservations are accepted, but you can request a table by the semi-circular window overlooking the Plain and wait until it becomes available.

Crown Colony Pizza

What: Walk-up sandwich stand

Where: The ground floor of Crown Colony House

Price Range: $

Also known as Crown Colony Provisions, this stand serves up sandwich (club and roast beef) and seafood salad platters as well as pizza and fries combos. There's plenty of seating in a large open club-like room at the other end of which is a broad, handsome bar dispensing a wide range of beers on draft. If you're just stopping in for a beer, look for the comfy leather sofas in a side room — a great place to take a load off.

Shopping in Crown Colony and Egypt

My favorite shop here is **Edge of Africa,** opposite Crown Colony House, where you will find some nice African crafts and some sharp looking safari hats. There is also a good selection of clothing and toys aimed at the youngest visitors. Also nice is the **Golden Scarab,** in Egypt, offering replicas of Egyptian antiquities, some of them quite nice. In addition, you can pick up the requisite "I survived Montu" t-shirt as you exit the ride. **Photo ops** with the Clydesdales are offered from time to time at the Clydesdale Hamlet

Guided Tours

Busch Gardens Africa offers a number of special tours in addition to the *Serengeti Safari Tour* (see Crown Colony and Egypt, above). These offer special perks, behind-the-scenes access, and up-close encounters with some of its animal charges. There is a hefty extra charge for these special experiences, but if you have the budget I think you'll find it money well spent. The fees given below (which do not include tax) are in addition to regular park admission and only some tours offer very modest discounts to Passport holders. Prices were accurate at press time but are subject to change, so it's best to call prior to your visit to double check prices and availability. You can call toll-free at (888) 800-5447 and ask to be connected to the tour department. The direct line is (813) 984-4043. Tour tickets can also be purchased in the park at the Adventure Tour Center, to your left as you enter the park; at the Heart of Jungala, a small counter in the Tiger Lodge viewing pavilion in Jungala; at the Park Information counter in the entrance to Desert Grill in Timbuktu; and at the Edge of Africa shop in Crown Colony.

Children under five are not permitted on any animal interactions, although they can participate in other elements of some tours; bilingual guides can be arranged with prior notice.

Saving a Species Tour

This $45 45-minute tour adds a visit to the endangered white rhinos to the giraffe feeding of the *Serengeti Safari Tour*, described above. Participants also learn a bit about conservation efforts and the good work of the World Wildlife Fund, which gets a donation of $2 from the cost of the tour.

Sundowner Safari

This is an adults-only version of the *Serengeti Safari Tour*. It starts with a visit to the Crown Colony House for an abbreviated version of the *Brewmaster's Club* described earlier in the Bird Gardens section. Then it's off to feed the giraffes and visit the rhinos while knocking back a few more Anheuser-Busch brews. Presumably, they make sure no one is FUI (feeding under the influence). This 45-minute experience is $40 per over-21 head.

Animal Adventure Tour

This two-hour tour focuses on the animals of the park, with an emphasis on the newest additions to the Busch Gardens family. Consequently, the menu may change depending on who's given birth most recently. At each stop, you get a personal briefing from the keepers. The tour visits the Clydesdale stables and *Edge of Africa*. Then you climb aboard a truck for your own *Serengeti Safari Tour* (see above). From there, you visit the rhinos and the elephants. A stop at *Jambo Junction* might also be included. At most stops you will get to hand feed the animals and the tour guide will provide you with free ice-cold water during the tour.

There is just one *Animal Adventure Tour* each day, at 1:30 p.m. The tour, which is accessible to handicapped guests, costs $120 for all ages and is limited to seven people, so prior reservations are recommended. Otherwise, you can stop by the Expedition Africa shop to see if any slots are available. This tour is a sure-fire hit for animal lovers. If you are planning on taking the $34 *Serengeti Safari Tour* anyway, you may want to consider upgrading to this very special experience.

Heart of Jungala Tour

Here's a chance to get up close and almost personal with the tigers and orangutans of Jungala. There is just one one-hour tour a day at 2:00 p.m. and the fee is $34, a portion of which goes to the SeaWorld-Busch Gardens Conservation Fund.

The tour begins with a walk backstage to the subterranean quarters of the tigers who are not on display in the outdoor habitat. You will get to watch them being fed (blood popsicles, anyone?) in their cages while an extremely knowledgeable keeper explains the intricacies of caring for these magnificent beasts. Don't expect any "interaction." These are wild animals, after all, and no one at Busch Gardens touches them except when they've been anesthetized for veterinary. .

Next, it's off to the orangutan compound for a similar show and tell. Here the orang is behind glass and the keeper demonstrates the way the critter has been trained to respond to simple hand signals. A few of these are "tricks," but most have to do with making veterinary procedures easier on the keepers. Finally, you will get to meet two "Animal Ambassadors" from the bird kingdom, such as a golden conyer and a gaudily colored macaw.

Keeper for a Day

This is Busch Gardens Africa's ultimate animal encounter experience, not to mention the most costly. But the $350 you pay for this six and a half hour tour will probably seem worth it to animal and zoo fanatics. Because there is hard work involved, this one has some additional restrictions. Participants must be 13 years old and at least 52 inches tall and able to lift 15 pounds and climb a flight of stairs. You have to follow instructions, too, something not every tourist seems capable of doing. Your time is divided between caring for and feeding giraffes and antelopes in the morning and birds in the afternoon, all in the Serengeti Plain area of the park.

Guided Adventure Tour

This five-hour guided tour combines the animal encounters of the *Serengeti Safari Tour* with visits to *Edge of Africa* and the park's major rides and shows. Guests on this tour get front of the line access to several of the major coasters and the best seats in the house for the shows, as well as lunch at a "family favorite" restaurant (which means one of the more casual, cafeteria-style eateries). You also receive a 20% discount on all park merchandise and free stroller and wheelchair rental.

The tour costs $95 for adults and $85 for kids 5 to 9 and is limited to 15 people. Make a reservation before arriving or look for the "Guided Tour Adventure Center" in the entrance plaza to the park. Tours depart once a day at 10:20 a.m.

Thrill-Seekers Tour

This four-hour tour is for those who want to concentrate on the rides. For $75 (or $65 for kids 3 to 9), you get front of the line access to most of the major thrill rides and water rides as well as preferred seating for at least two shows, including *KaTonga*. Lunch at Crown Colony House is also included. Some people will no doubt find the VIP privileges worth the extra cost.

Elite Adventure Tour

This $200 all-day extravaganza is Busch Gardens' VIP tour and it can last as long as you wish, although at this price you'll probably want to arrive early and stay until the park closes. The Elite Adventure Tour offers the front of the line access, priority seating, and discounts of the *Guided Adventure Tour*, plus a free continental breakfast, lunch, and a free Fuji camera. This one must be booked at least 24 hours in advance, but large groups should book at least a week in advance.

Adventure Camps

If you really want to be nice to your kids, you won't just take them to Busch Gardens Africa, you'll leave them there. Busch Gardens operates a number of sleepover camps for kids from grade six through high school. There's even a program that takes college kids. With nifty names like Zooventures and Young Explorers, these camps last from three to nine days and cost from $800 to over $2,000. Housing is dorm style on Busch Gardens property.

And if you think it's unfair that kids have all the fun, ask about the Family Sleepovers that let adults tag along. For more information and to request a catalog of camp programs at all of the Busch parks (the SeaWorlds in Orlando, San Antonio, and San Diego also offer programs), call (877) 248-2267 or (813) 987-5252.

Above: It's a series of tubes.
(Adventure Island)

Right: A long way down.
(Gulf Scream, Adventure Island)

Below: A watery workout.
(Paradise Lagoon, Adventure
Island)

Chapter Seven

Adventure Island

BUSCH GARDENS AFRICA'S NEXT DOOR WATER PARK IS A WINNER, AND if your only shot at a water park is during a visit to Tampa, you shouldn't be disappointed. While Adventure Island can't match the exquisite theme-ing (let alone the dolphins!) of the newer Aquatica, it runs a not-too-distant second. The compact grounds are cunningly and beautifully landscaped. It's an older park, of course, so some of the trees have had a chance to grow and provide wonderfully shady areas.

Categories like this are slippery, but if Aquatica can be considered a "family park," Adventure Island appeals more to teens and young adults. That's largely because it's rides are, on the whole, zippier than those Aquatica has to offer. And, while the rides are extremely well designed, the emphasis here seems to be on the action rather than the aesthetics. It's a great place to sample the essence of the water park experience.

Before You Come

If you want to double-check any of the information given below, you can call (800) 800-5447 or (813) 987-5660.

You may also want to stop by the park's web site before you visit. There you will find the park's hours of operation during your visit, a complete accessibility guide for those with disabilities, information on day camps for young children, and any special offers that you might be able to take advantage of. The park's web site is:

www.adventureisland.com

When's the Best Time To Come?

Unlike Aquatica, Adventure Island is seasonal, which means it is closed during Tampa's cooler months. It's season runs from March to October, with limited openings in the early and late months of the season. After Labor Day, the park is typically open only on weekends.

The park has a devoted local following among school-aged teenagers and young adults. You might find the park less crowded on weekdays, when many of those in its prime target demographic are working, although I have found it busy on most days.

Getting There

Adventure Island is located at 1001 Malcolm McKinley Drive, Tampa 33674, right across the street from Busch Gardens Africa, two miles west of I-75 and two miles east of I-275. If you are going directly to Adventure Island from Orlando, take I-4 to I-75 north. Take Exit 265 (Fowler Avenue) and head west a few miles to McKinley Drive. Turn left and get in the left-hand lane. Look for the entrance to Adventure Island on your left. It's easy to miss if you're not careful and haven't remembered to get in the left-hand lane.

Opening and Closing Times

Park hours vary with the calendar. At the beginning (March) and end (September and October) the park will be open from 10:00 a.m. to 5:00 p.m. and usually only on weekends. As crowds grow and days lengthen during the warmer months, the weekend hours may extend from 9:00 a.m. to 8:00 p.m. The best way to know when the park will be open during your visit is to check the web site at the address given above.

One-Day Admission

At press time Adventure Island was offering a single one-day admission option, with no discounts, even for online purchases or Florida residents. The following prices include tax:

One Day Admission:

Adults:	$39.35
Children (3 to 9):	$37.22

Children under 3 are **free**.

Information on "Length of Stay" tickets, which combine two or more parks; the Orlando FlexTicket, which includes five or six parks; and "Passports" (annual passes), which also offer access to multiple parks, will be found in *Chapter One: Dive Right In!*

Arriving at Adventure Island

When you have turned into the main entrance, you will proceed up a winding, shaded, and beautifully landscaped drive to a ticket booth, where you will pay for parking. Parking is $6 per vehicle, motorcycles park **free**. Parking is free only if your Passport includes Adventure Island.

There is a very large and minimally shaded parking lot and if you arrive late in the morning, you may be far from the entrance, to which you must walk. At the park's main entrance, you will find a security check, ticket booths, electronic ticket kiosks, and an ATM.

Tip: Coolers larger than 16 quarts or more than 15 inches in length or width are not allowed in the park and it can be a long walk back to your car. See *Eating at Adventure Island*, below, for information on the Picnic Pavilion.

What To Expect

Everything said about Aquatica in the *What To Expect* section of *Chapter Four* holds true of Adventure Island, except that here there are no animals and there are more (and better) speed slides than at the Orlando park.

Good Things to Know About . . .

Once again, it's simplest to refer you to the *Good Things to Know About ...* sections of *Chapter One* and the Aquatica chapter. These notes apply specifically to Adventure Island.

Cabanas

You have two options for creating your own private space at Adventure Island. The Wave Pool Cabanas, situated as the name would suggest, overlooking the wave pool, come with a locker, a refrigerator, eight bottles of water and four souvenir towels. The charge is $150 for the day between Memorial Day and Labor Day, $125 at other times.

Less elaborate are Mango Joe's Chiki Huts, located behind the restaurant near the volleyball courts. They are simple, palapa-like shelters and come with a locker and four chaise lounges. They rent for $60 during peak times, $40 the rest of the season. Passport holders get a ten percent discount on both.

Day Camps

During the summer months, Adventure Island offers week-long (Monday to Friday) day camps for younger kids. There are two groups, Wave Makers for grades five and six and Hydra Heroes for grades seven and eight. Both camps run from 8:00 a.m. to 3:30 p.m. and cost $235. Passport holders receive a $10 discount. The focus is Adventure Island, but there are excursions elsewhere.

Lockers

Lockers are $8 and there is only one size. As at Aquatica, they allow in and out access all day long. You receive a $3 gift card when you return the key. However, it is redeemable only at Adventure Island, so one way or another you are paying $8. Best to cash it in towards a tall frosty before you head out of the park.

Rentals

A number of items are available for rent.

Beach umbrellas are $10.

Strollers and wheelchairs are $10.

Volleyballs are **free** with a photo ID or annual pass.

The admission price includes **free** use of inner tubes in designated areas of the park and life vests for all guests.

Towels

Adventure Island does *not* rent towels. You will either have to bring your own, borrow one from your hotel, or buy one at the park's gift shop — which is not a bad idea, actually, since they make a great souvenir.

Rides and Attractions at Adventure Island

Adventure Island is laid out in a sort of figure eight. I have described its attractions in the approximate order you would encounter them on a counterclockwise circumnavigation of the park.

Beach Areas

As you move from the entrance plaza and walk down the steps into the park proper, you see a delightful sandy expanse in front of you. It's ideal for sunning and relaxing (although not for picnicking) with its many lounge chairs. Many people prefer to spread a beach towel on the pristine white sands. The entire area is ringed by an ankle-deep stream so as you exit you can rinse the sand off your feet. Similar areas are dotted around the park.

Runaway Rapids

This series of five water slides is so ingeniously snaked through a simulated rocky canyon that you are hard-pressed to spot the flumes as you wend your way to the top. To the left are two child-sized slides on which parents and tots can descend together. To the right and higher up are the three adult flumes. Here, as at other slides in the park, red and green traffic lights regulate the flow of visitors down the slides.

You ride these slides on your back or sitting up; there are no mats or tubes used. As a result, they can get off to a slow start but they pick up speed as you hit the dips and turns about a third of the way down. Of the three adult slides, the one on the left seems the zippiest, while the one in the middle is the tamest. None of them are super scary, however, and most people should thoroughly enjoy the brief ride to the shallow pool below.

Wahoo Run

Adventure Island's newest ride is a twisty, turny mega slide designed for large rafts holding up to five riders. As you zip down 600 feet of corkscrewing blue tunnels at up to 15 feet per second, you pass under four waterfall curtains that guarantee a thorough drenching before you are deposited in a splash pool at the bottom. This is a great family ride.

Paradise Lagoon

This is a swimming pool with pizzazz. At one end, two short tubes (one slightly curved) let you slide down about 15 feet before dropping you from a height of about 3 feet into 10-foot-deep water. A short distance away, you can leap from an 8-foot-high rocky cliff, just like at the old swimmin' hole. Although the pool seems deep enough (10 feet), head-first dives are not allowed. At the pool's narrowest point, you can test your balance and coordination by trying to cross a series of inflated stepping stones while holding on to an overhead rope net.

Endless Surf

Adventure Island's 17,000-square-foot wave pool generates five-foot-high waves for body surfing as well as random choppiness for what is billed as a "storm-splashing environment." This is the smallest of the wave pools at the two parks reviewed here, with a correspondingly small lounging area at the beach end. Waves are set off in 10-minute cycles, with a digital clock at the deep end counting down the minutes until the next set of waves.

Fabian's Funport

Adventure Island's kiddie pool follows the formula perfectly. The ankle-to calf-deep pool is abuzz with spritzing and spraying water fountains, some of which let kids determine when they get doused. A raised play area features mini water slides and water cannons with just enough range to spray unwary adults at the pool's edge.

A unique touch here is an adjacent mini version of the wave pool, scaled down to toddler size. A raised seating area lets grown-ups relax while keeping an eagle eye on their busy charges.

Rambling Bayou

Adventure Island's version of the continuous looping river is delightful, with a few special touches — a dousing waterfall that is marvelously refreshing on a steamy day, followed by a gentle misting rain provided by overhead sprinklers.

Spike Zone

This is one of the nicest volleyball venues you're likely to find at a water park. In fact, these 11 "groomed" courts have hosted professional tournaments. Most of the play, however, is by amateurs. Even if you're not into competing, the layout makes it easy to watch.

Water Moccasin

Three translucent green tubes descend from this moderately high tower. The center one drops sharply to the splashdown pool, while the two other tubes curve right and left respectively for a corkscrew descent. This is a body slide (you ride lying down on your back) that offers the thrill of a speed slide in the middle tube and a rapidly accelerating descent through the others.

Key West Rapids

The tallest ride at Adventure Island attracts long lines due in part to slow loading times. Fortunately the wait is made easier to take by the spectacular view of next-door Busch Gardens. In the distance, past the loops and sworls of Montu, you can see the downtown Tampa skyline.

Here you pick up a single or two-rider tube at the bottom and climb up for a looping and swooping descent on a broad open-air flume. The ride is punctuated twice by rapids-like terraces where attendants (I call them the Rapids Rangers), regulate the flow of riders. Thanks to the two pauses, this ride never attains the speed of similar rides at the other parks, but it offers an enjoyable descent nonetheless.

Splash Attack

This is a more elaborate version of *Fabian's Funport* and draws an older crowd — kids from 8 to about 15. The multi-level play area (much like that found in Land of the Dragons at nearby Busch Gardens) is alive with spritzes, sprays, spouts, and hidden geysers that erupt to catch the unwary. A variety of ingenious hand-operated devices lets kids determine to some extent who gets doused and when. A huge bucket at the summit tips over every now and then, soaking everyone below. If your kids have done Aquatica and experienced *Walkabout Waters*, they'll find this a letdown, but if not, they'll think it's terrific fun.

Caribbean Corkscrew

This is a fiendishly clever little speed slide. Two steeply inclined enclosed tubes are twisted around each other like braided hair. As you descend, you pick up speed until you are deposited, slightly disoriented, in the long deceleration pool. Holding your nose is highly recommended for this one.

Riptide

Riptide adds the thrill of competition to the speed slide concept. A pair of twin enclosed speed slides, one red, one blue, take off from a single high platform. One pair of tubes swerves left, the other right, before rejoining for parallel splashdowns. No one knows who's winning until the final moments of the ride.

Gulf Scream

Right next to *Riptide*, these two slides offer a toned down speed slide experience and, by comparison, the ride down is leisurely. If you're uncertain about tackling *Riptide*, test your mettle here.

Aruba Tuba

Aruba Tuba shares a tower with the *Calypso Coaster*. As with *Key West Rapids*, you pick up your single or double tube at the entrance and climb to the top. This ride, as the name implies, descends through a tube that is mostly enclosed with a few brief openings to the sky. Periodically, you are plunged into total darkness, adding to the excitement generated by the speed, sudden turns, and sharp dips of the ride. All in all, one of Adventure Island's zippiest experiences. You emerge into a pool with a convenient exit into *Ramblin' Bayou*, just in case you feel a need for a marked change of pace.

Calypso Coaster

Unlike its sister ride, *Aruba Tuba*, *Calypso Coaster* is an open flume. It is also wider, allowing for more side-to-side motion at the expense of speed. But there's no drop-off in excitement as you are swooped high on the sides of the flume in the sharp turns you encounter on the way down. Of the two, I give *Aruba Tuba* slightly higher marks in the thrills department, but it's a very close call.

Everglides

Here's an interesting twist on an old idea. It is a slide — a speed slide in fact — but instead of descending on your back or in a tube, you sit upright on a heavy yellow, molded plastic gizmo that's a cross between a boogie board and a sled. As you sit in the ready position, held back from the steep precipice by a metal gate, you might start to have second thoughts. But then the gate drops, the platform tilts, and you are sent zipping down the slide. The best part of the ride is when you hit the water. Instead of slowing down quickly, you go skimming across the surface for about 20 yards before slowing to a stop. If you're doing it right, you'll hardly get wet. The major error to be made on this ride is placing your center of gravity too far back. If you do, you're liable to be flipped over backwards for a very unceremonious dunking.

Eating at Adventure Island

Adventure Island's rules on bringing food into the park are less restrictive than those at Aquatica, but the amount you can bring in is limited. Coolers coming into the park must be no larger than 16 quarts and no bigger than 15 inches long or wide — and they check at the gate. No glass containers or alcoholic beverages, of course. If you can get by with those restrictions, there are some nice places to picnic in the park. If you want a more elaborate picnic, you'll have to use the Picnic Pavilion outside the park. To reach it, turn to the left as you exit the park and follow the sidewalk.

For those who don't want to pack their own lunch, there are two casual eateries in the park. There are also a number of small stands offering sweet snacks and cooling soft beverages. Some even serve beer.

Surfside Cafe

What: Cafeteria and walk-up windows
Where: Near the park entrance
Price Range: $

Located to your right as you enter the park, Surfside is an unprepossessing looking cafeteria whose main serving line is a long open window in the side of the building. Turn the corner and you'll find more walk-up windows.

Pizza combos are the main attraction here, but there are also turkey wraps and sandwiches along with pulled pork BBQ. Kids will probably appreciate the Beach Dog Combo, which is a jumbo hot dog and fries to which chili or cheese can be added for a modest sum. For even younger kids, there are kiddie meals served in a souvenir beach bucket ready to take to the park's sandy areas.

The name is a bit misleading, but the utilitarian seating area, some of it shaded, does look out over the Beach area to Runaway Rapids and Paradise Lagoon. No beer is served here.

Mango Joe's Cafe

What: Cafeteria and bar
Where: In the center of the park

Price Range: $

Burgers are the big offering here, with the Better, Better Bacon Cheese-burger the top of the line. All burger platters are served with lettuce and tomato and a side of fries.

There are also sandwiches, wraps, and salads, with the Buffalo chicken wrap a standout. The most elaborate offering is Joe's Fiesta Shrimp Salad, which includes shrimp and crab tossed together in a "zesty citrus vinaigrette dressing." They also serve the same kid's meals found at the Surfside Cafe.

There is a separate bar, the **Bayou Beach Club**, in the spacious, shaded seating area under a Caribbean-style shed roof. It serves up a variety of Busch beers on tap as well as turkey legs. Nearby, flat-screen TVs are tuned to a sports network, but without sound.

Although the serving lines are nothing to write home about, Mango Joe's has a pleasantly friendly air about it and many people seem to hang out here for long periods of time (could it be that bar?). It's my choice for dining at Adventure Island.

Shopping at Adventure Island

Shopping at this small park consists entirely of the fairly small **Island Surf Shop**, which tries to cover all the bases. You can stock up on items like sunscreen, sunglasses, broad brimmed hats, and waterproof wallets, if you forgot to bring them. There is also a decent collection of swimwear for both men and women, most of it chosen to appeal to the younger visitor. The choices for young kids are especially fun. There are some nice beach towels and waterproof disposable cameras.

Also on offer here and not readily found elsewhere is footwear especially designed for water sports. A sort of cross between a sock and a sneaker, they are ideal for water park wear.

Index

This Index lists rides, attractions, and restaurants mentioned in the text, along with other topics of interest. Where appropriate, the location of each entry is indicated by the following abbreviations: (AI) – Adventure Island; (Aq) – Aquatica; (BG) – Busch Gardens Africa; (DC) – Discovery Cove; (GV) – Grande Vista; (PO) – Peabody Orlando; (RO) – Renaissance Orlando; (SC) – Rosen Shingle Creek; (SW) – SeaWorld.

Other Books from The Intrepid Traveler

The Intrepid Traveler publishes money-saving, horizon expanding travel how-to and guidebooks dedicated to helping its readers make world travel an integral part of their everyday lives.

For more information, visit our web site, where you will find a complete catalog, the latest news about our books, travel articles from around the world, Internet travel resources, and more:

http://www.IntrepidTraveler.com

If you love theme parks, you'll love zoos. *America's Best Zoos: A Travel Guide for Fans and Families* provides in-depth reviews of the country's 60 best zoos, plus information on scores more. Arranged geographically to inspire road trips, this is a must-have reference for your next family vacation.

http://www.americasbestzoos.com

If you are interested in becoming a home-based travel agent, visit the Home-Based Travel Agent Resource Center at:

http://www.HomeTravelAgency.com

For this book's companion volumes, *Universal Orlando: The Ultimate Guide To The Ultimate Theme Park Adventure, The Hassle-Free Walt Disney World Vacation, Hidden Mickeys: A Field Guide To Walt Disney World's Best Kept Secrets,* and *The Walt Disney World Trivia Book* (Vols. 1 and 2), plus updates to all our Orlando guidebooks, visit:

http://www.TheOtherOrlando.com